CHERYL D. BROUSSARD

The Black Woman's
Guide to Starting Her
Own Business

VIKING

VIKING
Published by the Penguin Group
Penguin Books USA Inc., 375 Hudson Street,
New York, New York 10014, U.S.A.
Penguin Books Ltd, 27 Wrights Lane,
London W8 5TZ, England
Penguin Books Australia Ltd, Ringwood,
Victoria, Australia
Penguin Books Canada Ltd, 10 Alcorn Avenue,
Toronto, Ontario, Canada M4V 3B2
Penguin Books (N.Z.) Ltd, 182–190 Wairau Road,
Auckland 10, New Zealand

Penguin Books Ltd, Registered Offices:
Harmondsworth, Middlesex, England

First published in 1997 by Viking Penguin,
a division of Penguin Books USA Inc.

1  3  5  7  9  10  8  6  4  2

Sister CEO™ is a trademark of Cheryl D. Broussard Corp.

*Publisher's Note*
This publication is designed to provide accurate and authoritative information
with regard to the subject matter covered. It is sold with the understanding that
the publisher is not engaged in rendering legal, accounting, or other professional service. If legal advice or other expert assistance is required, the service
of a competent professional person should be sought.

LIBRARY OF CONGRESS CATALOGING IN PUBLICATION DATA
Broussard, Cheryl D.
Sister CEO: the Black woman's guide to starting her own business/Cheryl D. Broussard.
p.  cm.
ISBN 0 670 87144 3 (alk. paper)
1. New business enterprises—Management.   2. Afro-American women executives.
3. Afro-American business enterprises.   I. Title.
HD62.5.B764   1997
658.1'14—dc20      96–21093

This book is printed on acid-free paper.

Printed in the United States of America
Set in ITC Garamond Light.
Designed by Kathryn Parise

# Dedication

*I dedicate this book
to my mother, Gwendolyn J. Reid,
and my grandmother, Leola Clinton,
who will always be my role models and Sister CEOs*

*And
to my high-spirited son, Hasan, who
loves me unconditionally and who always
keeps me on my toes.*

*Thank you.*

# Acknowledgments

Writing a book is similar to running a successful business: it takes a team effort to bring the product to market. *Sister CEO* would not have been possible without the efforts of my team of family members, friends, and coworkers. Thank you for your help and encouragement.

To my son, Hasan: Your love is my strength. Nothing is more important to me.

To my assistants Melanie Austria and Shirley Jackson: Thank you for sharing my vision and working so hard to bring it to fruition. I am fortunate to have each of you in my life.

To Mary Ellen Butler, my editorial assistant: Thank you for your insightful editing expertise.

To Autry Henderson, my assistant at Broussard & Douglas, Inc.: Thank you for being my confidante, guardian angel, and true sister-friend. Your daily encouraging words and positive energy kept me going when the road seemed unsteady. You are the best!

To John Douglas, my business partner: Thank you for supporting me during my time off from our projects to write this book. I am so grateful for our friendship.

To Madeleine Morel and Barbara Lowenstein, my literary agents: Thank you for believing in me.

To Wendy Wolf and her staff at Viking Penguin: Thank you for trusting me so completely with this book.

To Shirese Battles and John Broussard: Thank you for being

there when I needed help with Hasan. Knowing he was safe and in good hands allowed me to focus on writing this book.

To Gwendolyn J. Reid and Theodore Douglas, my mother and father: Thank you for being wonderparents. I love you.

To family and friends Leola and Hugh Clinton, Donna and Donald Shaw, Loraine Binion, Maybelle Broussard, Antoinette Broussard, Louise and Frank Brown, Reuben Brown, Sheila and Herb Fajors, Emma and Jim Hill, Jeanette Hood, Valerie Irons, and Elvin Tyler: Thank you for your faith in me. I am blessed to have each of you in my life.

To Imani Kei and Ozzie Lyles, my massage therapists: Thank you for your healing hands.

To the administrative assistants, secretaries, and receptionists: Thank you for your critical role in arranging the all-important interviews.

To clients of Broussard & Douglas, Inc.: Thank you for patiently waiting and allowing me to complete my book projects.

To Bert Garey: Thank you for allowing me to write in your beautiful and spiritual home in Irish Beach. It was there that my thoughts were able to freely flow. I will always consider the place my writing home.

To the Sister CEOs who took time from their busy schedules to speak with me: Thank you for your inspirational stories and for showing me that I needed to write this book to help all black women become empowered.

# Contents

## Part One
### Dreaming the Dream
### 1

## Part Two
### Nuts and Bolts
### 71

# Contents

# Introduction

## CONTROLLING YOUR DESTINY

> The girls and women of our race must not be afraid to take hold of business endeavor and . . . wring success out of a number of business opportunities that lie at their very doors.
>
> MADAM C. J. WALKER (1912)
> *first black self-made millionaire*

African American women throughout the country are waking up and taking control of their own destinies by starting their own businesses. The role models are plentiful—yet you would never know it if you were to read a business magazine about up-and-coming entrepreneurs. In *Sister CEO* you will read about women who look "just like you" and who are having fun, making tons of money, and succeeding in their own enterprises.

This is a tremendous time to be your own boss. The opportunities are out there for the taking. There are not only role models but real programs that will help you get started; they can teach you the skills, help you get financing, offer technical support, and connect you to a network of other self-starters on their way to becoming successful Sister CEOs.

With the precarious state of the economy, affirmative action disappearing, and the job market transforming before our eyes, being a Sister CEO is fast becoming a necessity, not just an option—because it is black women who all too often are bearing the brunt of "downsizing" and "outsourcing." It's a fact that you will never probably get paid what you are really worth if you work in corporate America. And even you professional "girlfriends" out there earning six figures: don't think for a second you're immune to losing your job. Companies today are becoming lean and mean and getting rid of the "fat" people with high incomes and major benefits.

The competition is fierce and there are plenty of folks in line waiting to step right in and work for half your salary. Regardless of who you are and what type of career you currently have, you can do better for yourself in a business of your own. With the improvements in technology, starting a part-time business from home is relatively easy. And you don't need to reinvent the wheel. Ask yourself: Can the skill you provide to your employer be turned into a sideline business? When Elaine W. Bryant, Sister CEO of E.W. Bryant & Associates, a part-time management consulting business in Tallahassee, Florida, asked herself that question, it was a resounding yes.

Bryant, a director of the Florida Department of Law Enforcement, is a tough sister with the right attitude and stamina to succeed. Her full-time job enables her to network and meet the right people who can later be an asset to her consulting firm. She commands up to $10,000 for a four-day seminar teaching corporations how to run their human resources department. With numbers like these, it's just a matter of time before Bryant will turn her part-time consulting practice into a full-time one.

I can already hear the "yeah, but"s rummaging through your mind—the voices of your two favorite sisters, "Ms Doubt" and "Ms Fear." They always show up when you make major changes or improvements in your life. Elaine Bryant and the other Sister CEOs interviewed for this book had the same sisters; they just didn't allow them to prevent them from living their dreams. You can succeed in this too.

While I have written this book in a fun and inspiring manner, starting your own business is a serious undertaking, particularly when borrowing money against your home or using credit cards to finance the start-up cost. In this instance you run the risk of losing your home or damaging your credit report if the business runs into difficulties. But if you plan, do your homework, and think ahead, owning your own business can make the risk worth taking.

Madam C. J. Walker, Rose Morgan, Sara Breedlove—these are the names of only a few pioneering Sister CEOs. There are many more, because entrepreneurship is in the blood of every black woman in this country. Think back to the days when you were growing up. Don't you remember Daddy's baby sister, Auntie Leola, frying chicken and making potato salad for the dinners she sold to the congregation for $3 after church on Sunday? Or what about your grandmother, who turned her kitchen into a beauty salon, charging $5 for a Press & Curl.

Black women have always had something on the side to bring in some extra money. But we have forgotten about these pioneering Sister CEOs. I'm not sure when it happened; maybe it was as we focused on breaking into the white/male corporate world. These women were our role models and should still be today. Let's not ignore them; instead, let's embrace them. It's time we look back and learn from their examples. They have already paved the way.

One of the most attractive ways black women can become self-empowered is through their own business. The majority of black women are underemployed, bored stiff, and trapped in jobs where only one-quarter or one-half of their skills are used. They've spent the last ten or twenty years on the same job, doing the same dull work, waiting for recognition and a promotion that never comes.

But your power is still there—you just need to draw it out *yourself* and not wait for someone to come along and reward you. *Sister CEO* will show you as a black women how you can:

1) use all your skills to build wealth, happiness, and independence while helping the black community at the same time.
2) promote yourself within your own business. Why should you wait for a promotion in your current job that may not come when you can earn as much or more in your own business within three to ten years. I have heard several black women state, "If I worked as hard for myself as I do for this company, I'd be rich." Well now! You can turn that dream into a reality by following the step-by-step advice in *Sister CEO*.
3) earn real money every day. The easiest way for companies to keep their cost of doing business down is by limiting what they pay their employees. Since black women are by all statistics the

lowest on the pay scale, there is slim chance that these women will ever earn big money—$75,000 or more—in their career. As a Sister CEO running your own business, your chances of reaching $75,000 a year or more are a lot greater.

4) gain the generous tax advantages that every small business-woman is entitled to, especially if she starts her business from home. Businessmen have long understood the significance of owing a business and its impact on their taxes. Since African American women have been far removed from this arena, many don't understand how owning a business will help them reduce their taxes, thereby putting more money into their pockets for their families as well as their businesses. *Sister CEO* will show you how.

5) improve your standard of living. Because many black women are single parents, they dream of being able to save money to provide a better living for their families. They want to be able to provide a good education and a home for their children and grandchildren. For a few black women this may be possible now, but not for the majority. If you, like so many, are in a low-paying job, living paycheck to paycheck every month, you'll learn here how easy it is to start a part-time business on the side while still maintaining your full-time job. You could improve your standard of living tenfold.

Today is the beginning of a new era for black women as we strive to reach the pinnacle of self-empowerment. Starting our own business is one of the avenues to help many of us reach the top. As black women take charge, not only will we build long-term wealth, but we'll increase our self-esteem, strengthen and give back to our communities, become role models for other black women and girls who desperately need to see successful and powerful sistahs, and possibly get written up in a book!

What will it take to get your business started? Knowledge, a strategic plan, commitment, perseverance, faith, trust, and action. By following the advice in *Sister CEO*, I can help you with the first two. The other traits you'll need to bring to the table. So sit back, relax, and enjoy *Sister CEO*. I hope you have as much fun reading it as I did writing it. "You go, girl!"

# Part One

## DREAMING THE DREAM

# Chapter 1

# A BUSINESS OF
# YOUR OWN

Surely you are not going to shut the door in my face. I am in
a business that is a credit to the womanhood of our race. I
started in business seven years ago with only $1.50.
                                            MADAM C. J. WALKER

If you picked up this book because you have a burning desire to
start your own business, you're in the right place. This book is different from other entrepreneurial books because I do more than
present theory. I tell the stories of many Sister CEOs throughout
the country who will serve as your role models. Their stories are so
uplifting, you'll want to immediately follow in their footsteps. I did.
After interviewing each of the women, I was more excited about
their businesses than about my own money management company. After talking with Sister CEO Catherine Hughes of Radio One,
I wanted to be in the radio business. The next day, I changed my
mind and wanted to go into the food catering business after
speaking with Sister CEO Norma Jean Darden of Spoonbread Inc.,
who is a cookbook author and caterer to the stars. Now I knew this
was an unlikely business for me, since I'm one of those sisters you
hear the brothers talking about. (And I'm not ashamed to admit
it—I'm not into cooking.) But it brings me to an important point
when starting a business: Whatever business *you* decide to start,
make sure you are passionate about the service or product you

offer. Otherwise you will not succeed. Notice I was tempted into those other fields, but I stuck with what I love—finance (and book writing!). Everyone on this planet has a purpose and once you find it, you will see your life change dramatically.

In this chapter, I'll help you find your purpose and turn your burning desire into action. You'll also meet Connie Harper, a fictional, "want-to-be" Sister CEO. She has the burning desire but not enough information to get started. I will present Connie in the earliest days of her dream of owning her own business. After she takes the Sister CEO Profile Quiz, we'll determine whether or not she's ready to be a Sister CEO and then identify the right business for her by finding what she's passionate about doing. Her start-up business will be interwoven throughout the subsequent chapters.

It's important to hear from people still on the rise as well as to hear the advice of the "arrived" Sister CEOs. It places you right at the kitchen table, learning first-hand how these Sister CEOs turned their idea into a business.

If you've read other self-help books, I'm sure you've read that entrepreneurship isn't for everyone. I disagree. While it is true that not everyone has the initial expertise to run a business, if you are an intelligent person—and I assume you are because you bought this book—you can learn what you need to know to get started and to manage a business. There is an array of information available on "how to run a business." The public library and now even the Internet are overflowing with sources. And I've listed additional resources in the back of this book. I *can* guarantee that you *will* make mistakes, and you may even fail once or twice, but that's part of the game. When that happens, you pick yourself up, swallow your pride, and move on. If Sister CEOs Jameela Bragg of E-Scent-Ials Body Care shop and Kathryn Leary of The Leary Group allowed their setbacks to keep them down, you wouldn't be reading about them today. In chapter 16, you'll read how these and other Sister CEOs overcame their business setbacks and once again turned their companies into profitable enterprises.

## Are You Ready to Go It Alone?

Connie Harper, executive assistant at a local bank in Atlanta, has dreamed of owning her own business for a year now. She's been with the bank for over ten years. Promotions have not been forthcoming and now there is talk the bank may begin laying off employees over the next couple of months.

Connie was bitten by the entrepreneurial bug at a Black Expo conference, where she met black women and men selling products that ranged from the works of black artists to beautiful African clothing. After talking to some of the vendors, she realized it wasn't as difficult as she'd thought, and that maybe she *could* start the business of her dreams—a spa and bath products mail-order company. She even had a name ready: "Body St. Lucia," inspired by the name of the Caribbean island where she'd vacationed last summer. Connie recently read that home-based businesses are the wave of the future. Now, if she only could get started. Maybe she could start her business part-time at home.

Connie is now on her way to joining over 7 million women across the country who have decided to take control of their lives through entrepreneurship. Unfortunately, as African American women entrepreneurs, we're barely scratching the surface. Out of the 1 million businesses started in 1995, only 30,000 were started by African American women.

So we have a lot of catching up to do, and we're making a start, according to Etienne Le Grand, executive director of the San Francisco-based nonprofit Women's Initiative for Self-Employment (WISE). WISE trains low-to-moderate-income women in San Francisco and Oakland in how to start their own businesses, and the organization is seeing an influx of women of color into its program. "The interest in being more independent through being a business owner is increasing," says Le Grand. "The timing is right and the economy fuels it because jobs aren't as plentiful as they used to be, so people are looking for alternative ways to make a living." Le Grand is also seeing a jump in women between the ages of forty and sixty who are candidates for early retirement packages from downsizing corporations. They are entering the program to assess their skills, think through their business ideas, and evaluate their capacity to use a portion of their buy-out money as seed financing for their own businesses.

For women who don't have access to capital, WISE has a non-traditional-Criteria Micro-Lending Program. The loans are available as start-up capital and range between $500 and $5,000. What's non-traditional about the loan is that when WISE evaluates the application, it looks at a person's character and integrity as well as the amount of assets available for collateral.

Programs such as WISE are available in almost every major city. As a Sister CEO you must take advantage of every available resource out there to help you to become self-sufficient through self-employment. I will discuss these types of programs further in chapter 8 ("Money, Money, Money"), and have listed a few of them in the appendix. I also explain how to locate the program(s) nearest you.

## Do You Have What It Takes?

Starting a business doesn't happen overnight. It requires careful planning, well-thought-out strategies, confident skills, and the strength to succeed. First and foremost, you must have a strong desire and the motivation to succeed in your own business. Without these qualities in place it will be far too easy for you to give up when the going gets tough. You must also be able to take rejection. When you are in business there may be many days when the door is slammed shut in your face because you're black and a woman. But that's okay, because when one door shuts a bigger and better door will always open.

Stamina and the ability to work on five or more tasks simultaneously are other important skills you will need to have in running your own business. There will be days when you will feel overwhelmed and find it hard to juggle the gazillion things you need to do. But this is what comes with the territory of being a successful Sister CEO.

These are only a few of the skills that make a Sister CEO successful. I'll address more in forthcoming chapters, but you can now see if you have what it takes. Set aside some quiet time and take the soul-searching Sister CEO Profile Quiz that follows. Look over your answers. Do they discourage or motivate you? Are there more yes's than no's? Compare your answers with those of Connie Harper, the aspiring Sister CEO who is ready to begin her journey toward self-empowerment.

Are you ready to become a Sister CEO? If you have some doubt after taking the test, don't become discouraged. Feel free to expand on the yes/no answers, as Connie does. Continue reading on and take the quiz again after you've completed the book. You may find that your answers change once you have a better understanding of how to start your own business.

## SISTER CEO PROFILE QUIZ

|  | YES | NO |
|---|---|---|
| 1. Do you believe you can earn money in your own business? | _____ | _____ |
| 2. Are you an independent person, and not afraid to go in one direction while others go in another? | _____ | _____ |
| 3. Do you believe your past failures will not prevent success in your own business? | _____ | _____ |
| 4. Do you believe in yourself? | _____ | _____ |
| 5. Does the cost of starting a business scare you? | _____ | _____ |
| 6. Do you know how to set goals, and persist until you have achieved them, even if you make mistakes along the way? | _____ | _____ |
| 7. Are you able to persevere when the going gets tough? | _____ | _____ |
| 8. Are you an organized person? | _____ | _____ |
| 9. Are you afraid your family will complain about your business? | _____ | _____ |
| 10. Do you have knowledge or experience |  |  |

in the business you're thinking of
starting?

11. If not, are you willing to take time to
learn what is necessary to succeed? _____ _____

12. Are you willing to make changes in
your lifestyle? _____ _____

13. Do you have some ideas about
where to go to obtain professional
help to get your business up and
running? _____ _____

14. Are you wiling to make personal
sacrifices? _____ _____

15. Have you or any of your family
members ever been entrepreneurs? _____ _____

16. Are you willing to network and learn
from other Sister CEOs? _____ _____

17. Are you a good money manager? _____ _____

18. Are you willing to take your time, start
small, and expand as you go along? _____ _____

19. Do you have good "people" skills—
that is, can you communicate with
and direct others? _____ _____

20. If need be, are you flexible enough
to make swift changes in your business
goals if the market or economy
dictates? _____ _____

21. Do you have the desire, motivation,
drive, energy, and patience to make
your business work even if you're
earning less money initially? _____ _____

22. Do you have an optimistic attitude? _____ _____

## PROFILE SCORE SHEET

1. YES; without a doubt, I feel like I can earn money in my own
business.

2. YES; my mom said I always was hard-headed.
3. YES; my past failures are behind me. I will not allow them to stop me from succeeding in my own business.
4. YES; sometimes. I need a little movement in this area.
5. YES; like most people, I'm afraid to lose my hard-earned money too.
6. YES; I finished college—I'm proud to have accomplished that.
7. YES; I will believe in my business and I understand there will be up and down cycles.
8. YES; when I set a goal I make a detailed game plan to help me stay focused.
9. YES; but they'll stop complaining when the extra money starts rolling in.
10. NO; but I plan to gain the knowledge by visiting the public library and other small business centers in my city
11. YES; I will spend time at the public library researching my business idea. I'll also seek business advice from successful black women entrepreneurs in my area.
12. YES; talking on the phone and watching television will become less important.
13. YES; I'll start with small-business centers.
14. YES; I understand, in the beginning, it will be next to impossible to do it all.
15. YES; my grandfather used to own two grocery stores.
16. YES; I'll start with my sorority.
17. NO; money management is not one of my strengths. I'll seek outside consulting.
18. YES; In the beginning I'll start my business part-time and keep my full-time job. The money I make from the business will be reinvested back into the company for expansion.
19. YES; I think I do. I used to work in the customer service department at the bank.
20. YES; I will stay open to new business ideas.
21. YES; I will do whatever it takes.
22. YES; I always see the glass as half full instead of half empty.

## SISTER CEO SUCCESS STORY
### *Audrey Rice Oliver*
INTEGRATED BUSINESS SOLUTIONS, INC.
SAN RAMON, CALIFORNIA

Audrey Rice Oliver is Sister CEO extraordinaire and my hero, and a woman who doesn't believe in the word "No." When faced with a challenge, she finds a way around it. "You have to if you want to succeed in your own business," says Oliver. "I was a single mother raising three children, but I didn't allow that to deter me." After twenty-three years, the success she envisioned has finally arrived. Oliver is the CEO and founder of Integrated Business Solutions, Inc., a multimillion-dollar computer company that provides software development, management and technical consulting services, and systems integration to small and *Fortune* 500 companies.

"My parents taught me there was nothing that I could not accomplish if I put my mind to it," states Oliver. She continues to live and work by that philosophy. Her five-year-old firm employs 50 and has grown in revenues from $500,000 in 1989 to $10 million in 1995, with four offices in the San Francisco Bay area and Chicago.

Oliver decided entrepreneurship was for her after working several years as a secretary for the Denver Transportation Department. She was the first black woman to own and operate a men's shoe store in Denver, Colorado. She posted annual sales of $150,000. This venture helped her learn what a retail business is all about. Although she had to close it after three years when the economy slowed and major street construction occurred in front of her store, she still considers it a successful business because she gave it her all.

After the store closed she put her newly developed entrepreneurial skills into play when she returned to the Denver Transportation Department. There she developed a coloring book on transportation for school-age children—an idea that came to her after her children asked her what she did at work. Recognizing her creative work on this project, Oliver's supervisors chose her to head the minority business program for the Denver Regional Transportation District. This position took Oliver into a more sophisticated arena, where she quickly learned how to play with the "Big Boys." There she was responsible for teaching executives of minority- and women-owned businesses how to work with the federal government and its agencies.

After spending six years as a minority business specialist, Oliver was ready for a change. She left Denver for California to take a position as a customer information supervisor for the Alameda County Transit System, the bus company that serves Alameda and Contra Costa counties. In reality the job was a step down, but Oliver says that a Sister CEO sometimes finds it is necessary to take a step back in order to move forward. "It's a sacrifice," she says, "but it usually pays off in the long run." Oliver knew that it was just a matter of time before she would go into business for herself again. She was just waiting for the right moment. Two years later, in 1994, she was on the move again, and back into an area she knew best—as a minority business development coordinator for the East Bay Municipal Utility District (EBMUD) in Oakland, California. That's where she really got involved in computers and technology. She saw virtually no minorities nor women in the field of technology. After tracking the trends and networking with contractors, she knew it was the right time and the right place to be.

From this experience grew home-based Integrated Business Solutions, Inc. Although sole owner of the company, Oliver employed a person who knew a part of the business she did not— the technical side. Oliver is a firm believer that no one person knows everything, and that it is a mistake to go into business thinking you do. She advises Sister CEOs to understand what their strengths and weaknesses are and to surround themselves with the best people they can in areas where they are weak. She also advises entrepreneurs to start small and grow their businesses methodically. While growing her business, Oliver continued to work at EBMUD to support her family.

Oliver truly understands the problems a black woman faces trying to capitalize a business. When she walks into a bank they see her as black first, woman second, and businesswoman third, she says. When a white female goes into the bank, they see her as a woman first, a businessperson second, and a wife third. And although Oliver admits this problem will probably never go away, she advises women to remember what they had to do to get to where they are today. "We have always had to use every aspect of our resources available to us," she says. "We have succeeded, exceeded, and jumped over every obstacle that other people couldn't endure."

Oliver believes that as Sister CEOs we need to reconnect with our spiritual intuition and principles and use them in our everyday lives—that these are the strengths of African Americans that have kept our families together and that can help our businesses survive as well.

## *Oliver's Advice to Sister CEOs:*

- Put yourself into a business mode and envision yourself in business. Don't worry if you don't have all the pieces in place.
- Become centered and focused on what you like and really want to do. If you don't know how to do something, then engage the services of someone who does. Become a risk taker. Don't believe in the word "No." If you run into a challenge, find a way to get around it.
- Find a niche and fill it—you'll find more opportunities. Oliver's shoe store catered only to men, carrying large sizes and unique imported shoes from Europe. Because of her specialty, she had famous athletes and entertainers as customers.
- Start your business from home and grow it slowly and methodically. If at all possible, obtain a start-up grant. Otherwise, begin saving money today from your 9–5 job to help you capitalize your venture.
- Research, research, research. Understand the business you want to go into inside and out.
- Reconnect with your feminine and spiritual intuition and principles. They're a Sister CEO's greatest strength. Use them positively to empower yourself and your business.

Oliver is right. In spite of the many barriers placed before the African American community, we are a strong group of people who have excelled in so many areas that it's beyond belief. That's why it is important that you read history books to learn about black men and women entrepreneurs, past and present. Let their accomplishments *then* motivate you *now*.

If you haven't taken the Sister CEO Profile Quiz on pages 7–9, take the time to do it now. It's the first of a series of action steps below designed to get you into the entrepreneuring mode. You'll be asked to take similar action steps after reading each chapter.

While you may have the personality to be a Sister CEO, let's see if you have what it takes to succeed. In the next chapter I will explain the traits and skills that are advantageous for a successful Sister CEO.

## Sister CEO Action Steps

1. Take the Sister CEO Profile Quiz: assess whether you are ready to become a Sister CEO.
2. Determine what are your best skills and consider partnering with someone who has skills you do not have.
3. Take Sister CEO Audrey Oliver's advice and begin to immediately put yourself into a business mode. Envision yourself owning a successful company.
4. Learn not to take rejections personally—it comes with the territory when you start your own business. Just remember: when one door closes, a bigger and better door will always open.

# Chapter 2

## Turning Dreams into Reality

Jumping in water so deep you don't know if you can
swim—that's what being alive is for me.

QUINCY JONES,
*chairman and co-CEO Quincy Jones/*
*David Salzman Entertainment*

Since the early days of slavery, black women have had to possess an
ironclad will and determination in order to survive the atrocities
that were inflicted upon them and their families. Many have *had* to
jump into water so deep, not knowing whether they would survive.
And yet, they did survive. This strength has been passed down
through the generations, with all black women still possessing
these traits today. Wake up, my sisters, and tap into your history.
Transfer this "strength to dare" into starting a successful business
of your own.

This chapter defines what it takes for a Sister CEO to succeed. It
defines the raw materials you will need to turn your ideas into
income and your dreams into dollars.

Whenever I'm ready to give up on a project, I recall the story of
the late Colonel Sanders, founder of Kentucky Fried Chicken. In
case you have not heard it, let me share it with you now.

At the age of sixty-five, Colonel Sanders was broke, alone, and
angry about receiving his first Social Security check, which didn't
amount to very much money. He had a chicken recipe that every-

## SISTER CEO SUCCESS STORY
### *Catherine Hughes*
RADIO ONE, INC.
WASHINGTON, DC

Catherine Hughes, Chief Executive Officer of Radio One, Inc., understands what it takes to succeed as a Sister CEO. As a former teenaged mom, she's now building a media empire to the tune of nine radio stations in the Washington, DC; Baltimore; and Atlanta areas.

"Confidence in yourself and the ability to persevere is what it takes," says Hughes. "Don't get hung up on racism and sexism. You know they exist. You also can't take them personally. If you do, they become occupational hazards."

Hughes knows all too well about perseverance. When she was trying to obtain a bank loan to buy her first radio station, she was turned down by thirty-two lenders, who, by the way, were all men. On the thirty-third try, Hughes lucked out with a brand new woman banker at Chemical Bank. It was the banker's first day on the job when Hughes walked into her office. After hearing her story and reviewing all the necessary paperwork, the woman took a chance and gave Hughes a loan of $1.5 million. "I never entertained the thought of giving up," says Hughes. "After the twelfth 'No,' it then became a challenge, and I was even more determined." Hughes feels those "Nos" were a blessing in disguise because practice made perfect. After repeating her presentation so many times, she could practically say it in her sleep. By the time she reached banker No. 33, she was fired-up and passionate about why she needed the money. She was able to answer every question and concern the banker had.

Hughes was actually quite fortunate that it didn't take her longer to get the loan. For many entrepreneurs it does.

one seemed to love, so he thought that if he sold his recipe to restaurants and showed them how to cook it, he could make some money. Well, unfortunately, not everyone liked his idea. They laughed in his face. To make a long story short, Colonel Sanders heard the word "No" 1,009 times before he heard his first "Yes." The rest, as you know, is history.

Although neither you nor I may look like Colonel Sanders, the perseverance principle he used to become successful is one we can use as well. So, when you hear the word "No"—and let me tell you, you *will* many times—think of the stories of Catherine Hughes and Colonel Sanders, and take it as a challenge.

I started this chapter with the trait of perseverance to immediately instill in you a "can-do" attitude. But it isn't by any means the only trait a Sister CEO needs.

## The Soul of Your Business

Because entrepreneurship is a fairly new arena for black women, some think we need to imitate the traditional route that white people—mostly males—have taken to running a successful business. I beg to differ. As we look at corporate America today, it does not take a rocket scientist to see that something isn't working right. What is the problem? Companies have lost their soul—their purpose. Those who run these companies care more about the bottom line than about the people who work for them.

So while the Sister CEOs in this book have the traditional business traits, they also possess spiritual traits. Their businesses have a soul and a purpose. They understand the need to reach back into their culture and to stay rooted and connected to their spirituality. That is why they—and their businesses—*are* successful.

It has only been within the last couple of years that I have understood the important part spirituality plays in business. Coming from "Wall Street," which is the ultimate white-male-dominated industry, I thought I had to be just like "them." I ran my money-management firm with an iron fist, only to find myself losing my feminine way of thinking. Yes, I was making a lot of money, but something was missing. I didn't have a sense of purpose. And I realized that making a lot of money was not enough to fulfill me. It was only after turning to books such as *Transform Your Life*, by Rev. Dr. Barbara King, and *The Dynamic Laws of Prosperity*, by Catherine Ponder, that I began to understand the principle of spirituality and business.

I tell my story to help you avoid the mistake that I made when I started my business—without a purpose and disconnected from my spirituality. That is why I call this section "the soul of your business." I firmly believe that, for you to be a true Sister CEO, you must first possess the following four spiritual traits: Faith, a sense of Mission and Purpose, Passion, and Intuition. Let's look more closely at each of these traits and how you can put them into practice.

## FAITH

### *Faith in a Higher Spirit: Prerequisite to Success in Business*

Faith is at the heart of your ability to turn your dream of self-employment into a viable reality. It fuels the drive, determination, and dedication demanded of a Sister CEO to overcome the personal and financial challenges she faces as she gets started.

How do you go about developing the kind of the faith you'll need to become a successful Sister CEO? You begin with: **Faith in a higher spirit**.

The challenge of being in business can become insurmountable and require you to seek advice outside of yourself. "This is the period when you Let Go and Let God and turn your fear into Faith," eloquently states Rev. Dr. King, noted author, founder, and minister of the Hillside Chapel and Truth Center in Atlanta, Georgia.

There will come a time while you are in business that you will need to "Let Go and Let God." It may be after you have lost a major client or when you can't meet your payroll that you will need to tune in to the higher spirit. Have faith that whatever challenge you are facing, "Everything *Is* Gonna Be Alright," when you "Let Go and Let God."

17

# SISTER CEO SUCCESS STORY
## *Janice Bryant-Howroyd*
### ACT.1 PERSONNEL SERVICES
#### LOS ANGELES, CALIFORNIA

Janice Bryant-Howroyd thanks faith in the Higher Spirit for her business success. Seven years ago, Bryant-Howroyd dedicated her sixteen-year-old human resource firm to God. She has made a deliberate spiritual commitment to acknowledging God as the center of her life and to abiding by spiritual principles. "Since this dedication, I now have a purpose, different goals for the firm, and inner peace," she says.

Bryant-Howroyd is the founder and president of ACT.1 Personnel Services, the largest minority/woman-owned employment service in the United States, specializing in both temporary and full-time placement. Her firm has twenty-three offices throughout the West, with future plans to expand to the East. Her client list reads like a Who's Who in business, and includes Toyota, Price Waterhouse, and AT&T. She's won numerous small-business awards, and her firm has recorded annual revenues in 1995 of more than $36 million.

Right from the very beginning, Bryant-Howroyd operated ACT.1 with precise and strategic marketing and business plans. She immediately developed the mission motto, "Pride in Performance," a goal which she instills in her employees and stands by with an unconditional guarantee of satisfaction. "Our success is directly attributable to our integrity of service," says Bryant-Howroyd. "We pay attention to both of our clients—the hiring company and the applicant. A good fit ensures survival."

## *Bryant-Howroyd's Advice to Sister CEOs:*

- Begin on a small scale, using personal savings if possible. Once the business begins generating money, reinvest profits back into the company.
- Learn how to start and grow your business by participating in

18

women's self-employment programs. Bryant-Howroyd herself is a graduate of the American Women's Economic Development (AWED) Management Program. "The AWED program has fine-tuned my management skills so that I can position our company for consistent growth," says Bryant-Howroyd. "Our goals for the company, though realistic, are much larger now."

- Give back to the community. ACT.1 gives back with college scholarships. So far, the firm has awarded sixteen students four-year college scholarships to historically black universities.
- Help other people achieve success. "You can get anything out of your life as long as you help get others what they want."

### *Faith in Yourself: Putting Hope Back into Your Life*

As I have travelled across the country speaking to black women, it disturbs me immensely that so many of us are giving up on our dreams. Seeing ourselves financially secure and in a career of our choice seems impossible. Why? Because we are tired of struggling, our self-esteem is low, and we've lost hope. And we have every right to feel this way. Mainstream America has ignored or dismissed the contributions black women have made to this nation. If it were not for magazines such as *Essence, Ebony, Black Enterprise*, and others, the recognition of blacks as sheroes and heroes would be nonexistent.

However, as black women, we're a group of headstrong sistahs. Once we begin to put hope back into our lives, there is so much we can accomplish. An excellent book to read on black women and self-esteem is *In the Company of My Sisters*, by Julia R. Boyd. Her book renews the spirit of black women and reminds us of how wonderful we truly are. So, if you are feeling low and think that there is no way in heaven you could start a business, read Boyd's and several of the other wonderful books I have listed in the appendix about black women tapping into their spirit. Put hope back into your life.

Success in business comes when, deep within your soul, you know that no matter what, you can achieve whatever you set out to do. You must look within to find your strength. You must be your own number-one fan, cheering yourself all the way to the finish line. Lack of faith in yourself is thus the main obstacle to achieving your goals in your business and personal life.

Faith in yourself comes from acknowledging all of your achievements and how you accomplished them. What are some of the things that you have done that at one time just didn't seem possible?

- Are you successfully raising or have you successfully raised your children?
- Are you earning or have you earned a degree?
- Are you purchasing or have you purchased your own home?
- Are you losing or have you lost weight or stopped smoking?

Remember the stumbling blocks and challenges that you have conquered, no matter how small, and put that same power to work in your life to help you remove the mental barriers to achieving business success.

Once a mental barrier is conquered, it becomes easy to do what you thought you couldn't do. As you will see from the stories in this book, the greater rewards go to the women who broke their barriers. Just remember that someone is always doing what someone else said could not be done.

Right now, list the five things in your life you would like to achieve for yourself today.

1. _____
2. _____
3. _____
4. _____
5. _____

List the five things you must *do* in order to make them happen.

1. _____
2. _____

3. _____

4. _____

5. _____

As you are raising your level of self-confidence to become a Sister CEO, be sure to build a support network. Recognize that every so often you'll need a booster shot of faith to keep your spirits and rekindle your enthusiasm.

Start with your family and friends for a pat on the back. Read inspirational stories about people who have faced and overcome similar obstacles. Network with other successful black women and ask how they overcame their initial insecurities. Challenges are lessons we must learn. When we begin to understand this, we can then move forward.

## A SENSE OF MISSION AND PURPOSE

> Everyone has a purpose in life . . . a unique gift or special talent to give to others. And when we blend this unique talent with service to others, we experience the ecstasy and exultation of our own spirit, which is the ultimate goal of all goals.
>
> DEEPAK CHOPRA, *author*

### What is your purpose?

The seventh law in *The Seven Spiritual Laws of Success*, by noted spiritualist Deepak Chopra, is the law of Dharma, which also means "Purpose in Life." According to this law, you are a special and unique person who has been put on this planet for a specific purpose. There is something that you can do better than anyone else. And once you discover that unique talent, you can combine it with your work and service to mankind to create unlimited wealth and abundance.

The demands of entrepreneurship require focus. And to find that focus you must take time to discover your purpose. Why start a business doing something you really don't enjoy? Ask yourself the following question: If you had no time constraints and money wasn't an issue, what would you do? From the answer you may find the type of business that is right for you. In the next chapter you'll learn how to find the right type of business for you, but now I want you to begin thinking about why you are here and what unique talents you have that you can share with others.

I also strongly suggest that your purpose be greater than just making money. We've "been there and done that" in the '80s, when we concentrated on success rather than fulfillment. Our visions of wealth and "keeping up with the Joneses" drove us to ignore our inner callings and to sell out to the highest bidder. Now we're paying the price. How many six-figure-income folks do you know who are stressed out, burned out, and on the fast track to nowhere? It's not worth the sacrifice. You'd better be darned sure you like what you are doing because, as a Sister CEO, you'll be working harder than you ever have before.

To stimulate your thinking on what your purpose might be, let me share with you my statement of purpose: *To empower African Americans economically by sharing financial and business information through my writings and speeches. And to teach them to become financially independent through entrepreneurship.*

As you can see, my purpose is specific and clear. So now when I find myself overwhelmed by projects, I stop and read this statement and ask myself whether a project fits into my purpose. If it doesn't, I eliminate it immediately.

Now it's your turn. Before you go one step further, write a brief statement of your purpose:

_____

_____

_____

Don't worry, your purpose is not written in stone. Life ebbs and flows, and you may need to modify it over time. More than likely you'll change it several times. The more you work with it, the sharper and more honed it will become. Soon it will be a unique definition of who you are. But, more importantly, your purpose will excite you and kindle the passion to make your dreams come true.

### Mission Statement

You're probably asking what the difference is between your purpose and a mission statement. In reality, not much. But for right now, I am using the mission statement in the specific context of a business. Most small businesses and corporations have a mission statement to define the aims and goals of the company. Top management wants to make sure everyone is on the same page, so to speak. A mission statement does build camaraderie among employees, boosts morale, and gives everyone a sense of purpose in working for the firm.

*Black Enterprise* magazine has a great mission statement. While visiting their headquarters in New York City, I spotted the statement on a plaque in an employee's office. It reads: "Our mission is to educate, inspire, and uplift our readers, and to show them how to thrive professionally, economically, and even spiritually." Regardless of whether you are Sister CEO of a one-person firm or have 1,200 employees, your business should have a mission statement. It gives your company direction and focus. Write your mission statement so that it clearly states what product or service you are offering, who your customers are, the goals of the company, and the quality of service and guarantee the firm will stand by. If you haven't started your business yet, write the mission statement based on what you would like your company to stand for. In fact, writing out this statement beforehand will actually help you to focus in on and create your ideal business.

Write your company's mission statement below:

_____

_____

_____

## PASSION

Purpose and passion together are a Sister CEO's secret weapon. The trick is to focus on the purpose and let it invoke your passion. For without passion for the product or service you offer, it's difficult to turn your business into a success. When you are passionate about your business, you are focused, intentional, and determined. Your mind, body, and heart all are moving in one direction toward the same goal. You feel energized and inspired.

We all have passion within us and the capacity to feel this intense emotional excitement. It's deep within the seeds of our soul. However, few of us *act* on our passions. Black women have buried their passions. We've allowed society to extinguish our spark of passion for fear of being labeled too aggressive. Instead we conform to their rules. For so many generations we have been a "let's get to it, get down to work, stop dreaming" group of women. As a result, we've stifled our passion and creativity. As a Sister CEO, you must rediscover the necessary tools to unlock your passion. Passion and dreams go hand in hand. Engage yourself in passionate thinking. It will turn your dreams into reality and propel your company to new heights.

Dorothy Brunson, Sister CEO of Brunson Communications, Inc., and owner of three television stations, admits to being a workaholic with a passion for business. For Brunson, being a Sister CEO is as exciting and challenging as being a great dancer or top-rated football player. "I love the feeling of winning," she says. "For me it's a thrill to be able to decipher an industry and make a profit. The black community would be healthier if successful business people were treated like sheroes and heroes and made into role models."

**INTUITION**

The final spiritual trait Sister CEOs employ in business is intuition. They make a habit of following their "hunches," "gut," or "mother wit" in business dealings. Barbara Bates, Sister CEO of Bates Designs, Inc., is learning to access her intuition and notes that it takes practice and lots of attention to listen to that quiet inner voice. "If I had not listened ten years ago, I would not have quit my secretarial job to pursue Barbara Bates Designs."

## SISTER CEO SUCCESS STORY
### *Barbara Bates*
#### BARBARA BATES DESIGNS
##### CHICAGO, ILLINOIS

Barbara Bates, fashion designer to such noted celebrities as Oprah Winfrey, Whitney Houston, Michael Jordan, Scottie Pippen, the Winans, and Sinbad, loves what she does and is happy she followed her "gut" in 1986. Unhappy and working as a secretary in corporate America, she knew she had a flair for design when her colleagues wanted her to make them clothes. "By wearing my own designs to work I was my own best advertisement," she recalls. Bates never had to worry about getting clients. She sold her clothes on the side in the women's bathroom. "Sometimes I literally sold clothes off my back."

Three months after leaving her job, and with the support of family and friends—and an uncanny sense of direction—Bates opened Barbara Bates Designs. The company has grown from four seamstresses to a staff of eighteen, exchanged cramped working quarters for a spacious 3,000-square-foot studio on Chicago's Gold Coast, and is a $1 million plus company with five-year annual sales projections of over $5 million.

From the very beginning Bates trusted her intuition. "I understand that building a successful business is very much like constructing a quality garment," she says. "Each requires hard work sparked with creativity, respect for valuable resources and the knowledge of how best to use them, an attention to detail that is unwavering, and a clear vision of what the market not only wants but also needs."

### *Bates's Advice to Sister CEOs:*

- Really believe in yourself, stay true to yourself, and follow your feminine intuition. Start your business right now. Keep going after what you want. Don't wait until everything is perfect. If you do, you'll never start. "People are always amazed that I'm a

25

fashion designer and I don't even sew. Just because you may not be an expert in the area doesn't mean you can't start a business in it. You can either find a partner or hire out."

- Love what you do. "Don't start a business thinking you'll become rich overnight. It won't happen. You must enjoy the business in order to stick with it."
- Have a strong business person on your staff, especially an accountant.
- Be your own best fan. There will be periods when you will want to give up, particularly when you're unable to meet your payroll. Bates remembers the many times when she was faced with that dilemma. "It was during this time I was given strength to think of creative ways to get my product out on the market and to bring in new money. Several times I pawned my jewelry. You just have to weather through it."
- Grow the business slowly and don't depend on bank loans when you're first starting out. Prove you are a successful business and then they will be ready to talk to you.
- Get yourself into an exercise program to relieve the stress of running your business.
- Get emotional support. "My girlfriends were always there for me when I needed support."

## The Traditional Traits: the Four A's of Success

While the spiritual traits bring soul into your business, the traditional traits pay the bills. They are the driving force behind your company's ability to make money. What are the four A's of success? **Attitude, ambition, assertiveness,** and **action**. These traits are the raw materials that make a Sister CEO. Alone, however, any one or two of the four A's are generally insufficient to create a successful Sister CEO. Fused, the four A's are a force of consequence.

## ATTITUDE

Yes, you *can* program yourself to become a successful Sister CEO.

You first begin with your attitude. Many of us undermine our chances for success by getting stuck in old negative-thinking habits. We have been so conditioned to think negatively that it has become an epidemic, and, worse, most of us are not aware that we're doing it.

But the good news is that positive-thinking habits are easily formed, and once they are set in our minds, we will find ourselves taking faster steps toward our goals and building success upon success in our business. We need only make the decision to program ourselves positively instead of negatively. The choice as to which way we want to go is pretty much left up to us.

Dr. Gwendolyn Goldsby Grant, Sister CEO, author, psychologist, and advice columnist for *Essence* magazine, says that too many black women program themselves for failure or they're too quick to accept the status quo. When we begin to accept failure for ourselves we develop a psychological blind spot—we don't see what we should be seeing. If you use this trait in your business, you'll see gloom and doom everywhere and won't notice the opportunities more positive competitors may be seizing. We have to consciously set our course for success. We also need to stay away from negative people, for they are contagious. Nothing can pull you down faster than a person that says, "Being a Sister CEO is crazy; you'll go broke."

Whenever you go against the grain, there's no shortage of people ready to put a hex on your potential success. So an important step in getting what you want is consciously to surround yourself with people who are positive.

A positive attitude has always been one of my strongest assets. I grew up in a family full of positive thinkers. My mother, grandmother, and aunts all had a "can-do" attitude that would knock your socks off. I never recall feeling as a child that there was anything I couldn't do. When I wrote my first book, *The Black Woman's Guide to Financial Independence*, I was told by several writers that major publishers would not touch the book because they consider African American book buyers to be a small market.

Yet, when I did my research and found there were 6 million black women in my target market, I didn't consider that to be *so* small. So my attitude was, well, if they aren't interested, I'll do it myself. So, instead of wasting precious energy and time sending out manuscripts to publishers, I bought a book on self-publishing and followed it step by step. Not once did the thought of not being able to do it enter my mind. When 30,000 copies of the book sold in three years, this project became a major boost to my attitude and confidence level—and the book was reissued by a major publisher! I don't tell you this story to boost my ego, but to show you the importance of a positive attitude—and how it can make a tremendous difference in whether or not you succeed or fail as a Sister CEO.

## AMBITION

> You've got to be hungry for it.
>
> LES BROWN, *author, motivational speaker*

Desire. Determination. Drive. . . . Ambition. Do you have the burning desire to start your own business? Are you so hungry for it you can virtually taste it? Are you willing to place all your energy, willpower, and effort behind your goal of becoming a Sister CEO? Once you start your business, will you be willing to sacrifice dinners out, vacations, new clothes? And last, are you willing to stand by your desire until it becomes the dominating obsession of your life, and stick with it until it becomes a reality? These are thought-provoking questions you need to ask yourself to determine if you have the ambition to run your own business.

Sister CEOs are ambitious and get mileage out of their ambition. They are cravers of end results. They don't necessarily crave the money they ultimately earn, but they are ambitious for something they consider worth striving for. They align their ambition with the other A's (attitude, assertiveness, and action) and go after what they want. These sistahs are willing to stretch themselves, bite the bullet, and put everything on the line.

Carol Jackson-Mouyjaris, Sister CEO of Biocosmetic Research Lab, manufacturer of Black Opal cosmetics, is standing by her desire to be the leader in the ethnic skin-care industry. In just two years after its introduction, the Black Opal line has a 33 percent share of the ethnic skin-care market, up from 7 percent in 1994—an astounding growth rate, averaging 250 percent per year.

---

## SISTER CEO SUCCESS STORY
### *Carol Jackson-Mouyjaris*
#### BIOCOSMETIC RESEARCH LAB
##### NEW YORK, NEW YORK

Carol Jackson-Mouyjaris, Sister CEO of Biocosmetic Research Lab, a manufacturer of beauty products—namely the Black Opal Skin Care Collection, the Black Opal Color Cosmetic line, and Black Opal for Men—is one of the most ambitious Sister CEOs profiled in this book. The three-year-old company had an estimated $8 million in sales in 1994.

Jackson-Mouyjaris, educated as an attorney, began her career as legal counsel to I. Natural, a chain of cosmetics stores. After observing the limited selection of cosmetics and skin-care products for black women, Jackson-Mouyjaris set out on a mission: to help black women take better care of their skin by offering a complete line of products made with their particular needs in mind.

Originally, Jackson-Mouyjaris's plans were to enter the cosmetics business. But after realizing the area was saturated, she shifted her focus to skin care. With the expertise of Dr. Cheryl Burgess, a certified dermatologist who treats skin disorders of black women and men, Jackson-Mouyjaris developed the Black Opal skin-care line for women and men.

Jackson-Mouyjaris, who started the business with personal savings, attributes her success to understanding her market and aggressively going after it. Prior to the launching of the Black Opal skin-care line, she spent four years studying market demographics and sizing up the competition. With the aid of research firms, she

---

conducted a series of consumer focus groups and in-home product tests.

After launch, she used advertising and an extensive mass-market distribution system to sell her products, and set prices affordable to her market. Her products are now sold in over 10,000 chain drug stores and discount variety stores, including Wal-Mart, Walgreen's, and Drug Emporium, at prices ranging from $5.95 to $11.95. Her media campaign includes advertising in black women's publications such as *Essence* and *Black Elegance*. The Black Opal for Men line was launched with a $2 million ad campaign starring Minnesota Vikings quarterback Warren Moon.

Now that she is recognized as a leader in the ethnic beauty market, Jackson-Mouyjaris is once again hoping to apply her Midas touch and reap the gold. With the debut of the Black Opal Color Cosmetics line, she is returning to her original dream of providing cosmetics to black women.

## ASSERTIVENESS

Assertiveness is the third traditional trait needed by Sister CEOs. I honestly believe this is a natural trait for black women. We had to be assertive in order to survive. But now many of us are afraid to assert ourselves for fear of being called a "Sapphire." We've allowed society to put a cap on our natural talent. Far too many of us don't earn anything near what we could in our careers because we are afraid to speak out. Yet being assertive is essential for black women in business. It is the "gutsiness" and "spunk" that will transform your home-grown business into a multimillion-dollar corporation.

Assertiveness alone is like attitude or ambition alone—not enough. Many black women are assertive but accomplish nothing. Guts without goals or guts without self-confidence usually leads to a mean-spirited black woman. However, when assertiveness combines with ambition and a positive mental attitude, an awesome trio exists. Here emerges the black woman with a can-do spirit, unwavering focus, and the guts to tread where others fear to tiptoe.

Black women need not apologize for their assertiveness. We must be forceful in order to succeed. Every time we speak up, we strengthen ourselves. Remember, we *do* come from a line of street-smart survivors.

## ACTION

> Don't put off until tomorrow what you can do today.
>
> BENJAMIN FRANKLIN

Up to this point, you know you have all the traits needed to become a Sister CEO. Now ask yourself, Am I a self-starter? Will I follow through on the steps I need to take to become a Sister CEO? Am I a woman who can get results, or I am just a talker?

All these questions have one aim: to find out if you are a woman of action. The most important trait a Sister CEO must have is the ability to take action.

Having an excellent idea for your business isn't enough. Millions of us toy with the ideas. We toy but don't try, or we don't try long enough to get the payoff. There is no real action, no long-range follow-through. Many of us talk, talk, and talk about making more money or having this great idea for a business, but we don't turn the words into business plans, a real product—or money. Instead we procrastinate and complain on and on about how we dislike our jobs or how we don't have enough money to get a business off the ground. We bury our ideas because we are afraid to act on them. And we pay for that decision over a lifetime by constantly telling ourselves, I coulda, woulda, shoulda. Like the boxer in the movie *On the Waterfront*, we say, "I coulda been a contender."

Sister CEOs who live their dreams are those who stop considering all the angles, weighing the pros and cons, and just go and do it. They understand that they can daydream about making more money, but if they aren't willing to stick their necks out and set things in motion, becoming financially empowered through their own efforts is an elusive dream. They may not always be "in the mood" when they begin, but they do it anyway. They know that without action there is no change. Without change there is no excitement. Without excitement life becomes dull and monotonous and we become boring.

These four traits are prerequisites for success in your own business, but you don't need all of them in full supply before you begin. Far too many black women have the misconception that they have to be in the right frame of mind before they can start. "I must feel more confident before I start my own business," they tell themselves. Does this sound like you? If it does, it's time for a change. You can't sit around waiting for your feelings and attitude to change *before* you act. Studies have shown that the most expedient way to change how you think about something is to take action. Once you set the wheels into motion, you will notice immediately that you feel better and you begin achieving your goals.

Yvette Lee Bowser, Sister CEO of Sister Lee Products, producer of the hit sitcom *Living Single*, advises black women to become doers and not to be afraid to act on their visions. Bowser isn't a newcomer to the TV business. She's been writing for television for over eight years. It was as an apprentice on the *Bill Cosby Show* that she won recognition for her work and subsequently became the producer of *It's a Different World*. If you want to write and produce television shows, you can't sit around waiting for someone to notice you. Bowser says, "You need to keep writing scripts, let people know you are out there, and learn everything you can about television production. Sometimes all it takes is for one person to recognize you. When that happens, you need to seize the opportunity and make the best of the opportunity."

Right now, make up your mind to turn your idea into a business. Give your idea value by immediately acting on it. Regardless of how good the idea is, unless you do something with it, you get absolutely nowhere. Take small steps. Spend a weekend in the public library researching your product or market, or make an appointment with a banker to discuss the different small business loan options that are available. With neither of these steps are you spending money, yet you're gaining valuable knowledge. Once you begin to take concrete steps, you'll have an enormous sense of satisfaction that will recharge and rev up your energy to take more steps.

---

# SISTER CEO SUCCESS FORMULA:

ATTITUDE + AMBITION + ASSERTIVENESS + ACTION =

SUCCESSFUL SISTER CEO

Imprint this success formula deep in your mind. Better yet, write it down on a 3 x 5 index card and carry it in your wallet. Pull it out when when your two favorite sistahs, Ms Doubt and Ms Fear, come to visit. Affirm to yourself that you *can* become a Sister CEO.

---

## What It Takes in a Nutshell

In this chapter I have tried to give you a honest assessment of what it takes to become a Sister CEO. I hope I haven't scared you away. The most important point to remember is that it takes commitment. You really must want to do this if you plan to be successful. It's a lot of hard work but it's fun work when you have a purpose, a passion for your product or service, a willingness to persevere, a hunger for it, and, last but not least, a willingness to take the necessary steps—*action*. Begin today to put these six lessons to work:

**Lesson 1:** Setbacks prepare the way for comebacks. Sister CEOs who have extraordinary success don't crumble when they stumble. They know the difference between a delay and a defect, a detour and a denial. When they hear the word "No," it is a given that they can turn it into a "Yes."

**Lesson 2:** Have faith and count your blessings. When you're self-employed you need to maximize the positive aspects of your business and minimize any of the negatives. Once you begin to focus on all that isn't right about your business, it disheartens your spirit and dries up your creative juices. I firmly believe "like mind attracts like." Think of a time when you were in a negative state of mind. (It happens to the best of us.) Didn't you notice how everything seemed to be going wrong that day? It was because you were putting out negative vibes and they were being returned right back to you. How often have you walked into a retail store to make a purchase, or made a call to a business, and girlfriend behind the counter or on the phone had an "attitude problem"? Were you immediately turned off? Most people are, including your clients and customers, who probably won't return to your place of business. In spite of the challenges your business may be facing, make every effort to look daily at the brighter side. And be sure to teach your employees to do the same as well. It's a win–win situation for everyone.

**Lesson 3:** Live by the persistence principle. Sister CEOs who have the winning edge are tenacious in the pursuit of their goals. They understand that talent alone doesn't guarantee success. But, if it's combined with skill, it gives you the ability to persevere, which leads to success.

**Lesson 4:** Maintain your sense of humor. Try not to take everything so seriously. Use the therapy of laughter to lift your sagging spirits and to reduce any inner feelings of discouragement. Many black women, myself included, have "take charge," controlling, and perfectionist personalities, which are excellent traits for Sister CEOs. But sometimes when "stuff" is going every which way, these traits can get in the way and be detrimental to your business. If this is the case, step back and look for the humor in it, and laugh. You'll definitely feel better. It will also help you to release your tension, regain your focus, and get you back on your track toward success.

**Lesson 5:** Seize all opportunities regardless of the risks. A key ingredient of being a Sister CEO is having the ability to take a risk and plunge right in. Sometimes it may be necessary for you to put everything on the line and go for it. It may mean refinancing your house, or doing your own hair and nails for a year, in order to save money for the start-up capital to get your business off the ground.

**Lesson 6:** Get rid of Excusitis. We all have dreams, hopes, and aspirations for ourselves. However, fulfillment eludes many of us because we make excuses as to why it can't be done. Some of the common excuses we use for not starting our own business include: lack of time, worries about what other people will think and say, fear of failing, and the notion that we're too old. Most of our excuses are not valid and need to be put in their proper place. If you want to start a business, allow me to paraphrase the famous ad slogan for Nike shoes: "Get off your butt and Just Do It."

## Sister CEO Action Steps

1. List the five things in your life you would like to change today.
2. List the five things you must do to make the changes happen.
3. Write out your purpose. What are your unique talents or skills?
4. Write out a mission statement for your new or existing company. It will provide your business with direction and focus.
5. Write out two or more steps to take today to get your business started. For example, do research at the public library or call the women's self-employment program in your area for a free brochure.
6. Write down on a 3 x 5 index card the Sister CEO Success Formula (see page 33). Read it whenever you need to reinforce your commitment to be a Sister CEO.

# Chapter 3

## THE IDEAL BUSINESS FOR YOU TO START

To build the life you want, create the work you love.
MARSHA SINETAR, *author of*
DO WHAT YOU LOVE, THE MONEY WILL FOLLOW

Doing something you love and not having to answer to anyone but YOU! What could be better? Having meaningful work is basic to living an exciting and fulfilled life, but for many of us work means a dead-end job with little connection to who we are and what matters to us. One of the biggest complaints I hear from black women today is that they hate their jobs. Why? Because corporate America too often underutilizes your talents, keeping you from working at your fullest potential. This scenario doesn't look like it will change anytime soon. Therefore, *you* have to make the choice to make your work more challenging, stimulating, and joyful. *You* have to make the decision to turn your unique skills into money. *You* have the power to make yourself happy, regardless of your personal obstacles, age, past history, or past failures—and it's never too late to start.

The idea of starting a business is the dream of many black women who work 9 to 5. The key, though, is finding a business to suit your lifestyle and personality while it maximizes your existing experience and contacts. This will bring you professional and personal happiness.

## Loving What You Do Is the Key to Financial Success

Sister CEOs have discovered that starting their own businesses can be spiritually and financially therapeutic. Many set out initially in search of happiness, not money. But many learn that doing what they love can make them prosperous, too—and, ultimately, financially secure.

Successful Sister CEOs have found that owning their own company becomes a central part of their life. They actually look forward to going to their offices each day—whether it is in a smartly decorated suite on Madison Avenue or a small office in the corner of the bedroom. By owning their own company, they see themselves as appreciated, productive, creative, and contributing members of the community.

In this chapter you will learn how to dream again and find the business that will bring you satisfaction and fulfillment.

To discover the business you want to start, complete these two revealing exercises:

### DISCOVERING WHAT YOU LOVE TO DO: DREAM EXERCISES

### Exercise I: Discovering what you love to do
1. Write down as specifically as you can what your ultimate career and personal dreams are and what you want to accomplish in your life.
2. Write down what impact you want to have on the African American community.
3. Write down your financial dream.
4. Write down your fun dream.
5. Write down your spiritual dream.
6. Write down your family dream.

### Exercise II: Designing a business that makes you happy
1. Do you want your business to help you to grow and discover new things?
2. Are you willing to devote all, most, or some of your effort to this business?

3. Is it important that the business provide you with fun?
4. Do you want to work alone, or with a partner, or with several people?
5. Is it important that your business make a difference in the black community?
6. Is it important that you become rich?
7. Is it important that you spend a lot of time with family and friends?
8. List five things you are good at doing.
9. List your strengths/weaknesses.
10. List the skills and tools you have today that can help you earn money.
11. List ways you are willing to make owning your own business a reality.
12. List your favorite work activity.
13. List your favorite hobby activity.
14. List your favorite social activity.
15. List your favorite sport activity.
16. List your favorite education activity.
17. List your favorite recreation activity.
18. List your favorite indoor activity.
19. List your favorite outdoor activity.
20. If you're married, will your spouse give you the support you need for your business?
21. Are you a good organizer?
22. Are you good at keeping records?
23. Do you balance your checkbook?
24. Do you make decisions quickly?
25. Do you have a "stick-to-it" attitude?
26. Choose the phrase that best describes you;
    A) Not afraid to take risks
    B) Willing to take some risks
    C) Not willing to take any risks

Now that you have completed both exercises, you are one step closer to finding out what you love to do. Based on your answers, jot down five businesses you would consider starting. Get creative. Don't worry if the business seems silly or impossible. There may be a variety of businesses you could start based on that one idea. The key is to get your ideas on paper, while they are fresh in your mind so please do it right now. Later in the book you'll learn how to turn these ideas into real businesses.

The businesses I would like to start:

1. _____

2. _____

3. _____

4. _____

5. _____

## SISTER CEO SUCCESS STORY
### *Carol Columbus-Green*
#### LARACRIS INC.
##### CHICAGO, ILLINOIS

Carol Columbus-Green, Sister CEO and founder of Laracris Inc., loves her business to the tune of $3.5 million in annual sales. She is galvanizing the intimate apparel market with Aubergine Collections, a line of sexy, body-contouring lingerie, and BodySynchers activewear. A former professional model turned entrepreneur, Columbus-Green was inspired to start her business back in 1989 after she was unable to fit into a slinky velvet dress following the birth of her second child. "Even though I had lost the forty pounds I'd gained, I still had this little tummy," she says. When she checked department stores for girdles, all she found were large sizes and frumpy styles. She then decided to design her own and find a manufacturer. "They all laughed at me. They said, 'Forget it. Lace, colors, small sizes won't sell.' " But not one to give up easily, Columbus-Green, who didn't have a background in design or sewing, ignored their warnings. She decided that if no one would listen to her, she would strike out on her own. And that she did.

But not without doing her homework. After intensive market research, what she found was worse than she imagined. According to Columbus-Green, the industry was dominated by men who knew nothing about the needs of women or about control-type lingerie. The market consisted of basically two types of products: lingerie that offered no support, or unflattering and unattractive girdles. Columbus-Green knew this was an untapped market waiting to be mined.

Her instincts were right. With financial backing from her physician husband ($200,000), Columbus-Green hired a seamstress and bought yards of colorful spandex, lace, and elastic. With panty girdle in hand, she contacted the lingerie buyer at Marshall Field's department store, who was immediately impressed and ordered seventeen of them to test. At about the same time, a local newspaper ran a story about Columbus-Green and her lingerie. Several Marshall Field's customers stormed the lingerie department, and the store begged Columbus-Green for more. Today, her lingerie is sold at Neiman Marcus, Saks Fifth Avenue, Bloomingdale's, and Nordstrom. And if you don't want to go to the stores, you can find her lingerie on QVC, the popular home-shopping network, or directly from her mail-order catalog, *Inner Circle*.

She's been seen on the Oprah Winfrey show and on CNN. And her famous customers include the rap group Salt-n-Pepa, who wore the garments in one of their music videos, and Valerie Simpson of Ashford and Simpson.

Despite her success, Columbus-Green is still hungry, with big plans for expansion. International expansion, that is. She has a licensing deal with a Japanese company to produce and sell smaller-sized Aubergine shapewear to outlets in Japan, Taiwan, and Korea. She also has a new product: Complexion Perfection, which is a line of flesh-toned shapewear designed to complement fair-, medium-, and brown-skinned women.

Carol Columbus-Green is a true Sister CEO pulling out all the stops.

## Columbus-Green's Advice to Sister CEOs:

- First and foremost do your research and know your market. Talk to the owners of companies with similar products. They can provide you with good information to help get you started. (Columbus-Green contacted Carol Wior, creator of the Slim Suit body-slimming swimwear—a total stranger she had read about in a Chicago newspaper. "It took me a few days to get her on the phone, but I just kept calling," she says. "I used to sleep by the telephone! I guess she finally said, 'I better talk to this crazy person so she'll stop calling.' ")
- As black women we have a double negative, and people don't take us seriously. So don't start your business without a business plan. And make sure it is thorough. "My business plan was so good, the first banker thought I didn't do it."
- On money: "It's close to impossible to get a loan from a bank. I know I've been blessed. . . . Black women need to search out every avenue possible to obtain money."
- On children: "My children are my No. 1 priority. I take them to and pick them up from school and sometimes bring them to the office. Don't allow the fact that you have children stop you from starting a business. There is a way to do both and balance it out."
- Black women need to realize that when they are in business there will be tough times ahead. At that time, turn within and ask the higher spirit for assistance. Spirituality is very important in business.
- Black women need to network and help each other in business. And stop being so "catty." It causes divisiveness and we can't get ahead.
- Keep focused on your goals and never give up.

## Sister CEO Action Steps

1. Complete Exercise I: Discovering what you love to do.
2. Complete Exercise II: Designing a business that makes you happy.
3. Based on your answers from the exercises list five businesses you may want to start.

# Chapter 4

## GOALS—THE KEY TO YOUR BUSINESS SUCCESS

*Achieving the goal isn't half as important as setting it.*
ANTHONY ROBBINS,
*author, motivational speaker*

"I want to make a million dollars! I want to have a store in every state! I want to own my own bank! I want to be on the cover of *Black Enterprise* magazine and listed as one of its 100 most successful businesses!" When Sister CEOs launch their businesses, they usually have a specific goal in mind. It might be wealth, fame, or market domination. Regardless of what their goal is, they start with a clear picture of what they want to achieve in their business and personal life and then determine the steps they must take in order to make it happen.

Oftentimes, we get so caught up in the rat race that we have only two goals: to pay the rent and to keep our car from being repossessed. Sure, we would like more money and the respect of others, but few of us are prepared to commit the time or effort to write down our goals and draw out a strategic road map for our future.

I've been an advocate for setting and writing down goals for many years. When I work with clients and their money and speak to organizations on money management, I always emphasize the importance of having written goals, both personal and professional. It makes all the difference in the world when you have focus and know what direction to move in. It helps with managing money and it will also assist when you are running your own company.

Harriet Michel is president of the National Minority Supplier Development Council in New York City, an organization whose primary goal is to assist women- and minority-owned businesses in becoming suppliers to major corporations. Michel states that the single biggest factor working against black-owned companies is that they are not focused and specific. "You need to be very precise and know who you want to supply and what you want to supply," she says. "Also, people start businesses before they are ready. You need to spend twelve to eighteen months doing your research and setting goals."

I bet you've already read something about the value of setting written goals. Have you taken time to do it yet? If you're like most people, probably not. Studies have shown that less than 5 percent of successful business owners nationwide have taken time to write out their goals in detail and develop an action plan to realize them.

Why don't we take time to write out our goals? Three reasons: First, we fear we'll fail to reach them. If they are written down, someone else may see them and will know if we don't achieve them. The second reason that we don't commit our goals to paper is because we don't have any, or at least not clear ones. Is this the case with you? If so, then you must make a decision right now to begin your journey of goal-setting. What *would* you do if money were no object? If you *could* spend your life doing whatever you wanted, what would that be? If you were told you only have twelve months to live, what would you want to do, see, and achieve in that time? Many of these questions you answered in preceding exercises. That's okay; ask yourself again and see if you come up with the same answers. Later on in the chapter I'll take you through a goal-setting exercise in which you'll be able to list both your personal and business goals. I want you to really understand what it is you want out of life and how having your own business will help you achieve it.

The third reason many of us do not set written goals is that no one has instilled in us the importance of doing it. Take it from me, if you don't take the time to complete the goal-setting exercises in this book, you will have little chance of getting where you want to go. How can you, without a road map? Make completing the exercises a fun project. Open your mind, exercise your fantasies, and allow yourself to stretch your imagination to the fullest. Write down anything and everything that comes to your mind; don't allow any limitations to creep in and sabotage your dreams.

## Setting Your Goals

As a black woman entrepreneur, what do you expect to get out of owning your own business? Do you want to be rich and famous or do you simply want to bring in $500 a month to pay extra bills? You must get specific and know exactly what it is you want. How do you find out?

Well, you've done a lot of the work already in the preceding exercises. By now you should know your purpose, what you're passionate about, and what type of business you want to start. The next step is to write out two lists of goals: personal and business. But before you start identifying these goals, let's go over the six components it will take for them to succeed:

1. The goals should be in line with your purpose and your business mission statement. When you set goals with these in mind, you have a better understanding of what you want, both in your conscious mind and your subconscious mind as well. Once your mind is specifically geared toward a certain target, it will do everything in its power to help you reach it. Because your mind knows exactly what you want, it is drawn to people and opportunities that will help you. You'll also find that when you set goals with your purpose in mind, opportunities and people will suddenly appear out of nowhere to help you reach them.

2. To succeed at goal-setting, you must be specific. If you want to start a business this year, don't just say, "My goal is to start a business this year." Write down everything about the business you can think of. Know the type of product or service

you will offer. Its color and price. How many employees you want your company to have. Break it down in detail so you know exactly what you will be aiming for.

Your mind can work wonders. It will do whatever you command it to do. If you tell it that your goal is to start a business, it will do everything in its power to help you start the business. If, however, you send it mixed messages—that you want the business and yet there are all these reasons why you can't do it—your mind will work overtime to provide you with all the excuses in the world why you can't start the business. Basically, your mind will do whatever you tell it to do. So use this powerful machine to your advantage and tell it your specific objectives. Just watch how quickly your goals will materialize.

3. Of course, the goals must be realistic. Don't expect to become a millionaire after only one year in business. Yes, it could happen—remember the "pet rock"? But chances are slim. It's better to start the business with reasonable goals; you're more likely to stick with it.

4. The goals must be achievable. If you want to go to Africa next month and you haven't saved up a dime, I don't think that's going to happen unless you have a rich uncle somewhere. One of the few "don'ts" I have is: Don't set yourself up for failure by naming goals no one could realistically achieve. Life is hard enough already, and you'll be making it harder. Don't go there.

5. Ask yourself whether you are willing to make the necessary sacrifices. If you aren't, forget about achieving your goals. You won't be successful. It takes working smart and delaying gratification. You have to be committed.

6. Your goals must be measurable. You need to set goals that will allow you to check your progress toward them. For your intangible goals (those you cannot physically see), set up a scale to track your progress by time, income, or some other appropriate measure, such as the number of new customers your business acquires over the course of a year.

Now that we have the important points out of the way, let's have some real fun by writing out a list of our personal, business, and financial goals. This is and will forever be my favorite part of business planning. I've always enjoyed setting goals and seeing them turn into reality. It's a wonderful feeling to know that you are in control of the things that happen in your life.

At the beginning of every new year I spend at least an hour of quiet time alone writing out my personal goals and devising a plan to achieve them. In the past many of them have come true because I was focused and knew exactly what I wanted. For my business, my partner and I spend a day in our conference room mapping out our business goals and a strategic plan to reach them.

Many companies go way out to plan their business goals. They meet annually at a luxury hotel, retreat, or health spa to have a business planning session. It must be nice. Well, at least we have something to look forward to as we turn our businesses into multi-million-dollar corporations.

In order to plan effective goals you must set them in stages. First, think about long-term goals of five or more years. These are the things that you ultimately hope to achieve. The next level is the mid-range goals. These are goals you want to reach in one to five years. Finally, you will develop short-term goals of a year, a month, a week, and even of a day. If you follow this method, you'll begin with your ultimate goal and then work backward to see what steps you need to take in order to reach the top.

Let's get started formulating your goals right now. Do the following exercises with the perspective that these goals are not set in concrete. You can and should revisit them throughout the year so you can add, delete, or update them.

## LONG-TERM GOALS

First, find a new spiral notebook or three-ring binder with blank paper, and a quiet place where you can work uninterrupted for approximately one hour. If you can find a place outdoors, all the better. Being in nature tends to have a calming effect, helping you to think more clearly. On the top of the first sheet in your notebook write the words "long-term personal goals" and on the second sheet write "long-term business goals." On each sheet write down fifty things you want to own or accomplish in the next five to ten years. Don't worry about how much it will cost or what you think your chances of achieving them are. Don't think long and hard, just let your mind flow, and write. Don't stop until you have fifty down on each paper.

Now go back through both lists and number the ten most important goals on each, with number one being the most important and number ten the least important. These goals should be those accomplishments that will fulfill your ambitions and provide you with a real sense of achievement. Write the goals below and set a date you plan to reach it:

*My top ten long-term* personal *goals are:*

*Date I will achieve each goal:*

1. _____          _____
2. _____          _____
3. _____          _____
4. _____          _____
5. _____          _____
6. _____          _____
7. _____          _____
8. _____          _____
9. _____          _____
10. _____         _____

*My top ten long-term* business *goals are:*

*Date I will achieve each goal:*

1. _____          _____
2. _____          _____
3. _____          _____
4. _____          _____
5. _____          _____
6. _____          _____
7. _____          _____
8. _____          _____
9. _____          _____
10. _____         _____

## SHORT-TERM GOALS

Often, long-term goals seem so far away that they appear unreachable. To avoid becoming overwhelmed by this, break the goals down into short-term goals. This will make them seem more manageable and help you reach them more quickly.

What's also nice about short-term goals is that they encourage you to set priorities. For example, if your long-term business goal is to start a food catering business, your short-term goal could be to attend a seminar on trends in the food industry so that you can understand the types of foods you will need to prepare in your business. If your long-term personal goal is to attend the African American Women on Tour conference in Miami, Florida, your short-term goal could be to open a savings account earmarked for the conference and put fifty dollars in the account every time you get paid. By starting small and close to home you can inexpensively and quickly start off toward your ultimate goal.

Each short-term goal that you reach is another step up the ladder to achieving your top goal. Although your goal may seem far away, every step you take allows you to see where you are going much more clearly. The clearer your goals are, the closer they will seem.

Also, break your short-term goals down into daily goals to help keep yourself on track. Every day, write down a goal for that day. It must be something that will help you reach your major goal. Make it specific and reachable. Watch out too for activities that will *not* help you to reach your goals. For example, spend your lunch hour at the public library researching ideas for your business instead of going with your coworkers to the shopping mall across the street.

## FINANCIAL GOALS

Setting specific financial goals for your business as well as your personal life is extremely important. Get rid of your moneyphobia if you have one. It's *okay* to make a lot of money, and it's double okay to save it! Remember, we want our business to help us reach financial independence. Write out your financial goals below and continue to update when necessary.

## FINANCIAL GOALS EXERCISE

Business Income Goal for
(Name of Business)
1. By_____I want to earn $_____ per year.
   (Date)
2. By_____I want my business to earn $_____ per year.
   (Date)

## Pat Yourself on the Back

Whether long-term or short-term, reaching your goals is a monumental task and you deserve to reward yourself for achieving them. Especially the short-term goals. When you see yourself reaching these goals it gives you the confidence to move forward and reach for the others.

You don't have to go overboard and buy or do something extravagant. Make it simple and inexpensive; buy yourself a new pair of earrings or have a massage. When you hit the big goal, then it really is time to celebrate; but for now, make it a small gift to yourself. Sign a contract with yourself: As you write down specific short-term goals, also include the name of the small reward that will become due and payable once each goal is reached. The more challenging the goal, the larger the reward.

Rewarding yourself is an important step. It focuses your mind on the delightful outcome that reaching your goal will bring instead of all the hard work it will take to get you there.

## Keep Your Goals Alive

You should reassess your goals three to four times a year and adjust them if need be. Your life is in ever-changing motion, and as you move forward toward your goals, things will happen that may necessitate changing them. Some of the things may make it easier to reach your goals; others may make it harder. The key is to stay flexible and reprioritize your goals on a regular basis.

Each week, write your daily goals for the week in your journal, Daytimer, or your computer organizer. Look at them constantly and put pressure on yourself to achieve them. And remember, the clearer your goals are, the harder your mind will work on reaching them.

Another great way to reinforce your efforts is to visualize yourself reaching the goals. What you think is what you get. Visualization is the process of creating pictures in your mind, giving form to your thoughts so you can easily direct them toward a specific goal. "Seeing" yourself already in possession of your goal has a major impact on your subconscious mind. Successful athletes have used this technique for years to win major competitions, and studies have shown people with illnesses turn their lives around after visualizing themselves healthy and well. You can use this same technique to achieve your business and personal goals.

Following is a short course on the technique.

### *Four Short Steps to Visualization*

1. Choose the goal. Once again, I recommend that it be in line with your purpose or mission statement.
2. See the goal in your mind. You need to be relaxed for this step because it helps focus the picture more clearly. Think of it as similar to looking at a movie: you are on the outside looking at the big picture. Bring it into sharp focus. Enliven the color and notice the details. Make sure you are in the picture as well, or your subconscious mind will not know whom the picture is for.
3. Use all your senses in the visualized picture. Get right inside and feel it happening. Experience the joy and excitement of seeing your goals come alive. The more you put your emotion into the picture, the better the visualization works, because it is the emotional experience that imprints the movie on your mind and helps bring the image to life.
4. Believe that the visualization will work. If you don't believe that it will work, or if you have a negative attitude about it, the picture more than likely will not develop. Trust in your ability to visualize, and in the power of visualization. It works!

Are you now motivated to set your personal and business goals? Resolve now to set long- and short-term goals. You need direction and focus on your road to becoming a Sister CEO. For a recap, see the sixteen strategies on pages 54–55 for successful goal fulfillment.

## SISTER CEO SUCCESS STORY
### *Diane Richardson*
#### RCI FINANCIAL
##### LANHAM, MARYLAND

A major financial empire is slowly being built under the visionary and spirited leadership of Diane Richardson, Sister CEO of RCI Financial, a $10 million, 1,200-agent financial services firm whose mission is to break into the *Black Enterprise* 100 successful businesses list.

Richardson, a former banker and college basketball athlete, attributes her success to her spiritual commitment to God and family, and to her mission to train and educate people who know nothing about finances to become financial planners. "Most of our agents come from families who didn't talk about finances over the dinner table, or who know of someone in their family that retired broke!" Richardson says. "I understand, because I've been there. If it weren't for my basketball scholarship, I would not have had the opportunity to acquire an education, because my parents—like most of the folks I knew—didn't think about my college education until I was a senior in high school."

However, Richardson's move into entrepreneurship came out of the necessity to earn extra money to pay for therapy for her first daughter, who was born with cerebral palsy. While working for the Women's Bank in Washington, D.C., she began selling insurance and annuities part-time on commission during her lunch hour. After much success, she realized she could make more money if she devoted her efforts full-time to this venture, so she launched RCI Financial as a home-based business eleven years ago. Later her husband and brother joined the business as part-timers.

For Diane Richardson, the future looks even brighter. On the day of our interview, a bid from RCI Financial to buy a bank was approved. I think Richardson's goal of being on the *Black Enterprise* 100 list is not very far off.

## Richardson's Advice to Sister CEOs:

- Don't start a business without a business plan. You need it not only for your banker but to give you direction as well.
- Black women are naturals at selling something, yet too many are afraid to try it. If you are thinking of starting a business, get a sales job working on commission. It will prepare you for the ups and downs of owning your business and teach you to manage your money.
- Whatever business you start, develop a mission for it. The mission needs to have a focus on helping someone other than yourself.
- Always remember to thank God for your success. We begin and end each meeting with a prayer.
- To stay motivated, read positive-thinking and spiritual books. We buy them by the truckloads for our employees and have a company mandatory reading list. There were many days I wanted to give up, but my family kept me going. I was the first one to graduate from college and I couldn't let them down.
- Do your homework. Knowledge is what gives you confidence. When you have confidence, you become unstoppable and continue to persist.
- Start part-time. Don't jump in too fast. Grow the business slowly. We never had to borrow money for the business because we took our time and grew the business internally.
- Develop a relationship with a banker. It's important, because there will come a time when you will need to borrow money for expansion, and will need a banker. I send pizza and fruit baskets to my bankers to show my appreciation, and they love it.
- Have your finger on the pulse of your business. Go over the accounting books and sign the checks. There are too many opportunities for fraud in a small business.

> • Include your children in the business. The Asians do it. We need to teach our children about business. My son, nephew, and godson work in the business every summer.

## *Sister CEO Strategies for Successful Goal Fulfillment*

1. Set personal goals that are consistent with your purpose and business goals that are consistent with the company mission statement.
2. Be specific. Know exactly what you want, but at the same time allow flexibility to change your goals as your life changes.
3. Pledge yourself to attaining your goals. Don't adopt a wait-and-see attitude. Develop an action plan to lead you to success.
4. Give yourself a deadline. You need something to shoot for. Otherwise, your goals will languish forever in the back of your mind.
5. Break the goals down. A large goal can be intimidating, so break it down into small steps.
6. Be wary of roadblocks. Obstacles can and will stand in the way of achieving your goals. Expect them and design a "Plan B" to work through them.
7. Make your goals a priority. When a friend calls you to do something and you really don't have the time, tell her you're working on a major project right now.
8. Be enthusiastic and have a positive attitude toward achieving your goals.
9. Have both long-term goals and short-term goals. When you successfully reach your short-term goals, it motivates you even more to reach for the long-term goals.
10. Set no more than ten goals at a time. Any more than that will overwhelm you. When one goal has been realized, then add another.
11. Review your goals regularly to revise or update them.

12. Visualize success. Visualize yourself every day as the CEO of your own business.
13. Spend time every day doing something toward achieving your goals.
14. Network with other Sister CEOs. These women have goals similar to yours and can be a positive influence on you.
15. Don't make all your goals materialistic. Balance out your business and financial goals with goals for self-development and health.
16. Keep your eyes on the prize. Continue to stay focused and remember not to lose sight of your goal.

### *Sister CEO Action Steps*

1. Write out your ten personal long-term goals.
2. Write out your ten business long-term goals.
3. Determine your financial goals by completing the financial goal exercise.
5. When you achieve one of your goals, pat yourself on the back by rewarding yourself in a small way.
6. Visualize yourself achieving your goals.
7. Review the sixteen Sister CEO strategies for successful goal fulfillment.

# Chapter 5

# SISTERHOOD:
# NETWORKING FOR SUCCESS

When Sistahs Help Sistahs, We All Win.

Sister CEO Dolores Ratcliffe swears by the need for black women to network. When she first started her educational consulting firm, Corita Communications, Inc., she and five of her business colleagues cemented a pact that each would buy the others' goods or services. They vowed that if they couldn't satisfy each others' needs, they would use each others' clients. And only after exhausting these two levels would they do business outside of their network. During the first year of this agreement, the women's revenue increased by 20 percent.

That was thirteen years ago. Ratcliffe and her network of friends have now mushroomed into the Association of Black Women Entrepreneurs, a Los Angeles-based, 600-member, nationally renowned organization that offers training for current and wannabe Sister CEOs.

"Black women have to network, for no matter what you think, you cannot do it alone," says Ratcliffe. "When you are starting your business, this is not the time to be a 'prima donna,'" she says. "Share and receive information; it will help you to grow."

Within the last few years, networking has become a buzzword in the African American community, particularly among women. As black women finally begin to move into positions of power and influence in both the public and private sectors, many are coming together to open up opportunities for other black women. Jewel Jackson McCabe is Sister CEO of Jewel Jackson Associates, Inc., a strategic planning and communications firm, and is chair and founder of the National Coalition of 100 Black Women, a 7,000-member service organization. "Women must begin to support each other and be willing to share advice and resources," says McCabe.

Sisterhood is alive and kicking. Black women across the country are taking heed of Radcliffe's and McCabe's advice and are forming networking organizations to provide support and to nurture one another. As black women, we are a unique group. In business we share the "double whammy" syndrome, suffering both racial and gender discrimination. It's a challenge that every Sister CEO has complained of, but each has stated that, with the support of the sisterhood, they were able to obtain guidance for and solve many of the tough problems that were unique to their situation.

Sister CEOs today are no longer hesitating to leverage their clout and use their high-powered contacts. "We have to network and form organizations. It's the *only* strategy black women entrepreneurs have for survival and growth," says Radcliffe. "If one of our members is having a business problem, the organization will try to assist them in solving it. That's what networking is all about."

Drawing on the strength of their ancestors, the support of family and friends, and the nurturing of each other, Sister CEOs are challenging the odds and reinventing the rules. We are becoming major players behind the scenes and are changing the course of how we conduct business.

In the midst of writing this chapter, I spoke at the first Northern California Professional Black Women's Networking Brunch in my hometown, Oakland, California. The event was a phenomenal success. Over 200 beautiful, powerful, black women attended, each seeking alliances and sisterhood. Among them were politicians seeking election, a spiritual leader spreading the gospel of faith and empowerment, a local television news anchor and a radio announcer both dealing with racism and sexism on their jobs, a physician, and scores of sisters working 9–5 with dreams of starting their own business but needing support and encouragement.

The energy in the room that day was incredible. If a match had been lit I'm sure the spark would have ignited the atmosphere. It was a type of energy that was new to me; I had never felt it in any of the other women's seminars I had attended. These women were hungry for information. They wanted to connect with their sisters and support each other in fulfilling their oh-so-many unfulfilled dreams. It was a wonderful experience for me and I believe the other women walked out of the session with the same feeling of empowerment, camaraderie, and "I know I can do it" spirit that I felt. It's too bad I couldn't bottle up that intensity and give it to the women as they left. They will need to hold on to that motivation and that fighting spirit to succeed at whatever they want to do in life.

## Sisterhood Is Strength

Black women have networked socially since early times through such organizations as the Links and college sororities. We naturally reach out to nurture, and to be nurtured. Our strength and success lie in our ability to bond with each other.

A prime example of the economic power of networking black women is illustrated by the success of the highly acclaimed movie *Waiting to Exhale*. With the support of sisterhood, the movie grossed over $60 million in theatres alone. Articles in newspapers across the country reported how busloads and limousines full of black women saw the movie together, then attended *Waiting to Exhale* parties afterward to celebrate the monumental event. This is what I call black women wielding power . . . Green Power, that is. When black women begin to exert their Green Power in an organized fashion, we will see a change in the workplace for the betterment of black women. And the way for us to acquire more Green Power is by becoming Sister CEOs and establishing our own businesses.

As black women we must begin to pool our resources and our talent and begin networking on a business level. We need to become more strategic in our thinking and in our actions. When we network we must focus more attention on entrepreneurial and financial issues as part of our strategic agendas. Then, as we move into positions of power in greater numbers, these issues will already be at the top of the list.

Powerful black men understand this concept. Presently, a group of the nation's most prominent and affluent black men have come together in an organization called "The Network." Some of its key players include Earl Graves of *Black Enterprise* magazine, John H. Johnson of Johnson Publishing Company (publisher of *Ebony*), Robert L. Johnson of Black Entertainment Television, and several other top business leaders in corporate America. These men are the movers and shakers of the black business community. They are in positions of power to form pools of capital to open up business opportunities for black Americans that otherwise may have been stifled by America's traditional barriers to black progress.

When I searched for a black women's group of this magnitude there was none. Why? I'm not one to talk about my truly beautiful sisters, but some of that natural assertiveness I spoke about in chapter 2 we use against ourselves to hurt one another and to prevent one another from moving ahead. Envy and jealousy oftentimes rear their ugly heads in black women's organizations. Many of the businessmen I regularly talk to claim we women are more cutthroat than they are. This cattiness and back-stabbing doesn't go over well in the business arena. If black women want to get into positions of power, we must set aside our egos and begin to empower each other. Let's use the black men's network group as our role model. Let's learn how to play the game and form black women's business networks consisting of women in every major industry. Our goal in forming this organization would be to take black women to the next level, assisting and encouraging more of us to become economically empowered by providing each other with opportunities and role models. We can pool our resources (all we have to do is stay out of the shopping malls) to buy cable television stations or a hotel/convention center to hold our networking brunches and major sorority conventions. The opportunities are limitless. Sure, you can say, "I'll do this on my own." Yes, you can, but it's hard to go it alone. When you have the backing of Sister

CEOs in positions of power the task can move a lot more smoothly. That's the benefit of networking!

## How to Make Networking Work for You

One of the most successful black women's networking gatherings is the African American Women on Tour conference, produced since 1991 by Maria Carothers, Sister CEO of PromoTrends, a meeting management firm based in San Diego. (You can read Carothers's success profile at the end of this chapter.) This three-day conference attracts up to 4,000 women annually while touring major cities throughout the United States. It offers black women the opportunity to network, exchange information, and address the issues critical to their lives.

Carothers founded the conference after deciding that it was time to offer black women a gathering especially for them. This come as-you-are conference allows black women to reunite and take sisterhood to a whole other level.

The African American Women on Tour conference is only one of many networking opportunities for black women. Every year there are several Afrocentric conventions and expos throughout the United States featuring top black women speakers in the fields of business, education, finance, politics, health, career, and spiritual development. Here black women get to hobnob with movers and shakers, share information, make money for their businesses, and take an active role in promoting the growth and positive identity of African American culture, communities, and families. The mission for the majority of these networking conferences is to uplift, empower, and enhance the quality of life for black women everywhere through economic, intellectual, and spiritual development.

### NETWORKING THE RIGHT WAY

Networking works miracles, but it isn't by magic. The key issue in networking is understanding how to network and how to make these networking opportunities work for you. There is no any quick method, but there is a networking style that should be

60

followed when either attending a conference or compiling a list of people you want to let know you're in business.

Here are six networking tips to use at a conference for building your business:

1) **Have a goal in mind.** What is your objective in attending the conference? Are you looking for start-up capital to start a business? Are you there to market your product or service? Before you attend the conference map out a strategy and know exactly what you want to accomplish.

2) **Offer to conduct a seminar in your area of expertise or possibly be a facilitator.** Speaking in front of people is the No. 1 fear for many people, so conferences are always on the lookout for speakers. If you aren't afraid, get out there and toot your own horn. You'll become recognized as an expert at the same time you are marketing your business.

3) **Volunteer.** By volunteering to help out at the conference, you can network, sometimes mingle with celebrities, and get into the conference for free. Volunteers for the African American Women on Tour conference are allowed free entry on the days they volunteer.

4) **Become a vendor.** If your business sells a product or a service, consider setting up a vendor's booth. You'll be able to network and make money for your business by selling your products, or you can obtain leads for the service you offer.

5) **Attend the major functions.** The top echelons and VIPs usually attend the major luncheons and receptions. Once you are there don't just sit at the table the entire time talking with people you already know. Get up, "work" the room, and introduce yourself around. Make sure to have plenty of business cards on hand to exchange.

6) **Stay in touch.** The follow-up is the most overlooked part of networking. I'm a culprit as well. Don't allow those contacts' business cards to gather dust inside your desk drawer; use them. Send a letter, brochure, or a card letting them know more about your business and how you enjoyed meeting them at the conference. If they are a contact that can help in your business, put them in your computer database and send

61

out a monthly newsletter or press release about your business. The key is to keep your name in front of them. It may eventually lead to business down the road.

Here are four tips to building a networking list:

1) **Target your network.** Who are the contacts who can help you achieve your goal? Make up a list both of people you know and those you would like to meet who could possibly help you. Your contacts could be professional associates, community leaders, friends, and even family. Suppose you're interested in marketing your new children's computer software program nationwide. You have a number of options available for distribution: selling through retail stores, mail-order, conferences, sales representatives, or bookstores. Your networking objective then becomes to find people who can provide you with information and advice regarding the most effective options for your company. Your list of contacts would include bookstore owners, direct-sales representatives, children's toy store owners, and schools and educators.

2) **Determine what your contacts bring to the table.** After compiling your network list, gauge the value of each connection. For example, what is the person's professional interest? Who are their colleagues? What groups do they belong to? What are their special interests? You need to weigh your contacts and determine how much influence and interest they may have in helping you and your business. When you know this type of information you can network more selectively and thus more efficiently.

3) **Give in order to receive.** What can you offer your contacts in exchange for information or assistance? Start networking by providing each contact on your list something they can use or that they value. Consider bartering with your service or product in exchange for their help.

4) **Receive as well as give.** Are the contacts you have met offering anything in return to help move you closer to your goal? If you have referred two or three clients to a colleague and they have not reciprocated, you need to assess whether

that person is interested in networking or is just freeloading. For networking to be really effective, you should be trading information and leads back and forth. Don't waste time or your energy on people who don't understand the true meaning of networking.

## OTHER NETWORKING OPPORTUNITIES

When you are in business for yourself you want everyone to know it. So be prepared to network everywhere you are—on planes, trains, buses; at sporting events, churches, and political gatherings; in hair and nail salons—even the supermarket. There is no harm in striking up a conversation with a person and telling them about your products or services. People are always intrigued by people who run their own businesses. And even if they aren't interested in your product or service, they may know someone who is. So speak out and don't be afraid to let everyone know what you are doing. A successful business is really only a numbers game. The more people you talk to the higher your chances of selling your products or services.

### Networking on the Board

The boardroom is another superb place in which to network and make excellent business contacts. Being on a nonprofit or corporate board can arm you with valuable experience, skills, contacts, and prestige.

African American women have generally not been privy to being invited to serve on the boards of major corporations. The reason: racism and sexism, of course, which means we have been blocked from developing the proper connections needed to get us in. Unless you have been a major player in business, the *Fortune* 500 boardrooms traditionally have been off-limits. But that scenario is beginning to change. Greater diversity in the workplace results in growing opportunities for more people of color to serve on various major boards.

The way to secure a seat on a board is to know someone who is already there and who will nominate you as a potential board member. Start with your local community, professional, and non-

63

profit organizations as a volunteer—organizations such as the YWCA, YMCA, and Big Brothers and Big Sisters. They are always on the lookout for entrepreneurs and executives to volunteer their expertise and fill their boards. These boards consist of highly successful businesspeople who can help you penetrate corporate America's old-boy networks. You will be able to develop relationships with influential executives you might never meet otherwise. And if your goal is to become a member on a major corporate board, the smaller community and nonprofit boardrooms will serve as a catalyst and prepare you for the responsibilities of a larger board.

If you want to be nominated, learn how to market yourself and become an active participant in your community. Join professional organizations, write a column for the local newspaper, produce a community television show or radio program on the local stations, and volunteer your services for noteworthy causes. With enough publicity, people will get to know who you are and will nominate you to be a part of their team. Boards are looking for movers and shakers. They want someone who can get the job done.

### Sports Networking

Women today are more athletic and focused on getting into shape for overall health as well as physical fitness reasons. With more women involved in sports, there is additional opportunity to network in this arena. The gym, tennis and ski clubs, and team sports such as softball, basketball, football, and baseball are excellent avenues for women to network socially and professionally with both women and men.

White men have been networking and maneuvering business deals in the sports arena for years, particularly on the golf course, and black men are beginning to follow in their footsteps. Look at the success of the *Black Enterprise*/Pepsi Golf & Tennis Challenge. In just two years the event has drawn a crowd of over 900 professional African Americans. They meet every year over the Labor Day weekend at a luxury golf, tennis, and spa resort. Even if you aren't a golfer, however, there are still plenty of social opportunities to network and hobnob with entrepreneurs and executives.

To locate the sporting events or activities in your area, contact your gym or the local YWCA and YMCA.

### Networking Lists

One of the best networking lists available is put out by *Black Enterprise* magazine. The January issue always has a pull-out calender for the new year with a schedule of events on the other side. Every major black organizational conference is listed with its date, location, and a contact number to call for additional information.

Another list of the hot spots for networking African Americans appears in the national bestselling book *Success Runs in Our Race*, authored by George Fraser, a business colleague of mine and noted networking expert. Fraser calls for the revival of the Afrocentric communal spirit among black Americans who are seeking personal and professional success. He states that the time has come for black Americans to join together so that people who are already successful can collectively help those who are still struggling.

Here is a list of my favorite business networking conferences for Sister CEOs; information on how to contact the organizations appears in the appendix.

- African American Women on Tour
- Association of Black Women Entrepreneurs
- National Association of Black Women Entrepreneurs
- National Coalition of 100 Black Women
- *Black Enterprise* Entrepreneurs Conference
- Women of Color As Warriors of Light
- *Black Enterprise*/Pepsi Golf & Tennis Challenge
- National Black Nurses' Association
- Alpha Kappa Alpha Sorority
- Delta Sigma Theta Sorority, Inc.
- National Black MBA Association
- Sigma Gamma Rho Sorority, Inc.
- National Association of Black-Owned Broadcasters
- National Association of Black Journalists
- National Urban League, Inc.
- National Association for the Advancement of Colored People

- National Minority Supplier Development Council, Inc.
- National Baptist Convention of America, Inc.
- International Black Women's Congress
- *Essence* Awards and *Essence* Music Festival

## Are You Ready to Network Now?

If you still aren't convinced about whether or not you should network, let me share with you a personal story of how I lost $7,000 because of my lack of connections.

A couple of years ago I was asked to speak at a black women's expo in a major city. The honorarium offered to me to speak at the expo was $3,000 plus airfare and hotel. On the day of my talk I ran into a male business colleague who was to speak directly after me. As we waited backstage, our conversation shifted to the subject of money and how much we were getting paid to speak. And since men tend to equate money with power, my colleague proceeded to tell me he was getting paid $10,000 to speak because he knew the producer of the expo—who, by the way, was a man. Needless to say, I was floored. Here it was a black *women's* expo, I was addressing financial issues for black women, and was receiving $3,000, as opposed to my male counterpart, who was speaking on a more generic topic and was receiving $10,000. Something was definitely wrong with this picture.

First of all, black women should be the producers of a black women's expo. This particular expo drew a mostly female crowd of 50,000 or more over a three-day weekend. With an entry fee of $6 per person, we are talking big money here, my sistahs. This is the Green Power I spoke of earlier that we need to get a handle on to empower ourselves. I'm certain that if a woman had been producing this particular expo, there would not have been such a blatant inequity of fees paid to the speakers.

Unfortunately, it was too late to go back to the expo producer and ask for more money, but I did learn an expensive and valuable lesson that day. I now make it a point to know the producer of the expo or conference, the other speakers, and the amount of their honorariums before I agree on a fee. *The moral of the story:* Black women must Network! Network! Network! in order to reach any type of economic empowerment.

---

## SISTER CEO SUCCESS STORY
### *Maria D. Carothers*
#### PromoTrends/African American Women on Tour
##### San Diego, California

Maria D. Carothers, Sister CEO of PromoTrends, a five-year-old marketing and meeting management firm, knew early on she was destined to run her own business. She came from a line of pioneering entrepreneurs. Twenty years ago, Carothers's aunt owned the first gay club in Los Angeles, and her uncle was the owner of a retail store and a Louisiana chicken restaurant. "Seeing my family in their own businesses inspired me to want to be my own boss," states Carothers.

Raised in San Diego, Carothers began planning special and community events as early as junior high school. After receiving her Bachelor of Science degree from California State University she started her family.

With determination, Carothers went on to graduate school to study urban planning. Shortly afterwards she landed an internship with the Los Angeles Urban League, which she credits as the turning point of her career. It was here that Carothers gained experience in marketing, public relations, and event planning. She also found that she had a passion for bettering the quality of life of African Americans.

After seven years of perfecting her skills, Carothers opened the doors of PromoTrends, a marketing management company that developed various promotions and special events. Her most notable project was the coordination of *Essence* magazine's 1990 Cover Model Search. It was while working on this project that Carothers saw the vision of black women coming together to empower themselves. "I could see that black women were craving a moment just for them—for us," Carothers exclaims. Because of

---

her determination and perseverance, Carothers's dream came to fruition in 1991 with the success of her first black women's conference in San Diego. Now in its sixth year, the conference has expanded to five major cities and attracts up to 4,000 women annually. The two-day conference offers black women the opportunity to network and to learn from experts in business, health, education, and spiritual development. "This is a come-as-you-are kind of conference," says Carothers. "Attitudes are checked at the door, minds are unlocked, spirits are elevated, and sisterhood takes on a whole new dimension."

## Carothers's Advice to Sister CEOs:

- Make sure you understand how to manage your cash flow. I found this to be the most difficult. If you are unsure as to how to manage it, hire someone who can help you. Actually, the best thing to do is to computerize it. We use Quickbooks, a business software by the makers of Quicken.
- Managing family and business is stressful. You need the support of your spouse or significant other and family. Also take time to get away for a couple of days to recharge your energy.
- Network with other black women. And, never "dis" anyone. You never know when you might need that person's assistance in the future. And if word gets around, you may develop a negative reputation in the business world, which could have a detrimental effect on your business.

## Sister CEO Action Steps

1. **Business cards.** Print up an attractive and clear business card to let potential clients know the type of business you are in.
2. **Make out a list** of individuals with whom you have an interest in networking or developing a business relationship. Call them or send them a note or brochure about your business along with your business card.
3. **Plan to attend** one or two major black conferences or expos

per year. If your business has a product or service, consider renting a booth at the event.

4. **Offer to be a speaker.** Don't let my story sway you. Often conferences do not pay their speakers but may instead offer free publicity or the use of a booth without cost. Take it. Your objective is to let people know about your business and to become well-known in the community. Once you raise your business profile level, then you, too, can command a speaking fee of $10,000.

5. **Network every day.** Set a goal to tell at least three people about your business. Business is really a numbers game: the more people you expose to your business, the more success you will have.

# Part Two

## NUTS AND BOLTS

# Chapter 6

## THE ESSENTIALS

Until you get your business up and running, you'll do everything. You'll learn every job you have to hire for and trace every dollar that goes out. You'd better be the best-informed, best-qualified person in the place. Otherwise, you should be working for the one who is.

HARVEY MACKAY, *from BEWARE THE NAKED MAN WHO OFFERS YOU HIS SHIRT*

Starting a business for yourself can be an exciting and rewarding undertaking, or it can be sheer hell. How well a successful Sister CEO guides her business through good times or bad depends on the qualities and traits she possesses.

To survive as a Sister CEO, you must be willing to sacrifice your time and energy to make your small business work. Unfortunately, many enterprising entrepreneurs do not grasp how much time and effort they will need to give to their business. This explains why most businesses do not last longer than three years. As I've mentioned several times already, make sure whatever business you start is in a field you are passionate about. Then the sacrificing and the up and down periods will not create helter-skelter in your business and personal life.

For your company to last longer than three years you must first and foremost be absolutely certain that you are ready to dedicate yourself to it 100 percent. Then you must assess your start-up requirements so you will know how much income you are going to need to get your business off the ground.

## The Cost of Doing Business

Money problems are generally at the root of all business failures. During your first few years in business, lack of money will be your biggest hurdle. This was a rude awakening for me when I first started my company.

As a Sister CEO, I expected my first year of business to be profitable and that *of course* I would draw a six-figure salary. Boy, did *I* need a reality check! My firm *lost* money the first few years. And as for my salary—what salary? Luckily—or wisely—I had a cushion of money to fall back on to get me through the lean periods. Chapter 9, "Managing the Money," will get more into the specifics of having a money cushion. But for now, understand that it is absolutely essential to keep your start-up costs to a bare minimum.

While start-up costs vary depending on the type of business, the secret is to begin with the lowest cash investment and the lowest overhead possible. Most Sister CEOs start their companies on a minimal budget using their own money and lots of sweat equity. More than likely, you will need to go this route as well, since very few banks assist fledgling entrepreneurs with start-up loans.

For an idea of what costs are involved, take another look at Connie Harper, our aspiring Sister CEO who wants to start a mail-order body-care products business. If you recall, Connie is starting her business part-time out of her home, so her expenses as itemized in the chart on page 75 are less than those of a person starting a full-time business and leasing office space. Also, if your business provides a service rather than a product, your costs may be lower since you do not have to invest in an initial product inventory.

The costs listed for Connie Harper's business are only estimates. If ever there is a time for conservative realism, exercise it when planning for these costs. Often the start-up amount is twice the amount you plan on, and it takes twice as long to get the business up and running. So plan conservatively and possibly even add an additional 5–10 percent to the estimates in Connie's list.

For anyone who is considering a full-time business, quadruple the costs below and add leasing costs, which vary from state to state. Check with your local realtor for estimates on the cost of leased office space. This will give you a general idea of how much you will need to get started.

## *Start-up Expenses for Connie Harper*

| ITEM | COST | |
|---|---|---|
| Rent | 0 | |
| Initial inventory | $500–$1,000 | (To keep this cost low, get orders for your products from customers before you purchase your inventory) |
| Business cards/stationery | $150 | |
| Business supplies (computer software, file cabinets, office supplies) | $100 | |
| Advertising (newspaper ad, flyers, brochures, postage) | $150 | |
| Licenses/fees | $50–$100 | |
| Telephone (separate phone line in home) | $100 | |
| Professional services (accountant, legal) | $50–$100 | |
| Miscellaneous | $50 | |
| Salary | $0 | |
| TOTAL: | **$1,150–$1,750** | |

A word of advice for Sister CEOs planning to rent office space: Do not go overboard buying expensive office furniture and elaborately decorating your office space before your business is making a profit. Wait until you have a steady flow of clients and income. Otherwise you are just wasting valuable resources that could have been used to grow the business.

## How Much Money Do I Have?

To determine how much money you have to invest in a business, you must evaluate your own personal finances. The best way to do this is to complete a personal balance sheet (see below). Begin by listing all your assets and their value: house, car, jewelry, and so on. Next list all your debts: credit cards, mortgage, car loans, and so on. Now calculate the ratio between your total assets and total liabilities to determine your net worth and the degree of debt you are in. This ratio is called "Assets:Liabilities" and should be about 2:1, or, if you are like most folks living in America, 1:2. This is also called a Quick Ratio. If your assets exceed your liabilities, you are in good shape. If liabilities exceed assets, I recommend you pay off as much of your debt as possible before you begin your business. Too much credit card debt or too many outstanding loans can hamper your success. You will not be able to focus on the business because you will be too concerned every month with trying to meet all your credit obligations.

### *Personal Balance Sheet*

STATEMENT OF FINANCIAL CONDITION                                    DATE:_____

| ASSETS | AMOUNT |
|---|---|
| cash, savings and checking accounts | _____ |
| securities: stocks, bonds, mutual funds | _____ |
| real estate/home | _____ |
| cars | _____ |
| personal assets | _____ |
| life insurance cash value | _____ |
| other assets | _____ |
| TOTAL ASSETS **(1)** | _____ |

| LIABILITIES | |
|---|---|
| credit cards | _____ |
| real estate mortgage | _____ |
| monthly bills (expenses) | _____ |
| car loans | _____ |

| | |
|---|---|
| unpaid income taxes | ———— |
| secured loans | ———— |
| other loans | ———— |
| TOTAL LIABILITIES **(2)** | ———— |
| NET WORTH **(3)** (1 minus 2 = 3) | ———— |
| DEGREE OF DEBT **(4)** (2 minus 1 = 4) | ———— |

## Computerizing Your Business

For budding Sister CEOs, a high-tech office isn't a luxury anymore. It's a necessity. As a small-business owner you need to invest in technology more so than big businesses because you don't have the same type of support they have. Computers can give you that added boost. If you don't already own a computer, you should make investment in this equipment a critical part of your business plan because it can help cut costs and increase profitability.

Fortunately, technology designed with small businesses in mind is increasing—and it is cheaper than ever. Price wars have driven the cost of a "fully loaded" personal computer to under $2,000. Software developers are following suit. Software giant Microsoft Corporation is aggressively going after the small-business market with an array of software designed to meet small-business needs. In the appendix you will find a list of recommended software programs.

Here are ten ways a personal computer can give your business the edge:

1. **Accounting**: The No. 1 priority for any business—totaling the bottom line. There are several accounting packages available to accommodate the entrepreneur who is not an accountant. The best software simply asks the user to supply basic financial information, which the computer than enters in the traditional accounting categories. This makes it simple for Sister CEOs to do most of their bookkeeping and to track billing and cash flow more efficiently.

For a small, cash-based business, personal finance programs such as Quicken from Intuit, Inc., or Microsoft Money offer enough features to perform basic accounting. If your business is larger, with more information to track, consider a full-fledged accounting package like Quickbooks or Peachtree Accounting for Windows.

These programs will do basic financial reporting in the form of profit and loss statements, balance sheets, cash flow reports, and tax summaries. The reports really assist in keeping your business costs under control. Once you see the numbers you can pinpoint where your expenses are exceeding your targeted budget. Many of these programs will also allow you to write and print checks and provide other payroll capabilities.

2. **Customer service:** As a Sister CEO it is especially important to provide your customers with a personal touch. A well-planned database can help you incorporate your customer needs into your daily operations. For example, Connie Harper should keep a list of the names and addresses of her customers, what products they like, and the day of their last purchase. Her customers will love it when she sends them a reminder that it is time to buy more. Customers crave the personal attention they no longer get in larger retail and discount stores. This type of service will provide repeat business as well as referrals.

3. **Office management:** As your business grows you will need to implement an office management system on a database. Not only will you maintain your customer information but your employee files, company policies, business supplier information, office inventory, and insurance claims as well. If you are unsure how to set up a database system, the Black Data Processing Associates (see appendix) is available to help you out. This nonprofit organization provides a forum for black business owners who want to interact with black technology consultants. Their objective is to involve business owners in opportunities on the information superhighway, such as government contracting, international opportunities, and avenues for promoting products.

4. **Advertising:** Designing your own ad campaign isn't as complicated as you may think with the use of desktop publishing software. Many of the programs come with pre-designed layouts for flyers, brochures, and calendars. All you need to do is insert your company logo, ad copy, a few creative graphics, and that's it. With a laser printer, copier, and nice paper, you can print professional-quality flyers, brochures, business cards, and direct-mail pieces. Your customers will think you had a professional advertising agency create the campaign.

   And what's even better about desktop publishing is its flexibility. If your business needs change, you can instantaneously create new brochures and flyers without having to use an expensive printing company.

5. **Newsletters:** A newsletter is a great way to maintain communication with your clients and customers. My firm puts out a quarterly newsletter for all clients called *Invest in Yourself.* It provides tips on what new investments are available, how to select a stock, and other pertinent information on money. You can alert your customers to special promotions, new products, and general information about your business. And, if you followed the advice in item No. 2 and developed a database, you already have a ready-made mailing list.

   Another often overlooked idea is marketing your expertise to other professionals via a specialized newsletter. For example, if you own your own beauty salon, you can provide advice to independent hair stylists who would one day like to run their own shop and are hungry for information on how to do it. Your newsletter will also establish you as an expert in your field, and you may be able to obtain free publicity from media sources, which in turn will increase your exposure to potential clients.

6. **Managing projects:** When you are in business for yourself, your whole life may seem like a project. To organize it, consider time-management software programs. These programs have Daytimers, calendars, and "to do" lists to help you keep track of your daily activities.

7. **The World Wide Web:** When you run a small business— whether it is full-time, part-time, from your home, or from an office—you know that information plus communication equals power.

   That's where modems and online services come in. With a modem attached to your personal computer, you can turn it into a business entity capable of putting you on equal footing with your *Fortune* 500 competitors. Without leaving your chair, you can send e-mail, files, and faxes to customers and employees next door or around the world. Online services literally bring the world to your fingertips twenty-four hours a day, seven days a week.

   Some of the major players with information for small business owners are America Online, CompuServe, Microsoft Network, and AT&T Business Network. With most of these online services you can: connect to the Internet (the largest web of online services), tap the Small Business Administration's Entrepreneur's Forum, obtain business news, access stock market data, shop for office supplies, and find new clients by advertising on the Web.

   To obtain Afrocentric business information, try NetNoir Online, an online service available through America Online that provides business seminars, shopping, entertainment, and sports information for African Americans.

8. **Sales presentations:** Your computer can help you create colorful presentation slides with the use of presentation software. The software is designed for non-artists and is relatively easy to use. If you frequently give seminars on your specialty, you can create the presentation in slide form and take it on the road with you.

9. **Business planning:** Business planning for your company is essential. And now there are software programs available to lend a hand in this somewhat overwhelming project. The programs feature business plan templates for the budding entrepreneur as well as the established Sister CEO. By filling in the blanks, you are able to create a business plan tailored specifically for you. Business plans are covered in more depth in chapter 12.

10. **Legal advice:** Initially you may not have much money to spend on an attorney. If the legal issue is pretty straight-forward—such as a basic equipment lease, an employee's noncompete agreement, or a sales representative agreement—you can cut your costs by purchasing a software program that provides these and several other forms.

## Other High-Tech Tools

**Telephone:** Your telephone is your business lifeline. If you work from home, set up a separate business phone line and have an answering machine or voice-mail service to screen calls or take messages when you are not there. If you have young children, don't allow them to answer your business phone—it sounds unprofessional. With the proliferation of home-based businesses, the cost of a separate line has come down.

**Toll-free numbers:** An 800 number can be a windfall for your business. Once they were used exclusively by large companies or mail-order firms, but now they have become commonplace in small businesses.

Most long-distance and local telephone companies offer 800 services, and the rates have become extremely competitive. The set-up charge, if there is one, is usually nominal. Small businesses typically pay less than $20 per month for the basic 800 line service. Actual calls are billed on a per-minute basis. And, you don't need another phone line; you can hook the 800 number up to your existing business line.

As a Sister CEO, you want to make it very convenient for your customers to do business with you. The 800 number is a viable means toward that end. Because rates are competitive, shop around and negotiate for the best deal.

**Fax machines:** A fax (facsimile) machine has become a standard piece of equipment for small businesses. They speed up communication and provide an alternative to sending an important document through the mail. Home-office fax machines are much more sophisticated than in the past. You can now get a combination fax/copier machine at a relatively low price of a few hundred dollars at the office discount stores or ware-house-type stores.

## A Business from Home: The New American Workplace

A business from home is the new trend for the twenty-first century—brought about by factors such as corporate downsizing and women wanting to stay home with their young children. Veronica Smith, Sister CEO of Design Veronique, a manufacturer of post-operative compression garments for use by plastic surgery patients following a face-lift or liposuction, started her $1 million business from home. According to Smith, who lives in California, starting from home enabled her to keep the overhead low and gave her the flexibility and freedom she needed to care for her son.

According to the latest projections from *Entrepreneur* magazine on the status of home-based businesses, there are roughly 27.1 million Americans self-employed at home, and this trend is expected to increase fourfold by the year 2000. Certain businesses are great for starting from home; I've listed them in chapter 10.

### ADVANTAGES VS DISADVANTAGES OF A HOME-BASED BUSINESS

Starting your business from home has plenty of advantages and disadvantages. Let's start with the positives:

### *Advantages*

- Working from home allows you to keep the initial cost down, thereby allowing you to turn a profit sooner.
- If you are a single parent or a mother with children, a home-based business allows you to combine managing your business with family.
- You can turn personal expenses like rent and telephone costs into tax-deductible items.
- If you are unsure as to whether or not you want to start a busi-

ness, you can test your idea from home and keep your financial risk low.
- You set your own hours.
- You set your own salary.
- You set your own vacation schedule.
- You can work for your financial freedom instead of making someone else wealthy.
- You can build a business to leave to your children.

## *Disadvantages*

- Balancing your personal life with your business life is a major challenge. Sometimes it is difficult to stop working at 6 P.M., causing the fine line between work and your personal life to blur. To avoid this, it is necessary to have a set work schedule.
- Procrastination can set in. If you aren't disciplined you may have difficulty getting started without someone looking over your shoulder. Or you may find yourself running to the refrigerator every hour.
- Having children nearby can easily interfere with your work. While the motive for a women to start a business from home is to be with her children, unless it is planned carefully, I can guarantee you will not get much done.

Here are a few suggestions to help you avoid these problems and increase your odds of staying in business:

- Designate one area in your home as an office. Avoid the family room or your bedroom. You need to have one place in which you can work with minimal interruption.
- Keep business and personal time well-defined and separate. Rigidly define "work time."
- Establish a planning system. Use your computer planning software, personal organizers, or a plain three-ring binder.
- When you finish working at the end of the day, put away the papers you had been working on that day. You want to walk into a well-organized office the next day instead of the chaos from the previous day.

- When your business day is unfocused, it is easy to procrastinate. Before you leave your office write out a list of five tasks you want to complete the next day. This will help you to get over the procrastination syndrome.
- Promise yourself a short reward like a walk around the block after you complete a project.
- Involve your children in your work. If you have pre-schoolers staying at home and without a babysitter, set up a mini-area in the office where they can play and work on their own special projects. If your children are older, teach them to answer the phone and file folders, and pay them a salary. We need to expose black children to entrepreneurship as soon as possible.
- When you do not want to be interrupted, hang a "Do Not Disturb" sign on your office door. It may work, sometimes.

In addition, there are plenty of excellent reference books on starting home-based business. Several are listed in the appendix.

## Alternative Offices

When you need a real office but can't afford the cost of space, help and equipment, consider a small "incubator center" or space in an executive suite. They both can help you cut your costs while you grow your business.

### SMALL-BUSINESS "INCUBATOR" CENTERS: ONE-STOP SHOPPING

Government-subsidized entrepreneurial centers—called "incubator centers"—offer low-cost office space, shared clerical services and equipment, management training, and low-cost professional advice on how to run your business. Located throughout the United States and Canada, many of them are targeted as minority- and women-owned enterprises. Some of the incubators have also developed connections with bankers and venture capitalists. The office space is usually small, but utilities and the use of a conference room are usually included in the monthly rent. Phones, secretarial support, and access to office equipment are available for an additional fee. The subsidized office space rents at a reduced rate for three to five years. Once your business is up, running, and profitable, you graduate from the program and move on to set up shop in a commercial leased space.

You should research the incubator center as you would any office space. Key points to keep in mind include:

- The incubator's focus. If an incubator specializes in a particular industry and you are in a different field, you may not get all the benefits you need.
- The incubator's management. Does the manager have a hands-on business background and strong ties to local banks and the business community?
- The incubator's success ratio. If the incubator is more than three years old, ask how many companies have graduated and how many have failed.
- The word-of-mouth. Talk to the other business tenants in the incubator. Ask how they feel about the services and benefits they are getting.
- The type of support programs the incubator offers. Does it offer workshops and financial assistance programs to help you grow your business?
- Location. Make sure you choose an incubator that's in a good location for your business so you'll attract the right customers.
- The participation agreement. Does the incubator want a piece of your company? This is important information to know before you sign on the dotted line.

To find a small-business incubator in your area, contact your local Small Business Administration (SBA) office or chamber of commerce. I have also listed in the appendix incubators in several states.

## EXECUTIVE SUITES

Executive suites also fall in the space-and-service-sharing concept. They, too, are geared to businesses that need low-cost professional locations with furnished offices, conference rooms, phone service, and reception areas. Occasionally they will offer messenger services and health club options.

There are hundreds of executive suites throughout the country. Generally you pay two-thirds less than you'd pay elsewhere for similar office space. Many executive suites offer a flexible arrangement enabling the part-time Sister CEO to use an office a certain number of hours per week and the suite's business address for mail.

The first year I started my money management firm, my full-time office was located in a spare bedroom. I met with clients in an HQ executive suite that I leased for twenty hours a week. It was perfect. It allowed me to keep my costs down until the business made money.

When choosing an executive suite, follow the same guidelines you would when selecting regular office space, with location and parking for clients being the major factors to consider (see also below).

Leasing flexibility is another important factor. It is better to sign a month-to-month lease with an escape clause in case you have to move or cope with a cash flow crunch.

## Leasing Office/Retail Space

When you are ready to take the next step to renting an office space or your ambition is to open a restaurant or a retail store, it's important to understand how to select a location and negotiate the leasing contract.

Where you set up your business can have a tremendous impact on your success. How often have you heard the real estate adage, "Location, location, location"? It is equally true for the selection of a business site. A good location will do more for you than even the most ambitious advertising campaign. I know of one store in my city that sells unique items but that is located away from the main shopping area. As a result, the store often is empty when I visit. The writing is already on the wall. It's just a matter of time before the business will need to shut down for lack of customers.

The two major features to consider in locating your business are (1) the community you want to service and (2) the right location within that community.

## THE COMMUNITY

In the early 1900s there was a prosperous black community in Tulsa, Oklahoma, called "Black Wallstreet." It was a thriving business community consisting of 21 restaurants, 30 grocery stores, a hospital, a bank, a post office, libraries, schools, law offices, a half dozen private airplanes, and a bus system. Each dollar spent on "Black Wallstreet" circulated 36–100 times. It sometimes took a year for the currency to leave the community. Unfortunately, the model community was destroyed in 1921 by the Ku Klux Klan, who bombed and set fire to the town. There hasn't been a duplication since.

Today in the African American community, the majority of small businesses are owned and run by nonblacks. And the dollar barely circulates one time before leaving for the suburbs. We should own every nail salon, convenience store, and fast food restaurant in our shopping areas based on the amount of money we spend in these businesses. It really doesn't make sense for it to be otherwise.

Sister CEOs thinking about a retail or restaurant business should seriously consider going back into the community. There are several cities waiting with open arms to help you start a business in the inner city. They will help you find a location, give you a tax break if you hire city residents, and give you free rent for a couple of months. To learn more about these programs contact the office of small business and economic development in your city.

Whether or not you start your business in the black community, you still must carefully select the location. Here are a few location factors you need to think about:

- **Competitors.** Are there a number of similar type stores in the area? If so, how many? Visit the businesses to get an idea of the number of customers they are serving.
- **Access to customers.** Is a freeway or highway nearby? What

about public transportation? Your customers must have easy access to your business either by car or public transit.

- **Foot traffic.** For retail businesses foot traffic is a very important factor. There needs to be an ample supply. The way to gauge foot traffic is to stand out in front of the given location and count and interview the potential customers walking by. Select a few half-hour periods during the busiest hours of the day.
- **Parking.** Does the location provide easy, adequate parking and access for customers? Is it safe and well lit in the evenings? You want your customers to feel comfortable coming to your business.
- **History of the location.** What was the success or failure rate of the businesses that were previously at the location? Even if the businesses are different from your own, it is still a good idea to know why they failed or succeeded and the reasons they relocated.
- **Terms of the lease.** The amount of the lease can sometimes be the deciding factor in your choice of a location. The time to negotiate the leasing terms is before you sign the lease agreement.

When researching a business location, you should hire a real estate broker for assistance. They can help with locating the ideal location for your business as well as negotiating the contract. It's also absolutely essential to hire an attorney to look over the lease agreement before you sign on the dotted line.

## The Partnership Dilemma

Most of us aren't good at everything. In fact, if you're like most of the Sister CEOs I interviewed, many were whizzes at marketing their products or services, but had difficulty managing the administrative and financial end of the business. If that's the case for you, it may be advantageous to consider a partner. The key is to select the right partner(s).

A partner in business is not very different from a partner in marriage. In fact, you'll probably spend more time with your office "spouse" than with your marriage partner. So who you select is extremely important.

Like anything else in business, there are advantages as well as disadvantages in starting a business with a partner. Partners are great for feedback on new ideas. And when times are tough, it's your partner who will keep you motivated. In addition, a good partner can bring to the business contacts, customers, and skills you may lack or not enjoy mastering. A partner can pick up the slack if you are sick or out of town, and two or more people can usually get a business off the ground quicker than someone doing it alone. As you can clearly see, a partner adds productivity to a new business.

## FINDING THE RIGHT PARTNERS

The first step in identifying the right partner is to make a realistic assessment of your own strengths and weaknesses. What you don't want to do is to select someone similar to yourself. You want someone who has the strengths to offset your weaknesses. Next, determine and list what skills you want a potential partner to bring to the business. In all honesty, you want a partner who is as good as or better than you. *And, you must be willing to accept the fact that he or she is as good as or better than you!*

Your partner must be a visionary like yourself and must share the same vision you have for the company. In the initial stages, a new business takes a lot of sweat equity. If your partner isn't willing to put in the required blood, sweat, tears, and time, the business will not succeed. You want that person to be as excited about and committed to the business as you are. When a partner isn't totally committed, you will find one partner contributing more than the other and dissension will set in, causing the business to fall apart.

Other aspects to consider are the character, integrity, and trustworthiness of your potential partner. You can't be looking over your partner's shoulder all the time. Each must trust and respect each other's business decisions. Lack of faith in the other partner is a sure path to the demise of a partnership.

## YOUR SPOUSE AS PARTNER

Believe it or not, business relationships between spouses can work well. But there are some pitfalls. On the downside, you will be spending most of your waking hours together. While initially this may sound pretty good, eventually you may drive each other crazy. It's difficult to spend time with anyone day in and day out without sometimes getting a little tired of seeing them. Sister CEO Veronica Smith and her husband, George, purposely bought a large enough house so that they can each go their separate ways after they get home from the office. "George has his room and I have mine to unwind in for at least one hour after work," she says. "Then we spend the rest of the evening together and we don't talk about the business."

A married couple in business together can feel strain because there are more reasons for disagreements. Not only is there potential for clashing on personal matters, but on business matters as well. But for the right couple the positives far outweigh the negatives. When both spouses are involved in the business there is a complete view of the decision-making process, the ups and downs, and the pressures on the other spouse. There is also a built-in trust factor. You don't have to worry about your spouse ripping you off. That is, as long as the marriage isn't on shaky ground!

Another benefit to being in business together is the sharing of common goals, which generally leads to a stronger marital relationship. The struggles of the business are bound to bring a couple closer together. Plus, it's a lot of fun working with someone you enjoy being with.

Should you go into business with your spouse? That depends. First, both parties must love and respect each other. Second, there must be a clear understanding of who is responsible for what at home and in the business. And both parties must be in full agreement. One person cannot feel that they are being coerced or that they lack any type of decision-making power. Each spouse must contribute to the business. There can be a big problem if one spouse feels his or her contributions are unequal. Both must feel their talent is essential for the success of the business.

## YOUR FRIEND/RELATIVE AS PARTNER

Carefully tread water here if you are considering partnering with a friend or relative. There are plenty of horror stories about friends and family members falling out because of business disputes. The best advice is to treat this partnership just like any other. Make sure everyone understands their role in the business and be sure you have a written and legally binding agreement between all partners. Which brings me to the next section—preoperating agreements.

## PREOPERATING AGREEMENTS

Whether you partner with your spouse, friend, or relative, it makes good business sense to enter into the partnership with a written agreement stating what will happen to the business in the event of a split in the relationship. As part of this agreement, you could decide that the business would be sold and the money from the sale evenly divided. Or you could stipulate that one partner would have the opportunity to buy the other out. The key issue is that the agreement should map out a solution in case one partner no longer wants to be a part of the business. You don't want any surprises.

## Business Insurance 101

Although insurance can seem complicated, it pays to educate yourself about what kinds of coverage your business needs, how to shop for the best value, what your policies cover, and what they don't. Even more important, it pays to evaluate what risks your business faces and how can you reduce the risk of loss. In this section I'll cover the basic types of business insurance so that you are familiar with this important area, but before you make a business decision based on this information, consult further with a specialized insurance broker, tax adviser, or an attorney to obtain updated legal and sensible requirements information.

There are basically seven types of insurance Sister CEOs need:

1. Health
2. Disability
3. Liability, for the business
4. Automobile
5. Workers' Compensation
6. Business Interruption
7. Product Liability

**Health Insurance:** A good source of affordable group health insurance is through your industry trade and professional associations. If your spouse has health insurance through the job, continue on that policy.

If you have employees, health insurance to cover them can be very expensive. It may not be feasible to offer it until your company can really afford to. To get a general idea of the cost, contact an insurance broker who specializes in business health insurance.

**Disability insurance:** If you suddenly become ill or disabled, it could mean a rocky road for your company and personal finances. To prevent such chaos, Sister CEOs need to purchase disability. insurance. Although it's costly, it's worth it. Shop around and seek the advice of an insurance broker who works with several insurance companies.

**Liability insurance for business:** There are two reasons to purchase liability insurance—first, to protect your business in case someone gets hurt on your property, and second, to insure your expensive office equipment against theft. If your office is in your home, your homeowner policy may be enough to cover liability. Check with your insurance agent.

**Automobile insurance:** If you use your car for your business, or have company cars for employees, be sure to buy adequate insurance coverage for them.

**Workers' Compensation insurance:** Workers' Compensation insurance varies from state to state. This insurance pays the medical and other expenses of your employees if they are injured on the job. It is required by law in most states, and the rates vary from state to state.

How does it benefit your company? It provides coverage for the employee no matter who is at fault, so that an expensive employee injury doesn't drain your company's financial resources. Employees covered by Workers' Compensation cannot sue for more money unless they can prove you intentionally caused the accident.

**Business interruption insurance:** It is expensive, but business interruption insurance can safeguard your business against financial ruin because of a fire or other natural disaster. It is almost essential for businesses in California due to that state's relatively high incidence of earthquakes. The policies for this type of insurance differ. Some will pay your rent and day-to-day expenses. Others may cover your payroll. This insurance can be complicated. I suggest you seek the advice of an insurance broker.

**Product liability insurance:** This type of insurance covers deaths, accidents, or injuries that are caused by a defective product. While it is quite expensive, it sometimes is critical to the sale of the merchandise. For example, if your company manufactures children's toys, many of the national retail chains will insist that your company have product liability insurance before they will place an order. Food, medical drugs, and athletic equipment companies are also high-risk candidates for product liability insurance.

The laws covering product liability lawsuits are somewhat muddled, which raises the probability of your company being sued. A prime example involves a case in which a McDonald's franchise customer sued the corporation, claiming their coffee cup was defective, causing her to burn herself when the cup of coffee spilled in her lap.

This area requires close scrutiny and needs to be addressed by a professional. Consult with an insurance representative who is well-informed in product liability, as insurance premiums vary widely. If you belong to a trade organization, check with them as well; often they are able to negotiate a lower premium for their members. In the financial securities business, we are required to have extremely expensive "errors and omissions" insurance to cover client financial mistakes. Because of my company's business relationship with the Charles Schwab discount brokerage firm, we were able to obtain the insurance at a much lower premium.

## Business Estate Planning—Passing It On

It is important to keep the business in the family. Sister CEOs need to prepare their spouses and/or children to take over the business in case of their deaths.

The time to deal with this issue is while the founder of the company is still healthy enough to run the business. Otherwise, the business may face death-driven estate planning, in which the family will end up selling the business to pay estate taxes, which may cost upwards of 50 percent of the entire estate, depending on the state.

Business estate planning, although essential, can be costly. If the business has substantial assets, and the Sister CEO has many children, it may cost up to $100,000 to put the plan in place.

The plan is usually created by a team consisting of a tax attorney to handle the legal and estate investment, a certified public accountant to deal with federal and state taxes, and a financial adviser to manage the money investment.

A good idea is to write out an emergency plan detailing the new chain of command and management team. Name a successor immediately to avoid confusion among your employees and customers. If your business is in trouble, push your ego aside and get help. Denying the problems your business is facing will not help matters.

Loida Lewis, Sister CEO of TLC Beatrice International Holdings, the world's largest African American–owned business, understands all too well the importance of business estate planning. When her spouse, Reginald Lewis, unexpectedly died of a brain tumor at the age of fifty, he had not chosen his widow to succeed him. Instead he chose his half-brother, who was a former professional football player. With him in charge, the company was losing money. That's when Lewis stepped in. An attorney by training, she made herself chairman and CEO in order to protect her family's interest. She took immediate cost-cutting measures: She went in and got rid of the company jet, sold limousines, and reduced the number of employees from 5,000 to 4,500. She sold off four divisions of the company that were not making money, and relocated the main office from a lavish Manhattan office building to a less expensive one with one-third the space. Now that she is in charge, the company is making more money than ever.

# SISTER CEO SUCCESS STORY
## *Veronica C. Smith*
### DESIGN VERONIQUE
#### OAKLAND, CALIFORNIA

Veronica C. Smith, Sister CEO of Design Veronique, believes in turning a negative into a positive. Her $1 million company, a manufacturer of compression garments used by plastic surgery patients, began when her sister died of breast cancer. Smith, a trained fashion designer, seeing the need to help other women with breast cancer, started her part-time business designing mastectomy bras in a spare bedroom. As the popularity of the bras increased she began distributing them by mail-order. Eager to expand, but not sure into what, Smith was given the idea of compression-wear garments by a woman sales representative for her elastic distribution company. After talking it over with her physician sister who specializes in plastic surgery, Smith decided to go for it.

The company started with ten products, the first of which was a face mask designed for her sister's face-lift patients. After receiving an endorsement from another physician at a medical conference, sales suddenly took off. Today her company manufactures and sells over forty products (two of which have U.S. patents), and that number is steadily increasing.

As surgery procedures change, the need for different designs increases. Often Smith is asked by physicians to design a specific product. A firm believer in customer service, she gladly obliges. She's even gone international, with clients in Japan, Saudi Arabia, Brazil, Europe, Mexico, Australia, and Canada.

Smith also doesn't work alone. Her company employs fifteen people, one of whom is her husband George, a computer executive and a nonbeliever in the beginning. He came on board only after attending a medical conference in San Francisco. Seeing the potential market opportunities, he quit his job and is now the vice president of operations. "We're a great fit. I handle the marketing, sales, and finances and George handles the accounting and the computers," says Smith. "He's a definite asset to the company."

With sales increasing annually, and a new and larger office, Veronica Smith is destined to take Design Veronique to the stratosphere.

### Smith's Advice to Sister CEOs:

- In whatever business you start, have a strong desire to make a difference in the lives of your employees and the customers who buy or use your products or services.
- Manage the company using the team approach. Treat your employees with respect and they will reward you with a low turnover rate and loyalty.
- Become an avid reader and listen to audiotapes on business, finance, and marketing. Just because you know how to make a product doesn't mean you can run a business—you need to learn from others' mistakes.
- Customer service is important. People will pay for your service or product if they are treated well.
- If you offer a product, manufacture it yourself to preserve the quality control and the shipping and handling. Often we closed the sale because we had the products on site and were able to offer next-day product delivery.
- As part of your marketing strategy, purchase high-quality T-shirts, sweatshirts, and coffee mugs with your company name and logo and give them away to your customers and clients. People like getting things for free and it keeps your company name in front, building client loyalty.
- Revise and update your business and marketing plan every year.
- Become a visionary. If you have an idea, write it down—don't just keep it in your memory.
- Plan what you're going to do, study the market, be the best, become an expert at what you do and then execute the plan.

## Sister CEO Action Steps

1. Calculate your business start-up costs following the Connie Harper example.
2. Evaluate your personal finances by completing the personal balance sheet.
3. If you don't already own a computer, start shopping around and comparing prices. Next, open a savings account earmarked for the computer purchase and contribute $50 to $100 to it every month until you reach your goal.
4. Research the different software programs available for small businesses.
5. Get connected to the World Wide Web. You can't afford not to be a part of this new wave of information technology.
6. If you are already in business, call your local or long-distance phone company to inquire about a toll-free 800 number.
7. Set up your business in a spare room of your home to keep your overhead low.
8. Once the business is growing, consider a small business incubator program or an executive suite.
9. If you're planning to start a business with a partner, prepare a preoperating agreement.
10. Talk with an insurance broker about the various types of insurance you need for your business.

# Chapter 7

# LEGAL MATTERS

The mark of a millionaire is to seek counsel.

When you start a business, one of your most important decisions will be to choose the legal form under which your business will operate. Which form is right for you depends on the potential liability (the likelihood of your company being sued) of your business and the tax advantages you hope to achieve. Your business can be a sole proprietorship, general partnership, limited partnership, corporation, subchapter S corporation, or in some states a limited liability company (LLC). The chart on pages 102–103 compares the advantages and disadvantages of each legal form. If after reading this chapter you are still unclear which legal form is best for your business, it may be wise to discuss the options with an attorney or tax accountant.

## Sole Proprietorship

The simplest and least expensive business form is the sole proprietorship. In this form of organization, you alone own the business. Most small businesses just starting out are encouraged by small business consultants to choose this form until it becomes practical to enter into a partnership or to incorporate. The biggest disadvantage of this form of business is that the owner is fully liable for all business debts and lawsuits; the law, and any customers, don't distinguish between your personal and business assets. For example, if a client comes to your home office and falls on the sidewalk in front of your house, your home and all of your personal assets may be at stake in a lawsuit against your business. Therefore, to guard against potential lawsuits from your customers, you should purchase the liability insurance that was discussed in chapter 6, "Business Insurance 101."

Steps for establishing a sole proprietorship include:

- Deciding on a business name. In sole proprietorships and partnerships, you have the option of choosing a unique business name. If you aren't going to use your own name as the business name, (e.g., Connie Harper, doing business as [d/b/a] "Body St. Lucia"), you must register the business name by filing what's called a fictitious business statement with your, city, county, or state. In most states, you need only complete the fictitious business name statement and pay a registration fee to the county clerk. Some states also require you to place a fictitious name ad in a local newspaper, where it must run for three days. The cost to file a fictitious business name statement ranges from $10 to $100. To determine the procedure for your area contact your bank and ask what forms are needed to open a business account. If your state requires a fictitious business name statement, your bank may know how to obtain one.
- Opening a business checking account which is separated from your personal account(s). The bank also may require the fictitious business name statement, so be sure to call ahead of time.
- Applying for a Federal Tax ID number. This number can be obtained by filing form SS-4 with the Internal Revenue Service. You can use your Social Security number for a sole proprietorship, but it is more professional to have a special number for your business.
- Applying for a sales tax number, also known as a resale certificate. This is how your state tracks the amount of sales taxes

collected from you, your customers, and your vendors. When purchasing products wholesale, you will need to provide this number to the wholesaler so that he can sell you merchandise tax-free that you intend to resell. If you are in a service business and sell products, you are required to charge tax and will need a sales tax number. An example of this type of business is a hair braiding salon that also sells hair care products.

## Partnerships

If after reading the previous chapter, you decided to start a business with a partner, you'll proceed as you would in a sole proprietorship, except that all assets and liabilities are split among the partners. Thus, personal liability now extends to any of the partners. Now creditors or customers with judgments against the business can go after any or all of the partners' personal assets. This is why it is important to register the name of the partnership with your city or county and have a written agreement between partners outlining in concrete detail who will do what and to whom what is owed, and so on. All partners should purchase liability insurance.

You'll file a separate tax return for the partnership, which helps make claiming expenses easier. And moneywise, the partnership has an advantage in that banks will consider the assets of all partners to be used as collateral for a loan. In addition, selling partnerships can also be a method to raise money for the business.

### LIMITED PARTNERSHIPS

A limited partnership is similar to a general partnership except that it has two types of partners. The general partners have full personal responsibility for the partnership's liabilities in exchange for complete control and management of the business. The limited partners have liability limited to the amount of their investment, are not actively involved in the day-to-day running of the business, and are considered silent partners. Taking in limited partners is an excellent way to raise money without diluting your control of the business.

## Corporations

The legal corporation is the most advantageous form for a business because it is an autonomous legal entity that provides the ultimate protection from personal liability. Incorporating also is the most complex and expensive way to structure a business. But it is the best way to raise money from investors.

A corporation is owned by stockholders. There may be one stockholder owning all the shares or several owning various amount of shares. For the basic small business, there are two types of corporations. One is the C corporation, which is taxed twice by the Internal Revenue Service (IRS), who first taxes your profits and then taxes the dividends you pay out to your investors. The other is the subchapter S corporation, where the earnings and losses from the business are passed directly to the stockholders, who then pay the tax personally. The subchapter S corporation avoids double taxation.

Because the corporation is a separate legal entity, it will not dissolve upon the death of the officers of the business. It can be transferred from one party to another without upsetting the operation of the business.

### WHEN AND HOW SHOULD I INCORPORATE?

There really isn't an ideal time. Generally, experts have said that because of the expense of incorporating, it is better to wait until your business profits have reached five figures and exceed your personal income needs. However, seek out advice from your attorney and/or accountant. They can determine what's best for your particular business and tax situation.

Incorporating on your own has become relatively easy with legal self-help books and software, but it may not be legal in your state. If you're a novice in business, it may be wise to hire an attorney; if you incorporate incorrectly it will take more money to unincorporate yourself than to incorporate correctly in the first place.

# Limited Liability Company

The Limited Liability Company (LLC) is new and not available in every state. It is similar to a subchapter S corporation, with limited liability for the stockholders and taxable profits that pass through to the owners and not the business.

The LLC offers some advantages over the S corporation. For example, the S corporation can issue only one class of company stock, whereas LLCs can offer several classes of stock with different rights. The S corporation is also limited to a maximum of thirty-five shareholders, whereas an unlimited number of individuals, corporations, and partnerships may participate in an LLC.

## *Legal Forms of Business*

**SOLE PROPRIETORSHIP**

| *ADVANTAGES* | *DISADVANTAGES* |
| --- | --- |
| 1. Least expensive to establish | 1. Unlimited personal liability |
| 2. No double taxation | 2. Business terminated upon death |
| 3. Sole owner of business | 3. Ability to raise money is limited |
| 4. No legal requirements | |
| 5. Business losses are tax-deductible | |

**GENERAL PARTNERSHIP**

| *ADVANTAGES* | *DISADVANTAGES* |
| --- | --- |
| 1. Share ideas and workload | 1. Unlimited personal liability |
| 2. Easy to organize; less costly than a corporation | 2. Profits divided |
| 3. Access to more money for business | 3. Partnership ends upon death |
| 4. Losses are tax-deductible | |
| 5. Earnings from business taxed as personal income | |

**LIMITED PARTNERSHIP**

| *ADVANTAGES* | *DISADVANTAGES* |
| --- | --- |
| 1. General partners manage the business | 1. General partner has unlimited liability |
| 2. Limited partners liable only to amount of investment | 2. More legal regulations |

<table>
<tr><td>3. Earnings from business taxed as personal income</td><td>3. Limited partner(s) has no say in business</td></tr>
</table>

3. Earnings from business taxed as personal income

3. Limited partner(s) has no say in business

## CORPORATION

*ADVANTAGES*
1. Limited liability
2. Easier to raise money (through stock)
3. A separate legal entity
4. Tax benefits
5. Transferable ownership

*DISADVANTAGES*
1. Shareholders control business
2. Costs more to organize

3. Subject to double taxation
4. Regulated by states and IRS

## SUBCHAPTER S CORPORATION

*ADVANTAGES*
1. Same advantages of a corporation
2. Avoids double taxation

*DISADVANTAGES*
1. Regulated by state and IRS
2. Limited number of stockholders

## LIMITED LIABILITY COMPANY (LLC)

*ADVANTAGES*
1. Combination of business forms
2. Similar personal liability as corporation
3. Do not assume liability for business's debt
4. Tax advantages

*DISADVANTAGES*
1. Not available in all states
2. Tax requirements different in each state

## Business Licenses and Regulations

A business license is usually required by the city or county where your business will be located. The actual requirements vary from city to city and county to county. Some cities and counties do not require a business license, while others collect a business licensing fee annually. In addition to the licensing fee they may also receive a percentage of your gross sales and sales taxes. Home-based businesses that provide a professional service such as consulting may not need a business license. To find out what the licensing requirements are in your city, call the licensing bureau or the county registrar's or recorder's office.

## ZONING PERMITS

To run a business from your home—and do it legally—you will have to find out if your location is zoned for a home-based business. Not all types of businesses can be run from your home. For example, a business that has customers going in and out of your house will probably not be approved. Nor will a catering business. To determine if your business is allowed, first go to the county clerk's office to get a copy of the ordinances covering home-based businesses and read it carefully. You may even want to have your attorney take a look at it. Then check with the zoning office to see how your area is zoned. Also, if you live in an apartment, co-op, or condo, there may be restrictions on commercial use of your home; check your proprietary lease or with your landlord or building manager.

If your area isn't zoned for the type of business you want to start, consider the small incubator location instead.

## Patents

If you are like Sister CEO Veronica Smith and have designed an innovative product, it would behoove you to protect it with a patent. It's not an impossible feat and is actually easier than you might think.

The U.S. Patent and Trademark Office is now encouraging entrepreneurs to patent their products by reducing the filing fees for small businesses and individual inventors. The cost with outside legal advice is roughly $2,000 to $3,000, and the approval of the patent can take anywhere from eighteen to thirty-six months. But once it is patented it is protected for seventeen years.

Patents can make you a leader in your industry because no one else can use your design. And even if you don't plan to manufacture it yourself, you can license another company to manufacture it, sell the product, and receive a percentage of the sales.

Smith advises women with product ideas to work with a patent attorney who knows your industry. An attorney not only can assist you with obtaining the patent, but can advise you on how to protect your design from being stolen by another company. Patent infringement suits must be filed in federal courts and can be costly. For a patent application, contact the U.S. Patent and Trademark Office in Washington, D.C.

## *Sister CEO Action Steps*

1. Decide on the legal business form for your business.
2. Select a business name. If it is different from your name, file a fictitious business name statement.
3. Open a business checking account in the name of your business.
4. Obtain a business license from the county or city licensing bureau.
5. Apply for a Federal Tax ID Number.
6. Apply for a sales tax number/resale certificate.
7. If your business is home-based, obtain a copy of city ordinances.
8. Check with the zoning office to see if your home is zoned for your type of business.

# Chapter 8

# MONEY, MONEY, MONEY

---

*A sistah's true wealth is the good she does in this world.*

Every Sister CEO I talked to said scarcity of money was the biggest challenge she had to overcome to make her dream of owning her own business a reality. Most of the women had to use their own savings or borrow from family members. Myself included. Two years before my exit from Dean Witter I mapped out a plan to save two years of income to start my own business. It was tough, but I sacrificed dinners out, clothes, and expensive vacations. When I finally made the transition from employee to small-business owner, I had a nice nest egg to work with.

For most entrepreneurs, start-up money for a business is difficult to come by, and much more so for women of color, who generally are not taken seriously by the financial community. But today there are alternative sources and programs throughout the country providing start-up capital to help women establish their own businesses.

This chapter will cover some of the various ways to find money to start and grow your own business, from personal savings and credit cards to funding with venture capital and taking your company public. Remember the adage, "Where there is a will there is a way." Yes, there is a way; it may not be easy to find, but if it were, everyone would be doing it. With research, creative brainstorming, and lots of patience and persistence, you'll find there *is* money available for Sister CEOs to start their own businesses.

## Seed Capital: How Much Do I Need? Where Do I Go?

Plan on enough money to keep your company running for three to six months before you get any income out of it. Often your start-up costs exceed the amount you thought it would take, so it is actually a good idea to tack an additional 20 percent onto your expected costs—both one-time and monthly—and to work within that limit. For instance, if you have $5,000 to start with, you should keep your operating costs down to less than $1,000 a month while you are getting your business off the ground.

There are no fast rules that dictate the amount you need to start a business. As you saw with our business case study in chapter 6, the amount of money Connie Harper needed ranged from a high end of $1,750 to a low end of $1,150. A simple service business can be launched on a shoestring of under $500.

The secret to funding a start-up isn't to tap the best capital source you can, it's to tap *every* capital source you can. Sources can include: personal savings, family and friends, home equity loans, retirement savings, severance pay, credit cards, women's loan programs, banks, private investors, nonprofit foundations, the government (Small Business Administration), venture capital and going public.

## Going Personal

In most cases, starting a business using your own money is the only way to get your enterprise off the ground. And it may take some ingenious ways to make your start-up money. Cheryl and Nicky Moody, Sister CEOs of Found Treasures, a Washington, D.C.-based "wearable art" jewelry maker, have picked grapes at a winery, were au pairs to a wealthy family, and mounted butterflies in a museum in New York to save up the seed capital for their business, which now, by the way, makes jewelry for the

Hollywood elite. Bill and Camille Cosby are among their high-profile clients. Their jewelry has also been featured on the cover of *Essence* magazine and in major movies such as *Sister Act* and *Leonard, Part VI.*

Loan institutions and private investors take a dim view of risking their money for a proposed business unless the owners have a vested interest in the venture. You must be willing to commit some or all of your funds to start your business, because you're not likely to find anyone out there willing to fund 100 percent of a new company. If you do, find out what you are giving up in return for the money. A lender who takes that much risk is going to ask for a substantial return. It is likely that either the cost of the money (interest charged) will be high, or you will have to give up the majority ownership in the company. In that case, you would basically be an employee of the company.

By using your own money, you risk your own finances but you retain control of your company. And later, when you're ready to seek outside capital, you will look more attractive to lenders because of the confidence you have exhibited by investing and risking your own money. They're looking for people who are committed. Later in the chapter you'll read more about what traits lenders require to approve a loan.

## Loan Programs Specifically for Women

In Chicago, New York, Washington, D.C., San Francisco, and other major metropolitan areas in the United States you can find woman-only loan programs. These are loans which come directly from an agency with no bank participation. They are aimed specifically at women who generally cannot quality through the traditional financial channels and who have the toughest time convincing bankers to give them credit.

All Sister CEOs can apply for these programs, even if you receive Aid to Families with Dependent Children (AFDC). For example, the Women's Self-Employment Project (WSEP) and the Illinois Department of Public Aid have joined forces to create the Women's Business Initiative, a program that provides entrepreneurial business training, financial services, and microbusiness loans to Chicago women on welfare. "The goal of the Women's Business Initiative is to help poor women start businesses and work their way from welfare dependency to self-sufficiency," says Connie E. Evans, executive director of WSEP. The organization not only provides money but also teaches women how to run a business as well. Most participants are required to attend a series of business planning workshops to assess whether they are ready to become entrepreneurs. Participants must create an actual business plan in order to participate in the loan fund. For women already in business, WSEP also offers consulting services, mentor programs, and money for expansion.

Some of the loan programs are very original and creative. One in particular is called the Full Circle Fund, and is modeled after the Grameen Bank in Bangladesh. The fund blends peer support and nontraditional lending into a uniquely successful financial service. Full Circle Fund participants form circles of five women from the same community. The women select each other and they cannot be relatives or partners. They meet once every two weeks for support and assistance. Two women at a time can borrow money from the fund. They are required to make three loan payments over a six-week period before the other women can borrow money. The collateral used to back the loan is the peer support of the other women. In other words, if you don't make our loan repayments on time you get ripped by your fellow sistahs.

The nature of the other loans vary. For example, the Women's Initiative for Self-Employment (WISE) in the San Francisco Bay Area offers $500 research loans to test market your business idea. General start-up loans through WISE range from $100 to $25,000. Expansion loans go as high as $50,000. Usually your first loan is limited to $1,000 to $1,500. This must be paid off within one year and then you can go back for more. Interest rates can range from 10 to 15 percent. Creditwise, the programs are less stringent. If you haven't established credit, you can still qualify for a loan. If you have a bad credit history, you will need to explain why, show that you are correcting the problems that have affected your credit, and prove that the new loan will not make your debt load unmanageable.

See the appendix for the names and addresses of a few of the women-based programs in major cities.

## Small Business Administration Women's Program

The Small Business Administration is also beginning to see the viability of women-owned businesses. They have created a partnership with private business development organizations in rural and urban areas to provide start-up, management, and expansion training to socially and economically disdavantaged businesswomen. Currently there are fifty-five Women's Business Center Demonstration Project offices throughout the country. Call 800-U-ASK-SBA for a list of project sites in your area; see the appendix for the Internet connection.

## Other Support Organizations

Researching all money avenues is the only way to go. Several women's groups provide business advice but not funding. It's a great idea to join and network within these organizations; someone just may point you in the right direction. Contact the following:

- Association of Black Women Entrepreneurs, Los Angeles, CA, (213) 624-8639*
- National Association of Black Women Entrepreneurs, Detroit, MI, (810) 356-3686*
- National African-American Chamber of Commerce, Dallas, TX, (214) 871-3060
- National Chamber of Commerce for Women, New York, NY, (212) 685-3454
- National Association of Women Business Owners, (800) 238-2233
- National Minority Supplier Development Council, New York, NY, (212) 944-2430*

*Organizations marked with asterisks are run by sistahs.

- Minority Business Development Agency, Washington, D.C., (202) 482-4547*
- National Association of Women's Business Advocates, Chicago, IL, (312) 814-7176

## Credit Cards

None of the women I interviewed used credit cards for start-up capital, but many entrepreneurs today are finding this a viable source of money. The interest rates are high, but it is a way to get several thousand dollars quickly without the hassle of dealing with paperwork—as long as you don't go above your credit limit. One of the most famous African Americans to use this method is comedian Robert Townsend. With $60,000 from his credit cards, he financed his first movie, *Hollywood Shuffle*.

If you have a job, there are many banks that will issue you a credit card with a $5,000 credit limit. Five or six cards can mean $30,000 in credit and can be much easier to get than a $30,000 loan from a bank. With so much competition among banks, you may be able to find an introductory single-digit credit card rate with a one-year time span. You can use the low-rate cards to start, and when the introductory rate expires, switch to a new low-rate card.

However, caution is absolutely necessary if you're going to go the credit card route. It should only be a short-term solution to raising capital. Be careful about how much you borrow and make sure you remain current on your payments. It's easy to get over-extended.

## Private Investors

Private investors, also known as "angels," are an excellent source of capital for Sister CEOs. The key is to find them. These investors range from friends and family to successful business owners who have a few thousand dollars to invest in someone like you.

In mainstream America, there are enterprise forums in which start-up entrepreneurs make presentations before a group of "angels." A prime example is the Microsoft Corporation. It's estimated that more than 1,000 early investors in Microsoft are now millionaires.

For family and friends, you know where to go. For wealthy and successful business owners, talk with your attorney, banker, or accountant. They can be an excellent source of referrals and tell you who may be interested in investing in small businesses. One caveat: "angels" want to make money, so many will want equity participation. In other words, you'll have to give up some control of your company for the capital. But, as my partner John Douglas pointed out to me, what's better—to have 50 percent of your own company or 100 percent of no company? I'll let you figure out the best answer.

## Banks

Banks are notorious for not financing mainstream small-business owners, so you *know* the odds of a Sister CEO getting money are definitely pretty small. But since I am not one to be pessimistic, I think you need to know how to go about finding money from a bank. If you recall the story of Cathy Hughes, Sister CEO of Radio One, Inc., it took thirty-two bank rejections before she landed a loan. So you see, it can be done. Especially if bankers like Emma C. Chappell, Sister CEO of United Bank of Philadelphia, has her way. Chappell's bank is three years old, with $95 million in assets. She hopes to pave the way for more minority and women entrepreneurs to receive money. As an entrepreneur who has been through the trenches herself, she understands. "Women and minorities have a more difficult time getting capital," she says. "That's why we created this bank."

Keep in mind, though, that banks will rarely help with start-up money. Your company needs to be up and running and looking for capital to expand before they'll sit down and talk with you.

### DEVELOP A BANKING RELATIONSHIP

Whether you are looking to borrow money or not, Sister CEOs must develop a relationship with a banker. It makes good business sense. And you never know when your business may suddenly take off or you need some fast cash to fund more production or expansion. Good bankers can also save you money in fees and enhance your business opportunities through their extensive personal contacts.

### *Where Do You Start?*

You can save yourself some valuable time by bypassing the banking mega-giants and heading straight for the local community bank in your area. These banks are equipped to meet small-business financial needs, offering accounts and services ranging from basic checking, savings, and payroll activities, to lines of credit, equipment loans, and investment plans.

These banks build their reputations on providing services for small businesses. That means if you want to get some personal attention and satisfy your banking needs, they can help. Plus, many offer special programs for women and minorities in business. According to Debra Kaplan, assistant vice president at the Bank of California, her bank will provide a loan as low as $10,000 and will take into account your business experience as opposed to the amount of collateral you have to offer.

## WHAT A BANKER WANTS TO KNOW

When a Sister CEO asks for a loan, this is what a banker wants to know:

- How much money do you want to borrow?
- Why do you want the money, and how will it be used?
- What is the primary source that will generate the funds to repay the loan, such as selling inventory or increasing your business?
- What is the secondary source of repayment in case the business fails?
- How will the loan be secured (collateral)?
- Who will guarantee the loan? (The bank wants you to take the bulk of the risk.)

113

To increase your odds of a banker saying "yes" to your loan proposal, follow these six banking lessons:

### Banking 101

1. Shop for a bank that targets woman entrepreneurs. Establish a strong relationship. Transfer all your accounts—personal and business—into the branch. Immediately introduce yourself to the branch manager and loan officer.
2. Before talking to any loan officer about money, understand clearly yourself what you need the money for and how much you need.
3. Get your financial house in order—personal as well as business. Pay off or down any of your credit cards and review your credit report before the bank does to clean up any possible mistakes. Have a thorough set of financial statements ready, such as your tax return and savings and checking account statements going back at least three years. Have your accountant assist you in compiling the information.
4. Be prepared to answer a lot of questions. The banker wants to know two basic things: do you really need the money, and how are you going to pay it back—in good times and bad. Think through every bad scenario that could happen to you or your business and have a strategic plan in place. We will cover more on planning in chapter 12, "Your Game Plan."
5. When calculating how much you will need to grow your company, be sure to add extra money to the initial loan amount as a reserve cushion. It may be difficult to go back to the bank later and ask for more money.
6. To help legitimize your business, include product samples, press clippings, promotional material, and any other supporting evidence with your loan application.

In spite of the negative publicity banks receive for not helping small-business owners, go ahead and apply anyway. What do you have to lose? It just may be *your* lucky day to get a supportive banker who wants to help you grow your business.

## Foundations: Hidden Wealth

An often overlooked source of money for a business is a non-profit foundation. All you need is (1) enough perseverance to sift through 32,000 private foundations and community-based non-profit organizations for one that matches your business or industry, and (2) the ability to prove that funding your enterprise will benefit the community the foundation serves.

Many foundations don't deal directly with entrepreneurs but contribute through incubators and small-business development centers (see chapter 6). The foundations that give money can only contribute if the recipient's business is working toward the foundation's charitable mission. For example, if your business will help rebuild an economically struggling community, plus provide jobs, you may qualify for a "Program-Related Investment" (PRI) grant or a low-interest loan.

To tap into these foundations, start at the public library. A good source is the *Encyclopedia of Associations* that lists nonprofit organizations throughout the country.

## Small Business Administration

The Small Business Administration (SBA) is another government agency that isn't quite user-friendly to entrepreneurs. Oftentimes it's been called the lender of last resort by small-business owners because of the arduous process it takes to get money.

The SBA can make direct loans to special small businesses. However, it is much more common for them to guarantee loans from commercial banks. The SBA will guarantee 75 percent of a bank loan up to $750,000 if other financing isn't available. You must show the SBA that you have tried every reasonable method to obtain financing from the traditional sources without any success before they will consider your application.

The SBA offers a wide range of loan programs for entrepreneurs. Below are the three main ones.

**1) General 7(a) guaranteed loan program.** This program doesn't use government money; money is loaned by the bank or other financial institution but guaranteed by the SBA for 75 percent of the value of the loan. The interest rates are negotiable between the borrower and the lender and pegged to the lowest prime rate as listed in the *Wall Street Journal*. For loans of less than seven years, the rate is 2.25 percent over prime. For loans of more than seven years, the rate is 2.75 percent over prime.

**2) The 8(a) participant loan program.** This program gives financial assistance to firms that are certified as minority- or women-owned. It is not available in all states. Check with the Small Business Administration in your area.

**3) The microloan program.** This loan is good for Sister CEOs just starting out. There are more than 200 microloan programs available through foundations, banks, and the SBA. The loan amounts range from less than $100 to a maximum of $25,000 and differ from traditional loans in that they are offered to low-income borrowers and require little or no collateral. The qualifications are less stringent and it isn't mandatory for you to have an excellent credit record and a high salary.

The qualifications to obtain a guarantee on a loan through the SBA are similar to those of a bank. The SBA is looking for a Sister CEO with management ability and experience in her field, a business plan, some of her own money invested in the business (anywhere from 20 to 50 percent of the loan amount), and the ability to repay the loan from the projected cash flow and profits.

## Venture Capital

Venture capital firms invest money in businesses and expect a handsome return on their investments. They provide capital, absorb the initial financing risk, and then sell stock when the business becomes profitable.

Venture capitalists are what's known as equity partners. They invest money in your company with the intention of receiving four to five times the amount back once the business is sold. Therefore, they examine potential companies with extreme care. This type of financing is for a Sister CEO who really has it going on in business.

Your company has to be financially together, already making headway in a proven or up-and-coming industry, and capable of extensive business growth. Most venture capitalists are only interested in projects requiring an investment of $250,000 or more.

According to JoAnn Price, Sister CEO of Fairview Capital Partners, an African American venture capital firm, "The time to talk to a venture capitalist is when you need a lot of money and your company is in a hot industry such as broadcasting, high technology, health care, manufacturing, or food. These are the companies that many venture capitalists are funding today."

Very few Sister CEO companies are receiving venture capital money, according to Liz Harris, vice president of UNC Partners, a venture capital firm based in Boston, Massachusetts. "It's unfortunate, but many black women business owners haven't yet reached this level of financing."

There are several types of venture capital firms. They include:

- **Traditional partnerships.** These are generally established by wealthy families who want to invest a portion of their investment portfolio in small businesses.
- **Professionally managed pools.** These operate like the traditional partnerships but are made up of institutional money.
- **Insurance companies.** These firms usually invest a portion of their assets in small businesses for the growth potential.
- **Manufacturing companies.** Many *Fortune* 500 companies have a venture capital arm of their business to invest in small businesses that produce new products for their industry. It's their way of staying abreast of the market.
- **Specialized Small Business Investment Corporations (SSBICs).** SSBICs have been a key source of financing for black companies. These are privately capitalized investment agencies licensed and regulated by the SBA and designed to aid minority-owned and minority-managed firms with equity funds from private and public capital. SSBICs are restricted in the amount of money they can loan a small-business owner. Currently that figure tops out at $1 million. To obtain a list of the SSBICs in the United States, contact your nearest SBA office.

Although your company may not be ready for venture capital financing, it is still an area you should become familiar with in order to take your company into the multimillion-dollar level when the times comes. And now there is more help to take you there. Over the past several years there has been an increase in African American venture capital firms like Fairview Capital Partners and UNC Partners that are interested in funding black-owned companies. For a listing of other African American–run venture capital firms, contact the National Association of Investment Companies (NAIC), Washington, D.C., (202) 289-4336. The list can be purchased for a fee.

## Going Public

When you have been in business for a while and need money to grow, you can consider raising money by "going public" and selling stock in your company to be traded over the nation's securities exchanges.

This is a relatively new avenue for African American businesses. However, it is beginning to open up. Johnson Products, maker of Ultra Sheen, was one of the first black-owned businesses to trade on a major stock exchange. Since its buyout by another company, it is no longer traded on the exchange. Black Entertainment Television (BET) currently trades on the New York Stock Exchange.

Although going public can be an excellent way to obtain a large sum of capital, it is a long, complex, and expensive process. However, when you ask small-business owners who are now multimillionaires whether it was worth it to take their company public, you'll hear a resounding yes.

### WHEN TO TAKE YOUR COMPANY PUBLIC

Companies that go public usually expect to sell shares worth $1 million to $10 million. The money is used to pay off debt, buy new equipment, or purchase an office building. Going public also allows the owner of the business to "cash in" part of her investment in the business. She can sell part of her stock either during the initial public offering (IPO) of the stock, or at a later time.

Going public is also good for your employees. You can offer stock options as part of their benefits package, or even give them shares outright. The more profitable the company becomes, the more their stock will be worth—an added incentive for them to work hard to help improve the company's bottom line.

Going public also has disadvantages. First of all, when your company goes public you are no longer calling all the shots. Your shareholders have a major say in how the business is run. Second, your business operations become public. All financial and management information must be available to the general public. This regulation is enforced by the Securities and Exchange Commission (SEC), the government agency that regulates the offering and sale of public stocks. The SEC requires all public firms to disclose certain information to potential investors to enable them to make an intelligent investment decision. You will need to disclose your company's sales and profits, as well as the salaries paid to the top executives in the firm. Your company will not only need to report this information in the beginning of the IPO, but in quarterly and annual reports as well.

## SCOR—THE NEW WAY TO GO PUBLIC

SCOR—the Small Corporate Offering Registration program—is the latest kind of equity financing for small businesses. This program, available in forty-one states, allows a company to raise up to $5 million by selling common stock directly to the public for at least $5 per share. It's a do-it-yourself form of underwriting and it costs about $20,000 to complete. The SCOR guidelines fall under federal regulations A and D 504.

With Regulation D 504, you must file registration documents with the state securities office or department of corporations. The state office is not required to register the offering with the SEC. Companies under this regulation can raise up to $1 million in securities sales within a one-year period. You are required to provide an offering circular to each potential investor.

With Regulation A, the state must inform the SEC of the offering.

However, for securities sales of up to $5 million, the SEC is not required to register the public offering.

Even though the process is set up to be less bureaucratic and isn't nearly as complicated as the initial public offering (IPO), going public is still serious business. You must understand and follow the regulations to avoid costly blunders for your business. Before making any decisions to take your company public, talk with a securities attorney, an investment banker, and an accountant. In the appendix are listed the major African American investment banking firms and SCOR resources.

Money will continue to be a major issue throughout the life of your business. Stay abreast of the latest financing available for small businesses by networking with other business owners and attending conferences such as the *Black Enterprise* Entrepreneurs Conference and the Dow Jones Conference on Black Entrepreneurism. Both conferences hold special seminars on all aspects of finding money for your business.

*Sister CEO Action Steps*

1. Calculate the amount of seed money you need for your business.
2. Contact a women's loan program in your area to take a business planning class.
3. Develop a relationship with your banker and ask about their policy on business loans.
3. Visit your local Small Business Administration to obtain their small-business loan packet.
4. Call the National Association of Investment Companies (NAIC) for a listing of African American–run venture capital firms.

# Chapter 9

# MANAGING THE MONEY

Let money compound on money and work for you.
BENJAMIN FRANKLIN

Cash flow management is every entrepreneur's nightmare. Even for the financially astute, it's one of the toughest challenges every small business owner faces. Most have experienced a cash flow crisis at one time or another. Unfortunately, it's part of the learning process of being a Sister CEO.

How do business owners get into a cash flow slump? It can happen in a couple of ways. First, entrepreneurs spend so much time trying to get new business that they neglect to monitor the money coming in and going out. Second, when business is going strong and cash is flowing rapidly, they don't set aside any money for a rainy day, when sales decrease. These are both big mistakes! Take it from me and the other Sister CEOs who went through the school of hard knocks and have experienced cash flow crunches—believe me they aren't fun. One rule of thumb is, *Plan on everything in a start-up business to take twice as long and cost twice as much as you expect.*

In a nutshell: Stay lean and mean, trim your expenses to the bare minimum, and run your company as efficiently as possible.

## Where Do You Start?

Keep good financial records. A small business that fails to keep complete and accurate financial records places its long-term success and continuance in grave, grave danger.

Maintaining good day-to-day records provides the financial data that help you operate your business more efficiently, thus increasing the profitability of your company. Your records will enable you to identify all your business assets, liabilities, income, and expenses and help you pinpoint the strong and weak areas of your business. If there is a cash flow problem, you'll be able to see it before it turns into a major catastrophe.

Good records are also crucial for the preparation of current financial statements, such as the income statement (profit or loss) and the cash flow projection. These statements will present you with a complete picture of your total operation. You'll know exactly when you are in the red or in the black, and in what areas you need to make major financial changes. These statements are also essential if you are planning to apply for a business loan. Lenders will request them along with your business plan.

Good financial records are needed for the preparation of your business income taxes. Poor records often result in underpayment or overpayment of taxes. In addition, if you are audited by the IRS, you'll need accurate records to substantiate the expenses and income you claim on your income tax forms.

## Recordkeeping 101

Setting up the books for your business is priority No. 1. Don't even think about starting your business without a system in place. In this chapter, I'll set up the books of Connie Harper's Body St. Lucia and show you sample financial statements you can use to create statements for your business.

The system doesn't have to be complicated. In fact, it should be simple to use, easy to understand, reliable, accurate, consistent, and informational on a timely basis. You can design the system yourself, or use a computer. You should also hire an accountant to analyze the data. I'll cover selecting an accountant later in the chapter.

The two common forms of bookkeeping used by small businesses are single entry and double entry. If your business is small you may need only single entry bookkeeping. But if your business has to keep track of inventory, or you manufacture a product, the preferred method is double entry. It provides better cross-checking of income and expenses, giving you a more accurate picture of the financial condition of your business.

## CASH VERSUS ACCRUAL

For either double entry or single entry bookkeeping, there are two methods of keeping track of your cash flow: cash and accrual.

If you make an entry in your books when you actually receive the money or pay a bill, you are using the cash method. If you offer your clients or customers credit (they can pay later), and you include that income in your books before you get paid, you're using the accrual method. The IRS actually requires small businesses with inventory to use the accrual method. At year-end you are required to count your inventory on hand, even though it hasn't been paid for. Therefore, Body St. Lucia will use the accrual method because Connie will maintain an inventory of her beauty products.

As a service business you can select either method, although the IRS stipulates that once you have begun using the accrual method you cannot switch back to the cash method without filing a special application for approval to change.

## RECORDS TO KEEP

Your business will generate four basic types of records that you will need to track:

- Sales records
- Cash receipts
- Cash disbursements
- Accounts receivable

Sales records include all income from the sales of products or services. You can group them into one category or into sub-categories of different product lines so you can track which product is doing well and which isn't.

Cash receipts account for all monies generated through cash sales and through collection from your accounts receivable. This is actual income your business has received; it doesn't include money from your sales records unless you have a cash and carry business (when you make the sale you get paid immediately). In that case, your cash receipts should match your sales records.

Cash disbursements are your operating expense records or accounts payable. Your disbursements should be made by check so that business expenses can be documented for tax purposes. If you do pay by cash, include a receipt or some other form of proof with your records. Also, keep all your cancelled checks and paid bills in a safe file to back up the records.

Accounts receivable is the money owed to your company for products or services rendered. If you extend a client or customer credit, allowing them to pay in thirty, sixty, or ninety days, you need to keep careful track of when payments are due. Maintain these records on a monthly basis so you age your receivables and determine the length of time your credit customers are taking to pay their bills. The recommended payment term is as soon as possible, minimum thirty days. Anything longer impairs your cash flow.

## PREPRINTED BOOKKEEPING JOURNALS/SOFTWARE PROGRAMS

To keep track of these accounts you can use two methods. If you own a computer, you can use several software programs, such as Quickbooks by Intuit or Peachtree Accounting. Both programs have templates for small businesses. Basically, you just fill in the blanks and the program will balance your income and expenses and create a financial statement for each account.

The second method is the simple paper and pencil technique. Most office supply office stores sell simple bookkeeping systems. These come in formats that are laid out for specific businesses—

retail store, professional service, and so on. They're quite simple to use because here, too, you fill in the blanks.

## Financial Statements

Summarizing your bookkeeping records into financial statements will give you important data about the state of your business. The two most common financial statements are the income statement (sometimes called a profit and loss statement) and the balance sheet. The information with which to compile the statements is drawn directly from your journal of business accounts.

These statements provide a wealth of information. By regularly preparing and reviewing them you will know how much income your business is generating, whether your business is profitable, which expenses are a problem, and who owes you money.

Review your financial statements weekly to gain a real grasp of what is happening in the day-to-day running of the business. Eventually you will begin to see the sales and cash flow pattern of your business.

### *Income Statement (P & L)*

#### BODY ST. LUCIA BODY & BATH PRODUCTS
##### PROFIT AND LOSS STATEMENT AS OF DECEMBER 31, 1997

**INCOME**

| | | |
|---|---|---|
| Sales | $900 | |
| (Returns & allowances) | (25) | |
| Net sales | | $875 |
| (Cost of goods sold) | (600) | |
| **Gross profit** | | **275** |
| Gross margin (gross profit/net sales) | | 31% |

**EXPENSES**

| | |
|---|---|
| Advertising | $100 |
| Auto | 50 |
| Bank charges | 72 |

| | |
|---|---:|
| Office supplies | 20 |
| Professional services | 0 |
| Taxes & licenses | 50 |
| Telephone | 30 |
| Travel & entertainment | 0 |
| Miscellaneous | 25 |
| **Total expenses** | **$347** |
| **Net profit/loss** | **$(72)** |

## THE PROFIT AND LOSS STATEMENT

An income statement is your scorecard on the financial performance of your business. It reflects when sales are made and when expenses are incurred and differs from a cash flow statement in that the income statement doesn't show when the money is collected or when expenses are paid. It does, however, show the projected profitability of the business over a specific time frame. The sample on pages 125–126 shows a typical income statement.

## THE BALANCE SHEET

A balance sheet is generated annually and is a summary of your company's assets, liabilities, and equity. This sheet shows what the business owns and what it owes. What you own is reported as assets. These include cash, accounts receivable, and inventory. What you owe is reported as liabilities. These are classified as current or long-term. Debts that are due in one year or less are current liabilities. Debts due beyond one year are long-term.

The balance sheet also includes the calculation of owner's equity. This is your yardstick of how much you have in the business. Investors who are interested in investing in your company will look at this number when making a decision. To calculate the amount, substract the total liabilities from total assets. A sample balance sheet is shown on page 127.

## Balance Sheet

### BODY ST. LUCIA
### BALANCE SHEET
### DECEMBER 31, 1997

**Current Assets**

| | | |
|---|---|---|
| Cash | $200 | |
| Accounts receivable | 0 | |
| Inventory | 300 | |
| Total current assets | | $500 |

**Fixed Assets**

| | | |
|---|---|---|
| Computer | 2,000 | |
| Fax machine | 200 | |
| Printer | 300 | |
| Total fixed assets | | 2,500 |

**Liabilities**

| | | |
|---|---|---|
| Current liabilities | | |
| Accounts payable | 100 | |
| Sales taxes | 50 | |
| Total current liabilities | | 150 |

| | | |
|---|---|---|
| **Long-term liabilities** | 0 | |
| **Total long-term liabilities** | | 0 |

| | | |
|---|---|---|
| **Owner's equity** | | **2,350** |
| **Total liabilities and owner's equity** | | **$2,500** |

## Managing Your Cash Flow

Cash flow means business survival and it is one of the most misunderstood concepts among small-business owners. The way it generally works is: as sales go up, cash (meaning cash on hand) goes down, because you are spending more money on inventory and labor. It's crucial that you manage what comes in as tightly as what goes out. If you're selling a lot of products or services and not collecting the money promptly and watching your expenses, you will find your business quickly facing a cash flow problem.

Another reason why you want to keep a tight rein on your

finances is because sales of your product or service can be cyclical and seasonal—not all companies make (or should expect to make) the same percentage of return, or even generate the same revenues, every month year in, year out.

Here are five cash control strategies:

1. Create a monthly budget for your sales and expenses. It's a blueprint for your business and what you hope to achieve over a month's time. Start by forecasting how much in sales you expect for that month. For example, if you're selling a service, price out the fees you forecast and build your expected expenses around that figure. See page 129 for a sample budget.

2. Once you have a budget, begin tracking your cash flow. Make sure you know where your money stands at all times. Set aside time daily or weekly to update yourself on billings and collections. When you see more outflow than income, immediately nip it in the bud.

3. If your business is product-oriented like Body St. Lucia, maintain a low inventory. That's money wasting away just sitting on the shelf. Purchase products only when inventory is low.

4. Collect your money. If you offer credit to your customers to pay at a later date, bill promptly and continue to follow up when the bill isn't paid. The government and large corporations are notorious for not paying small businesses on time. Many have gone under waiting for money to come in. If you provide services or products to either of these entities, make sure you have a two to three months' money cushion to tap into when their payments are late. Ideally, try to have clients or customers prepay all or a portion of the total price before they receive the service or products.

5. Ax your overhead. Look for savings in every area, especially office supplies, advertising, postage, and the phone bill. These are areas where expenses can easily get out of hand.

## *Budget*

### BODY ST. LUCIA
### CASH FLOW/BUDGET STATEMENT
### MONTH_____ , **199**__

| | ACTUAL (A) | BUDGET (B) | OVER/UNDER (C) | %(c/b x 100) |
|---|---|---|---|---|
| Cash sales | $100 | $200 | $100 | −50% |
| | | | | |
| Receivables | | | | |
| Other income | | | | |
| Total income | 100 | | | |
| Expenses | | | | |
| Cost of goods | 50 | 50 | | |
| Advertising | 25 | 100 | 75 | +75% |
| Office supplies | 30 | 25 | 5 | −20% |
| | | | | |
| Total expenses | 105 | 175 | 70 | +40% |
| | | | | |
| Ending cash balance | $−5 | | | −10% |

**Note:** Body St. Lucia lost money this month because sales were down and products were purchased with the expectation of selling out at the end of the month.

## Tax Planning

Before opening your business, you should have a clear understanding of all your local, state, and federal tax obligations, when you have to make payments, and what deductions you can claim on your income tax forms. Because of the complexity of the tax laws, it is essential to seek advice from an accountant or tax attorney familiar with your type of business. The federal government is also a good source of information. The IRS publishes a free tax guide for small businesses each year.

## Should I Hire a Certified Public Accountant (CPA)?

Doing your own books is the surest way to understand how your business really works. However, business tax law changes constantly. As a Sister CEO, you probably won't have time to run your business and stay abreast of the changes. The wisest course to take is to do your own bookkeeping while your business is small, and also hire a CPA periodically to analyze the financial statements, to coordinate tax planning, and to complete yearly tax returns. As your business grows, you'll hire a CPA who will work with you year-round. However, continue to monitor the cash flow yourself and sign off on all outgoing checks. Despite their stature and income, Sister CEOs Anita Baker and Oprah Winfrey sign all outgoing checks. Anita Baker even does the payroll.

### Sister CEO Action Steps

1. Top priority: Before you sell any products or provide a service, set up an accounting system.
2. Create a monthly business budget.
3. Carefully monitor your business's cash flow. Track the inflow and outflow of all monies daily. Compare the actual figures with your budget.
4. Build up a money cushion for the lean months.
5. Obtain the free *Tax Guide for Small Businesses* from the IRS.
6. Hire the services of a CPA.

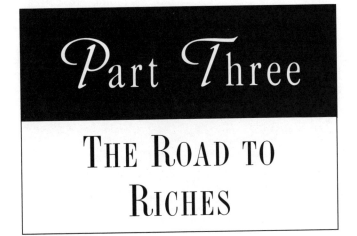

# Part Three

## THE ROAD TO
## RICHES

# Chapter 10

## FAST-GROWING BUSINESSES MADE FOR YOU

Seventy-five percent of all self-made millionaires achieved their wealth by owning their own businesses.

*USA TODAY*

In chapter 3, "The Ideal Business for You to Start," you learned that in order to be successful and become wealthy in your own business, you need to be passionate about or at least have a strong interest in the industry you select. I hope that by now you have completed the exercises in that chapter, and that you have a general idea of what business you would like to start. But if you still don't have a clue as to what business you can start on a shoestring budget, this chapter is for you.

Don't fall for the usual trap and let lack of money stop you. Nor do you have to quit your "day" job. You can start part-time right at home without risking your life's savings. The time to start: **NOW! Don't wait any longer!** Black women must seize the opportunity today. If it's economic freedom you want, then you owe it to yourself to start a business where *you* can decide how much money you make and what days and hours you will work—**you're the boss.** If it's a corner office you want, with "CEO" behind your name on the door, build the office around it!

In this chapter, I'll take a look at the four basic types of businesses today: product business, service business, mail-order business, and retail storefront. I'll give you starting-up ideas in each of those areas. I'll tell you a few Sister CEOs success stories for each business type. All of the businesses except the retail store/restaurant can be started right out of your home. For the business ideas, I scoured a slew of magazines and books; so can you! Several are take-offs of other businesses but with an ethnic twist. If none of the businesses suit your fancy, then design your own. Never limit your imagination!

The four worst words an entrepreneur can say are "I think I'll wait." If you have a unique idea for a business, what are you waiting for? More opportunities are lost, more years wasted, more lives unfulfilled by those four little words. Rest assured, if you don't like the freedom and the reward of being your boss, you can always go back to where you are now. But chances are, you'll be having too much fun to ever look back. Become bold and get it started.

The entrepreneurs that are wealthy today are leaders in their field. They, too, had a unique business idea. The only difference is that they did something with it. They took it and ran with it. When you have a business idea that isn't like anything out there, you need to quickly move forward on it to gain a strong market share. You want to be the major player—before your competition comes knocking at your door with knock-offs of your products.

## Market Trends

When selecting a business, it is important to look for trends in the marketplace. In today's fast-moving economic climate, you must get a handle on the changing markets that will affect the way you do business. You can either stay on top of the trends or fall behind the competition. You need to always have your antenna up, scouting for business opportunities. Your company really has to know where it is going and have a vision of the future that matches where the world is going. According to *Entrepreneur* magazine, the following industries and businesses are predicted to grow in the twenty-first century:

- Education
- Entertainment
- Health care (mental, physical, and cosmetic)
- Spirituality
- Ethnic-related concepts
- Self-discovery
- Personal services
- Financial security
- Personal safety and security

How to research trends will be covered in depth in the chapter on marketing. For now, I want you to think of today's trends as you read through the lists of business ideas in this chapter. Trends are always changing, so read with an open mind.

## Before Taking the Plunge

In addition to understanding the market trends affecting your selected business, you must also assess its potential for success. You don't want to spend precious time and money on a business that isn't feasible. For each business you are considering, ask yourself the following questions:

- **Start-up costs:** What are the out-of-pocket costs to start this business?
- **Income potential:** How much money can you *really* make in the business?
- **Growth potential:** Who are your competitiors? Is there room for growth or is the market saturated?
- **Recession resistance:** Will the business have peaks and valleys based on the economy?
- **Market appeal:** Does your product appeal to the mass market or to a specific niche?
- **Expansion potential:** What are the chances of expanding your product or service offering? Increasing your number of clients or customers?

- **Absentee ownership:** Can you take a vacation without worrying about a drop in your income?
- **Anxiety level:** Will this business create a lot of anxiety, and are you willing to go through it?
- **Time factor:** How much time will it take to get the business up and running, and do you have the time?
- **Lifestyle impact:** How much will this business impact your life and family time?
- **Pressure level:** Will the business constantly keep you on the edge?
- **Success ratio:** What is the success/failure ratio of this type of business?
- **Satisfaction factor:** Will this business help you reach your goals?

These questions are food for thought and will help you evaluate your business choices and expectations. Don't expect clear-cut answers. Some of the businesses will have both positive and negative traits. It's just a matter of deciding which traits are the most important to you, regardless of whether they are positive or negative.

## The Four Directions

### PRODUCT BUSINESS

In a *product* business you either make or buy products which you sell to others for a profit. The products can cover the range of all goods: jewelry, clothing (ethnic or not), food items, art, cosmetics, greeting cards, and so on. To sell these products you may run a store, a gallery, or a mail-order business, exhibit at trade shows, have customers at your own home, or use one of many other types of outlets.

The product business is my favorite. I believe it is better to build a business by offering an array of products, so customers can continue to come back for different ones. Repeat business is a built-in annuity. Certain product businesses are even recession proof. No matter what's happening in the economy, people will continue to buy the product. Cosmetics, toiletries, and vitamins fall into this category. Jewelry, cosmetics, and African clothing are popular and have proven successful for Sister CEOs in this category.

Here is one list of possible product businesses for you to consider. I've broken them down into the following categories: artistic/creative, high-tech, food, and spirituality. But remember— this is just a starting point! If your idea isn't here, it doesn't mean it isn't good; it means it's original.

### Artistic/Creative
- African American literature and books on tape.
- Paper goods: Afrocentric/people of color theme stationery.
- Self-published books: Start out writing about what you know.
- Niche publisher of other authors' work in a specific category, such as black romance novels.
- Unique children's clothes.
- Imported or handmade/ethnic clothing.
- Multicultural greeting cards: Margot Dashiell, Sister CEO of Frederick Douglass Designs in Berkeley, California, states that the greeting card business is becoming more competitive, but there is still room for opportunity.
- Afrocentric/multicultural home decorations: African sculptures, wall hangings, and furniture are big.
- Cosmetics/perfumes (homemade or commercial): natural scents and ingredients not tested on animals are in vogue.
- Black art/books/toys/memorabilia: many of these are becoming collector's items. Raid your great-great grandmother's attic to unearth some priceless treasures.
- Aromatherapy oils, potpourri, candles.
- Full-figured clothes, lingerie: the average woman today wears a size 14, yet designer professional clothes only go up to a size 12. Here's a market waiting to be tapped.
- Furniture: Cheryl Riley, Sister CEO of Right Angle Designs in San Francisco, California, designs avant-garde furniture bought by well-known entertainers.
- Flowers, even out of your own garden.

- Handpainted T-shirts, tablecloths, shower curtains with an ethnic theme: black folks love color, at least I do. If you're a good artist with an eye for color, consider this business. You can sell by mail-order, in specialty boutiques, and in a vendor booth at an expo.
- Clothes "for rent"—a lending service.
- Clothes which you select and deliver specially to the customer.
- Magazine/newspaper publisher—with a special niche: African Americans and money, black full-figured women, African American children, etc.
- Specialty newsletter: black women and beauty, healthy soul food, etc.
- Beauty products using natural products from the motherland and other third world countries, such as shea butter from Africa.
- Health products such as vitamins, aloe vera, iron, and calcium for postmenopausal black women who don't want to take hormone replacement therapy.
- Import/export business: Sell products from Africa, the Caribbean, Puerto Rico.
- City guidemaps to the historic and cultural events of African Americans: Sister CEO Angela Dorsey and spouse Thomas Dorsey of Go Ware Travel in Hayward, California, create colorful souvenir "soul of" guides to Atlanta, Los Angeles, and Oakland/San Francisco. The guides provide useful information for any traveler in that city.
- Importing or making herbal teas.

### High-tech

This is an area in dire need of African American input. If you look at the computer games for children and software for adults that are currently on the market, seldom do you see black characters. Young women in college should consider degrees in computer science to get into this untapped market.

- CD-ROM software games with an ethnic twist: ABCs or math skills game using black children as the main characters.

- Software programs geared toward people of color—business, financial, health issues, etc.

## Food

Food is an industry black women should dominate. Our mothers and grandmothers made sweet potato pies, peach cobblers, and fried chicken for eons without getting paid. Now it is time for black women to turn their culinary skills into profit with the following businesses:

- Specialty foods from your family: desserts such as sweet potato pies, peach cobblers, cheesecakes, pound cakes.
- Specialty foods from your region: pralines, gumbo, cajun-style food from Louisiana, sauces from the Caribbean, low-fat soul food.
- Catering business, specializing in vegetarian, low-fat, and nutritious foods.
- Prepackaged bean soups with seasoning. Can be sold through grocery stores and mail-order.
- Gourmet kitchenware sold through cooking house parties; instead of selling plastic bowls and containers, have a cooking party using the pots and pans you are selling, then serve the food. Your guests will attribute their good meal to the equipment used—it's a good sales strategy.
- Specially packaged herbs and spices for gourmet gift shops and through mail-order catalogs.
- Newsletter for African American connoisseurs.

## Spirituality

Spirituality is a billion-dollar industry today and expected to grow even more as anxiety-stricken, stressed-out baby boomers search for faith, values, purpose, and the meaning of life. Sistahs today are reading books such as *In the Spirit* by Susan Taylor of *Essence* magazine, and *Act of Faith* by Iyvala Vanzant. And, they are hungry for more. The market is wide open and there is plenty more room for publications of this nature; for example:

- Inspirational messages on audio cassettes, videotapes, books, and CDs; can be sold practically anywhere—at stores, mail-order, seminars, and retreats.

- Meditation tapes and books; easy to produce. Consider making and selling your own.

---

## SISTER CEO SUCCESS STORY
### *Jeri Hubbard*
### J. AND H. CO., LTD.
SOMERDALE, NEW JERSEY

**Product:** Ethnic rag dolls.

**How I Did It:** I started the business on a whim. In 1993, I was living in Los Angeles and was invited to a birthday party. I didn't know what to get as a gift and didn't want to spend a lot of money, so I made a boy doll with a cute little inscription attached that read, "This is the man you've always wanted!" Everyone in the party loved it and wanted one of their own.

In 1994, I displayed my dolls at the African American Women on Tour Conference, where a friend bought one of the dolls. It just happened that he was on his way to interview with Vogue Butterick Patterns. He took the doll into the interview; they loved it and gave me a contract. Now I'm hoping to expand into housewares, house accessories, and write a children's book on how to make a rag doll.

**Start-Up Money:** $300

**Earnings:** $50,000 (1994)

**Sister CEO Advice:** Seek out information on starting your own business and read books and magazines on your specific product to identify your competitors.

---

## SISTER CEO SUCCESS STORY
### *Brenda Winstead*
#### Damali Afrikan Wear
##### WASHINGTON, D.C.

**Product:** "New Afrikan" style tailored clothes made of colorful African mud cloth, hand-painted linens, and intricate hand-woven fabrics from West Africa.

**How I Did It:** I first started part-time with an art gallery. On a trip to West Africa I was really impressed with how the women were dressed. A year later, I went back and purchased clothes to sell in the U.S. At my first showing, I sold out. I knew then that this was the right business for me.

As business grew, I decided I wanted to design my own clothes. So on my trips back to Africa I bought mud cloth and other African fabrics instead of clothes. I'm not a sewer but I began experimenting and piecing the African cloths together in an intricate design and hired an outside contractor to sew the pieces together. After several successful shows and back-up money from refinancing my house, I quit my job as a night manager in a restaurant to design clothes full-time.

**Start-Up Money:** $7,000-$10,000 (from her savings)

**Earnings:** $80,000 (1995)

**Sister CEO Advice:** Start a business in a field you enjoy. Study your industry. Have a business plan, keep your business records straight, and make financial projections. If you don't handle your cash flow correctly it will really cripple your business. You need perseverance—it takes time for people to get to know you.

## SISTER CEO SUCCESS STORY
### *Sheila Hill-Fajors*
#### FAJORIAN FINE ART GALLERY
##### SAN LEANDRO, CALIFORNIA

**Product:** African American fine art; original and limited-edition paintings, sculptures.

**How I Did It:** I started the business a year ago part-time because of my love for black art. I have collected it for over twenty years. After researching the market, I found that most of the original paintings by African Americans were purchased by white Americans. They understood the investment in art concept—it is so deeply rooted in the European culture. They think nothing of spending $20,000 for an original piece of work. I wanted to bring the concept to the black community.

Many artists need someone to market their work. I started by representing one artist, but since have expanded to other artists. I host six art shows a year out of my home and set up personal appointments. Next year my goal is to expand into ethnic artifacts, sculptures, unique home accessories, and wearable art, and, eventually to own an exclusive bed & breakfast catering to executives.

**Start-Up Money:** $8,000-$10,000

**Earnings:** Breakeven (1995)

**Sister CEO Advice:** It's important in this new era for black women to understand what is happening in the economy and not to depend on their jobs. They need to find out what their talents are and use them for their own company. Women who are interested in the black art industry should take art history classes, and become a docent at a museum. You need to understand the different qualities of art—original, limited edition, and posters. Decide on the type of art you want to represent and focus on a specific market niche.

## SERVICE BUSINESS

The service business arena is exploding. It's a $300 billion-plus industry, according to the U.S. Department of Commerce. The massive downsizing of corporate America is generating business opportunities for entrepreneurial start-ups right and left.

In a service business you generally perform some kind of personal service for your customers. The start-up cost is low to reasonable. You just need your personal expertise, telephone, and business stationery. Examples include:

- Hairbraiding salon or in your home: hairbraiding is big business today; as black women return to holistic health and natural living, many are adopting natural hairstyles.
- Home health care: In an era when hospital costs are skyrocketing and patients are discharged sooner, home health care is the fastest growing segment of the health service industry. The hottest opportunity is in newborn home postpartum care. With insurance companies cutting back on maternity coverage, new mothers are being discharged within twenty-four to forty-eight hours of giving birth and need help at home to adjust to their new responsibilities.

    Some states have passed laws requiring insurance companies to cover longer stays or offer visits by home-care nurses. On a national scale, the Newborns' and Mothers' Health Protection Act—which would require follow-up home care for hospital stays of less than forty-eight hours, is currently in the Senate for approval.

    Black women who are pediatricians or registered nurses with an expertise in perinatal care can either become postpartum care specialists or start an agency providing the service.
- Consulting and sales management training: companies are looking for experts in areas like diversity, financial, computers. Do you have expertise you can sell?
- Business consultant to physicians, dentists, and lawyers in private practice.

- Internet (online service): provide specialized information on the World Wide Web for African American women.
- Newsletters: contract out to write newsletters for black organizations and associations.
- Author book-tour guide: authors on tour in every city need a guide to escort them to their book signings and media events. You need a car and contacts in the publishing or bookselling field to start this business.
- Seminar speaker: hot topics are money, motivation, health, and how to start your own business.
- Travel consultant specializing in black women's retreats, conferences, and cruises. Patricia Yarbrough, Sister CEO of Blue World Travel, annually puts on a seven-day cruise to the Caribbean specifically for over 1,500 African Americans.
- Temporary employment agencies.
- Afrocentric home decorating/painting business: in the $31 billion interior design industry, there is a lack of diversity. Only 2 percent of all interior designers are black, yet when you visit the homes of many African Americans you will see their ethnic decorations. To start, experiment with your friends for free to get experience and build up your reputation.
- Women-of-color modeling agency: although there are several well-known African American models, none are managed by a black modeling firm. Why not? If you live in New York or Los Angeles and know something about modeling, research this idea further.
- Editorial/publishing services, helping authors and would-be authors shape materials for publication or self-publication. It can lead you to becoming a literary agent!
- Masseuse/reflexologist: as part of the back to health movement, women and men are "de-stressing" with weekly massages. If you are selective of your clientele you can turn your spare bedroom into a relaxing massage salon full of candles, soft light, soothing music, and aromatherapy fragrances.
- Sharing your expertise via a 1-900 number.
- Weight control specialist, food and fitness consultant specifically for black women. Black women have weight and health problems unique to them as compared to women

in mainstream America. Overweight, hypertension, fibroid tumors, anemia, and low birthweight of babies are but a few. Physicians specializing in weight control, registered dieticians, and fitness experts should consider starting businesses in this area.

- Sports teacher: teach golf and tennis lessons to women and children.
- Gardening/landscaping: if you love the outdoors, the gardening business is booming. This trend is also attributed to baby boomers. With dual incomers, neither has time to take care of the yard work. There are a lot of low-cost competitors in this field so you will need to specialize in order to stand out from the crowd. For example, if you live in warmer climates you can specialize in desert landscapes using cactus and succulents. Hotels, restaurants, and casinos are viable markets as well as homes.
- Spirituality retreats and conferences: black women love spirituality retreats. One of the largest retreats today is the Denver, Colorado–based Warriors of Light annual summer retreat. Over 100 black women meet in spiritually centered areas such as an Indian reservation in Oregon or red rock country in Sedona, Arizona.
- Video production.
- Repair service: Are you Ms Fix-It? Black women are a rarity in this field. If you enjoy handywoman work, you could profit by fixing appliances and other items for your girlfriends.
- Seminar promoter: the black expos and similar conferences bring in loads of people and profit. Seminars geared specifically to black women are big, such as African American Women on Tour, Brides of Distinction, Today's Black Woman.
- Medical claims processor: this is an ideal business for former medical and dental office managers. You will need a computer and you can start right from home.
- Services to senior citizens: as our population ages, many need help with paying bills, and taking care of Medicare, Social Security, and insurance issues.
- Special events planner: political fundraisers and theme events such as a fiftieth wedding anniversary are areas to explore.

- Grantwriting service: foundations and organizations are always looking for money and someone to write a proposal. Network within several organizations to get clients.
- Home/office cleaning business.
- Literary agent: There is a renaissance in black literature and nonfiction writing. Mainstream publishers are finally beginning to comprehend this lucrative market and are looking for more works from people of color. The only problem is that this field seems to be run by a relatively small group of people centered in New York, so it may be difficult breaking in initially. But if you're aggressive, ambitious, and highly motivated you can push your way in. There are small presses and great ones in every major city.
- Wardrobe consultant: if you have an eye for fashion, you can make upwards of $150 per hour as a wardrobe consultant to women too busy to do their own shopping.
- Tutoring: the adult market is heating up with so many people returning to school to update their skills. The best place to publicize your services is at the local colleges and universities.
- Job counseling consultant to laid-off employees or welfare recipients. Certain states have government programs geared to teaching women on welfare how to raise their level of self-esteem and find a job.
- Wedding makeup artist: to obtain clients, take out an ad in your local newspaper and set up a booth at conferences such as the Brides of Distinction expo, created by Sister CEO Dian Valentine of Oakland, California. Valentine holds two conferences a year, one in northern California and one in southern California, with plans to expand nationwide.
- Holiday decorating service: there is a holiday in every month. Individuals and retail stores are your best customers.
- Painting murals for individuals, businesses, and cities.
- Promotion/advertising specialist.
- Voiceovers for radio and television commercials. Women with careers in television and radio can do this on the side to bring in additional money.
- Desktop publishing/graphic artist: create brochures, busi-

ness stationery, menus, and invitations with your personal computer.

- Ghostwriter for celebrities with book publishing deals: celebrity tell-alls are money-makers in the publishing world. For a bigwig, you may make upwards of $250,000 or more to assist in writing their story.
- Closet, business, and home office organizer.
- Secretary/word processor.
- Foreign language translator (speaking and writing): as businesses go international, they need someone to translate documents and brochures from English to the language they have elected to do business in. High-technology businesses are good candidates for this service.

---

### SISTER CEO SUCCESS STORY
#### *Norma Jean Darden*
##### SPOONBREAD INC.
###### NEW YORK, NEW YORK

**Service:** Catering to celebrities.

**How I Did It:** I was catering for three years before I realized I was a caterer. After my sister and I wrote the cookbook *Spoonbread & Strawberry Wine*, we were asked by someone at the Public Broadcasting Service to make quiche. It cost us six dollars to prepare the quiche, and before you knew it we were being asked to cater parties for private clients. To learn more about the cooking business, I took caterering and pricing courses at the New School in New York City. It was there that I learned about pricing, renting kitchens, and networking with others in the business. My company now has seven chefs skilled in a variety of cuisines. Our specialty is healthy but traditional African American cuisine. We decided to change our menu when our faithful client Bill Cosby asked us to fix low-fat and vegetarian foods. Because of this we now have some wonderful clients, such as Ed Bradley of CBS News, Bryant Gumbel of the *Today Show*, Harry Belafonte, former Mayor David Dinkins

---

of New York, Revlon, Kraft Foods, General Mills, and the Rocke-feller Foundation. And, our food was also featured in Eddie Murphy's hit movie *Boomerang*.

**Start-Up Money:** $6.00

**Earnings:** Six figures

**Sister CEO Advice:** Never turn down a job. This is why we grew rapidly. We have catered as many as five affairs on the same night—and we have cooked for as many as 5,000 people per event. Also, change with the times to meet the needs of your clients. If we hadn't listened to Bill Cosby and changed our menu, we may not have been as successful as we are.

## SISTER CEO SUCCESS STORY
### *Cynthia R. Jones*
#### JONES WORLEY DESIGN INC.
##### ATLANTA, GEORGIA

**Service:** Graphic design consulting.

**How I Did It:** Ever since I was little girl, I enjoyed drawing, col-oring, and arts and crafts. I sold my first painting when I was fifteen years old, and while in college I designed projects for clients and professors for a fee. Being a Sister CEO has come relatively easy for me since I have always had the discipline, spirit, and intuitiveness to become an entrepreneur.

The desire to start my own business grew when I worked for two architectural firms and recognized that there were no African Amer-icans who are really focused or known for graphic designs. I knew then there was an untapped niche in something I loved doing. At the edge of twenty-nine, with a leap of faith, I took the ultimate plunge and resigned from my job to work with several other busi-ness associates to design and disseminate public health information in high-traffic facilities. I wasn't too worried about failing. I knew there were only two things that could happen to me. First, if things got too bad, I would have to move in with one of my relatives, and second, I would just have to get a job—neither option was that bad.

Because my business didn't make enough money to pay a salary, I supplemented my income for two years by providing graphic design consulting services to clients, including my previous employer. She contracted work from Barry K. Worley, a designer I had worked with at my first job out of college. After working on joint project, I asked Worley if he was interested in working together as a team. He was, so we sat down and discussed the goals of the firm and several other critical issues, particularly what would be the consequence of a partnership between an African American woman and a white man. After careful scrutiny, we decided to go for it. I am president and CEO of the company and own 65 percent of the company stock. Worley owns 35 percent. We have twelve full-time employees.

Over our six years in business we have worked on projects in the United States, Switzerland, Indonesia, and Denmark. And, most recently, we have been contracted for design services for the 1996 Olympic Games.

**Start-Up Money:** $1,200 combined—$850 from Jones and $350 from Worley.

**Earnings:** We are profitable each year.

**Sister CEO Advice:** Before you start your own business, work in the field. You can cultivate business relationships, meet other people in the same industry, improve and strengthen your technical skills, and learn how businesses operate internally.

For black women starting their own companies, just remember to stay focused—don't let other people deny you of your opportunities; most of us give up too soon, just a day before winning. You must be clear and confident and not allow people to discourage you. Make sure the people you have in your life who you think care about you really do care about you. You also must have an ever-changing positive attitude in what you do to become successful.

## MAIL-ORDER BUSINESS

While it isn't a get-rich-quick business, mail-order is one of the easiest businesses to start in your spare time. This $266 billion industry no longer consists of just the Sears (now defunct) and J.C. Penney catalogs, but includes an overwhelming array of specialty catalogs (*E Style*, a collaboration between *Ebony* magazine and Spiegel's, and *Essence By Mail* are examples), direct mail, home shopping networks (BET Shopping and QVC) and computer online shopping (America Online).

A mail-order company is a wonderful way to achieve your dream of owning your business, because the start-up cost required is low compared to other types of businesses. You can start a mail-order business with a just few hundred dollars. You may not become an *E Style*, but you'll be your own boss, you'll be small enough not to attract a lot of competition, and you could well earn $5,000 to $100,000 or more per year.

In mail order, finding the right product to sell is the key to a successful business. The majority of products listed in the product business list in this chapter can be turned into a mail-order business. Hair care, beauty products, women's and children's fashions, gardening supplies, home decorating items, jewelry, and food items such as spices, herbs, and sauces are hot products to sell.

Knowing the ins and outs, the postal regulations, and how to fulfill orders are important areas of information required to run a successful mail-order business. Several excellent books have been written on how to start and run a mail-order business; I have listed a few in the bibliography. Also check out the public library.

---

## SISTER CEO SUCCESS STORY
### *Wanakee*
#### VERIFEN COMPLEX
##### ISLAND PARK, NEW YORK

**Mail-Order Business:** Hair care products for African American women.

**How I Did It:** My business grew out of a personal frustration with my own hair and the hair products that were available to me. Black women couldn't grow their hair long! Through prayer I asked God to teach me how to grow it. Simultaneously, I met a chemist who customized a formula specifically for me. I started selling to a few people and word begin to spread that my chemist developed an extra conditioning product to help textured hair grow. Later, *Essence* magazine did an interview with me and it took off from there.

**Sister CEO Advice:** Stay abreast of all aspects of your business. I write and create the layout for ads and the brochures. What helped is my experience working as a fashion illustrator for a big department store. It really prepared me to deal with customers. It's really important to pay attention to those jobs even if they may seem menial. Look at what you can learn from them; you may not think about it at the time but those jobs help you in getting started with your own business.

Also, when starting out, obtain professional advice, especially from your attorney.

---

## RETAIL STORE/RESTAURANT BUSINESSES

Of the four types of businesses, the retail store or restaurant is the most expensive to start because it requires renting space, hiring employees, and buying inventory to fill the store—in other words, higher overhead. Therefore, when you start this type of business, you need to have or have access to capital to get it started and keep it going. The key word for small businesses today, retail as well as restaurants, is specialization. With so many retail stores and restaurants out there, you need to be different and set yourself apart from the crowd.

Black-owned restaurants such as Aunt Kizzy's Back Porch and Roscoe's Chicken and Waffles are popular in the African American community. Even though they are located in Los Angeles and Oakland, many people from the East Coast, Midwest, and South are familiar with the restaurants and, when visiting in the area, will make it a point to patronize them. Why? Because they stand out from the crowd. They serve good food with a down-home feeling and, just as important, they offer good service. And the fact that they are black-owned plays a major factor. Most African Americans take pride in helping another small business succeed. With so few black-owned businesses struggling to survive, we have a strong desire to do all we can to keep them in business—that is, as long as they provide good products and good services.

Another restaurant worth mentioning is the One City Cafe in New York City, even though it is no longer open and was not black-owned. The restaurant was unique because, in addition to serving good food, it only hired unemployed, formerly homeless people who had a strong desire to make improvements in their lives. Customers benefited as well. The elderly and the disabled were able to use food stamps to pay for their meals. It was a business that made a sound responsibility statement.

So, if you have access to $50,000 or more in capital to start a business, you may want to consider the following ideas:

- Upscale but casual Afrocentric theme restaurant: this could turn into a franchise opportunity.
- Bookstore specializing in literature by and about people of color.
- Children's educational toy store.
- Designer consignment shop. Sistahs are always looking good; we spend plenty of money on clothes and have closets full of items we barely wear. There should be at least one black women-owned consignment shop in every major town to help us empty out our closets.
- Health food store: seldom have I seen a health food store in

the black community, among the McDonald's, Taco Bells, and Burger Kings, which we *can* find. There should be someone teaching African Americans the right foods to eat and the correct vitamins to take to balance out the non-nutritious foods so many of us eat.

- Beauty supply store: studies by Target Publishing, a Chicago research firm, found that out of the $1.3 billion spent annually on beauty supplies, black women spend $427 million on beauty and hair care products. Definitely not pocket change, yet when I visit beauty supply stores located in the inner cities around the country, the majority are owned by other enterprising minorities who know a good thing when they see it. What's up with this? Budding Sister CEOs need to look heavily into this business. With all the money we're spending in it, we definitely should own the industry.

- Nail salons: same scenario as the beauty supply store—a ton of black women customers getting their nails done by nonblack nail stylists. Please forgive if I offend anyone, but, in my opinion, businesses with a major black clientele should be run by African Americans so that the money stays in the community.

- Bath and linen store: the comforts of home are high on the agenda for most women today. The bedroom and the bathroom have become the favored rooms in the house, and people are spending oodles of money to decorate them. Big comforters, nice towels, and fragranced soaps are only a few of the big-selling home luxuries.

- Coffee or tea bar: these are the new singles' gathering grounds. Instead of meeting for a drink after work, many are making dates for a cup of coffee or tea. Coffee bars can also be found in major bookstores. Some have a monthly singles night. So, ladies, if you're looking to hook up with someone special, open your own coffee bar. You just may find Mr. Right.

- Day spas: a European luxury for hundreds of years is now finding its way here to the States as aging baby boomers look for ways to stay young and healthy with alternative health practices. The spas provide aromatherapy, massages, herbal medicinal baths, facials, and cosmetic makeovers along with focusing on healing the mind.

---

## SISTER CEO SUCCESS STORY
### *Clara Villarosa*
#### HUE-MAN EXPERIENCE BOOKSTORE
##### DENVER, COLORADO

**Retail Business:** Bookstore specializing in African American literature and fine art prints.

**How I Did It:** In 1984 I started my business with my significant other and a woman shareholder after I became bored with working as a psychotherapist in corporate America. I found I was so busy fixing others' stuff, I decided to fix my own stuff. I needed a challenge, plus I wanted to be in control of my career. So, with money from my savings, I opened up the Hue-Man Experience bookstore. At the time, there weren't enough places for black authors to display their work.

**Start-Up Money:** $10,000

**Earnings:** $400,000 a year

**Sister CEO Advice:** Being a black woman entrepreneur does open doors for you because there are so few who are perceived as successful. Use and maximize your work experience in starting your business. As a psychotherapist, I found the skills that were required—gathering information, problem solving, developing treatment plans and implementing them—were useful in writing up my business plan. You must have a business plan. Black women must stretch themselves and learn to analyze and solve problems. Many of us don't have these skills because we were never taught them. Also, be careful when starting a business with a partner. Know your business partner well because it is like a marriage. You need to be able to work with each other's habits.

---

## Now Do You Know What Business You Want to Start?

I hope that out of this huge list of business ideas you were able to find one you're excited about starting. If you didn't, then as I said earlier, design your own. Start a business you like and give it all you've got. Not only will you be a happy camper, but you may become rich, too!

### *Sister CEO Action Steps*

1. Decide which business type you want to start: Product, service, mail-order, or retail/restaurant.
2. Select one to three of the businesses in that particular list and ask yourself the "Before Taking the Plunge" questions on pages 135–136, to see if any are a feasible business for you.
3. Based on the business you select, head for the public library to do some extensive research before shelling out any of your hard-earned money.
4. Talk to people who've done what you want to do already (ask to speak to the store owner, talk to the person who sent you the mailing, etc.).
5. For inspiration, read the Sister CEO success stories again and again. Starting your own business isn't impossible. You can do it just like the Sister CEOs in this book.

# Chapter 11

## FRANCHISING

*Failure is a word I don't accept.*
JOHN H. JOHNSON

African American small-business owners have long been interested in—and good at—the franchising industry. And it stands to reason, since *Entrepreneur* magazine says franchising is one of the fastest growing sectors of American business, with a bright future in the twenty-first century. The difficulties of starting a business are oftentimes insurmountable to many novice entrepreneurs, which is the reason owning a franchise appears so appetizing. The idea of starting a business with the financial, marketing, and managerial support of a big company seems like an ideal opportunity for an entrepreneur seeking a somewhat low-risk way to start a business.

While many African Americans see franchising as a way to achieve the American dream of owning their own business, the industry has unfortunately not yet welcomed us with open arms. It has long been a white preserve; only recently have black people been allowed on the the playing field. And in small numbers at that. Minorities make up just 9.5 percent of all franchisees, with African American women a meager 1 percent of that, according to the International Franchise Association (IFA), a leading trade group.

Yet there's hope ahead. As the franchising industry matures, it sees African American and women small-business owners as the last fields to conquer for potential growth for their companies. Many of

the major firms are organizing minority business development programs to assist potential franchisees with start-up costs. The key is
finding a company that is truly sincere. "There are companies that
*talk* and those that *do*," says Terrian Barnes-Bryant, an African
American and IFA vice president for research for minority and
women's affairs.

For the first-time Sister CEO, the $800 billion industry offers
the best of both worlds. First and foremost, there's no need to reinvent the wheel. You're building a business from scratch, but you
have the support of a franchisor who has helped others to start the
same operation 20, 200, or maybe even 2,000 times before. You're
purchasing years of experience and the proven methods of the
franchisor. You're in business *for* yourself, but not *by* yourself.

"Once you find a company that is willing to walk their talk, success can be achieved," says megafranchisee Valerie Daniels-Carter,
Sister CEO of V & J Foods, Inc., owner of thirty-seven Burger King
outlets and one of the three franchise businesses included on the
annual *Black Enterprise* 100 top African American Companies list.
Daniels-Carter shares her "how she did it" advice—and why she
feels black women today need to consider franchises as a means to
becoming a Sister CEO—at the end of this chapter. Let's talk now
about the benefits of owning a franchise.

## How Does a Franchise Work?

A franchise is a predetermined and analyzed marketing method
used to distribute goods or services. It is set up by the franchisor
(parent company). As a franchise owner, you become a distribution
partner by paying anywhere from $1,000 to over $100,000—plus
royalties and advertising fees—to use the franchisor's trademark,
business formula, and advertising, as well as to profit from its business expertise. In return, the franchisor gets a cut of your sales—
anywhere from 2 to 30 percent, depending on the business.

For the money you invest in the franchise, you get instant name
recognition from the parent company's national advertising campaign, product group buying power, and tried-and-true training.
Okay, you may say, this sounds great, so what's the catch?

The catch is money. First-time women business owners may have difficulty raising enough capital to purchase one of the more expensive fast-food franchises and therefore may want to seek out one of the many cheaper franchises. The start-up cost for a McDonald's, for example, is around $500,000, and for a Burger King around $400,000. Although, you won't need to come up with all this money, you will need about $150,000 for them to even consider your application. On the other hand, Computertots, a franchise that teaches children how to use computers, has a start-up cost of approximately $40,000. (Check out the list below for additional franchises that are low-cost and have implemented programs to assist women and minorities.) One caveat though: never select a franchise based only on the start-up cost. This goes back to the basic rule of starting a business in something you love.

### *Franchises*

These franchises target specific markets with their products or services, or are actively seeking women and minorities:

| FRANCHISOR | LOCATION | TYPE | FEE | START-UP COSTS |
|---|---|---|---|---|
| Accent Hair Salons, Inc. | Dayton, OH | Hair salons | $20,000 | $140,000 |
| American Leak Detection | Palm Springs, CA | Water, sewer, gas leak detection | $45,000 | $85,000 |
| Blimpie Int'l, Inc. | Atlanta, GA | Fast food | $18,000 | $100,000–$150,000 |
| Computertots | Great Falls, VA | Children's computer classes | $25,900 | $31,700–$37,000 |
| Coverall North America | San Diego, CA | Commercial cleaning | $3,250–$3,600 | $33,600–37,100 |
| D&K Enterprises Inc. | Carrollton, TX | Personalized children's books | $100 | $2,500–$4,995 |

| FRANCHISOR | LOCATION | TYPE | FEE | START-UP COSTS |
|---|---|---|---|---|
| GNC Franchising, Inc. | Pittsburgh, PA | Retail nutrition stores | $25,000 | $100,000–$125,000 |
| Goodyear Tire Centers | Akron, OH | Tires & automotive services | $15,000 | $100,000+ |
| Jackson Hewitt Tax Service | Virginia Beach, VA | Computerized tax services | $17,500 | $30,000 |
| KFC Corp. | Louisville, KY | Fast food | $25,000 | $125,000 |
| Lawn Doctor, Inc. | Holmdel, NJ | Automated lawn care | $0 | $22,500 |
| Mail Boxes Etc. | San Diego, CA | Postal, business, and communications services | $24,950 | $95,000–$125,000 |
| O.P.E.N. America, Inc. | Phoenix, AZ | Commercial cleaning | $3,900 | $4,400 |
| Padgett Business Services | Athens, GA | Tax services | $22,500 | $50,000 |
| P.J.'S USA, Inc. | New Orleans, LA | Retail coffee | $16,000 | $120,000 |
| RACS Int'l, Inc. | Indianapolis, IN | Commercial cleaning | $3,500–$32,560 | $900–$11,600 |
| Subway Salads & Sandwiches | Milford, CT | Fast food | $10,000 | $74,600–$199,300 |
| The Southland Corp. (7-Eleven) | Dallas, TX | Retail convenience stores | $80,000 | $13,000–$223,700 |
| Travel Network | Englewood Cliffs, NJ | Travel agency | $9,995–29,000 | $1,000–$75,000 |
| Wendy's Int'l, Inc. | Dublin, OH | Fast food | $25,000 | $250,000 |

Source: U.S. Small Business Administration

159

Later in the chapter we'll cover more on how to select a franchise. Now, let's spell out the pros and cons of owning a franchise. As with any new business, owning a franchise has advantages and disadvantages and will take total commitment on your part to make it a success. To help you make the decision whether you should consider a franchise, bear in mind the following pros and cons:

## PROS

- **Image:** There's no need to create an image from scratch. You buy into an existing identity in the marketplace via trademarks, logos, advertising, etc.
- **Lower risk:** A sample of the business is already up and running. The franchisor has a business system in place you can implement. They know the costs of covering equipment, inventory, grand-opening expenses, and other major factors.
- **Training:** The franchisor provides initial and ongoing training in all aspects of the business, from accounting procedures to learning about the industry.

## CONS

- **Tight Control:** Franchisors keep a tight rein on their franchisees by requiring them to conform to their way of doing business. They tell you what to sell and how to sell it. The guidance you initially welcomed may seem like a hindrance once you've been in business for awhile. If you are a Sister CEO who likes to make her own decisions and doesn't like taking orders from above, a franchise may prove too restrictive for you.
- **Hours:** A franchise cannot be a part-time business. The franchisor wants and expects you to give 110 percent total commitment.
- **Royalties and fees:** The start-up costs include an up-front franchise fee plus royalty and advertising fees as a percentage of gross sales. The additional capital required pays for the beginning equipment, supplies, and possibly the real estate of the franchise location.

## Selecting a Franchise

If after a thorough self-analysis you decide franchising is for you, the next step is to find the right franchise opportunity and scrutinize it with a fine-tooth comb. It can mean the difference between your franchise succeeding or failing. As you diligently research, ask yourself the following questions of each franchisor you are considering:

- Are there African Americans in management? You need a support network to identify with. Ideally a franchisor's management team should include women and people of color.
- How many of the franchisees are African Americans? Franchise attorneys recommend that you interview franchisees in communities similar to yours. Ask how they like being in the franchise. Would they do it again? Is the franchisor supportive? Even though their success or failure isn't indicative of yours, their responses will give you a general sense of how the franchise works. Most franchisees will share information—excluding their net profits—as long as you're not planning to open a business in their area.
- Where are the franchises owned by African Americans? Are they only in the inner cities? If so, are they there by choice or because it was the only available site offered to them? You should be offered the same widespread choice of possible locations as everyone else. Franchises in poorer neighborhoods tend to have lower sales per customer, pay higher insurance costs, and face more potential crime than their more affluent counterparts, thereby lowering the possible success ratio of the franchise.
- Does the franchise have a minority franchisee association? If not, is there a general franchise association or advisory committee? What is its purpose? Is it successful in dealing with management? Are the franchisees able to solve problems through the committees?

## Evaluating the Franchise

First, request a copy of the Uniform Franchise Offering Circular from the franchise corporate office. This important document is required by federal law and contains information about the franchisor and its product or service; franchise fees, royalties, and other costs; the background of the principals; information on any pending or past bankruptcy or litigation against the company; franchisee's required investment; franchisee rights and obligations; franchisor obligations and restrictions; termination of franchise; and the franchisor's financial statements. It must also include the contract. Focus on the following:

1. **Earnings.** If the franchisor claims a specific amount of earnings, ask for proof or evidence and study such claims carefully. Are the earnings based on franchisee- or company-owned stores? Where are those stores located? Get comparable financial information for operations located in areas similar to the territory you have in mind. You want to compare apples with apples.

2. **The failure rate.** The Franchise Offering Circular must disclose a list of the people in your state who have left the company (voluntarily and involuntarily) over the past twelve months. Investigate further about their departures. If the franchisor isn't willing to share that information, try to find the former franchisees for their explanation on the matter. You want to know how well they were treated by upper management and whether they made or lost money on the business and on the sale of the business.

3. **Encroachment.** The document should also spell out your territory in clear terms with provisions that another franchise cannot encroach on your terrain. Some franchisors are boldly erecting competing stores down the block and around the corner from their older outlets.

4. **Current experiences.** Request names and visit current franchisees to get their feedback on the pluses and minuses of going with the franchise. Also visit franchisees that are not on the list to get another perspective. Often the franchisor

will pass along only the names of their up-and-coming or more successful franchises. Ask the franchisees what their biggest problem has been with the company and the business. Ask if they are making the kind of money they had expected. Ask about the time commitment it takes to run the business. This will help you see if your expectations are realistic.

Five years ago, when Carolyn Smalls-Holiday, Sister CEO of two Chicago area Subway (fast food) franchises, was thinking of buying a franchise, she went to the only black-owned franchise in the city to seek advice. After talking with the owner, Smalls-Holiday was able to get a much better feel of how much money she could make in her own franchise.

5. **Litigation pattern.** Has there been a pattern of lawsuits against the franchisor from African American– and women-owned franchisees? If so, this may indicate a big problem. Talk to the franchisor's attorney and get the details on the lawsuits.

6. **The specifics.** Get a detailed description of the initial and ongoing training the company will provide. Find out how long the company has been in business. Is it on a fast growth track? In addition, nail down the cost of doing business. How much are royalties? How much are the major expenses—business license, lease, insurance, etc? What are the termination rights? Franchise contracts generally run ten to twenty years and then must be renewed. You need a clear understanding of what happens when your contract is up. Will you have the right to keep the franchise, and, if so, on what terms? The specifics must be worked out way before you sign any papers. There's too much money at stake for you to wait for surprises from the head honchos.

7. **Hiring a professional.** To avoid making any major mistakes and to make a solid business decision, hire an accountant and an attorney who are savvy in the ways of franchises. If you want to do some analysis on your own, most libraries carry a copy of *Franchise: Dollars & Sense—A Guide for Evaluating Franchises and Projecting Franchise Earnings*, by Warren Lewis. The book analyzes the earnings of various franchisors.

Membership in a franchise organization has major benefits. As a member of the American Franchise Association (312-431-0545) and the American Association of Franchisees and Dealers (800-733-9858), you will be provided with a list of franchise lawyers. Plan to spend around $3,000 in legal fees for a review of the Uniform Franchise Offering Circular, the contract, incorporation of the business, and state filings.

## Money for the Franchise

Paying for the franchise will be your most monumental headache. As you saw earlier, buying a major franchise like a McDonald's may be financially prohibitive not only because you must shell out big bucks for the franchise fee, but because you need substantial additional capital as well to pay for inventory, rent, and other expenses.

Fortunately, franchisees have a significant advantage over other start-up companies searching for money. First of all, they have more avenues to pursue—such as financing provided by the franchisor or by the franchisee selling the outlet that is available. Second, banks aren't quite as reluctant to finance new franchisees, because franchise systems that have been in existence for a while have a track record to show. The bank can easily check out their performance.

The Small Business Administration is also a potential financier. Their LowDoc loan program is geared toward small-business owners seeking under $100,000. The loan process is easier, too. It's a two-page application and the approval time is usually less than two weeks.

As with any other business loan, you'll need to immerse yourself in the lending process. The better you understand the process and the more prepared you are, the better your chances of securing a loan. Lenders want you to prepare a business plan, be creditworthy, and put up a percentage of the money you need—typically 25 percent or more plus collateral.

Personal assets, particularly equity in your home, are also a common source of money for franchisees. The good news: the interest on the loan is tax-deductible. The bad news: if your business runs into financial problems or fails, you could lose your house.

The most desirable financing is offered by the franchisor. They can assist in several ways: by waiving start-up fees until your business is generating money, by leasing equipment to you, by arranging outside financing, or by loaning you money outright. When they do provide money, the interest rate is usually higher than a bank's but the terms are more lenient. You may negotiate for a longer payback time than the traditional three to five years of a typical business loan. And, franchisors raring to sign you up may accept a less than perfect credit history report or lower net worth.

Sister CEO Smalls-Holiday recommends that aspiring Sister CEOs develop a business relationship with their accountant, who may be privy to information on city and state loan programs for small-business owners. Her accountant helped her find the money to purchase her first franchise.

## Franchise Your Own Business

While many of you may not be in a position to start your own franchise system today, when you venture out on your own, you need to set your sights higher for the future. Why? Because when you analyze the financial statements of a franchisor, *they're* the ones making the real money.

African Americans have yet to enter this lucrative side of the business. (In my research, I only uncovered two African American franchisors, Accent Hair Salons and RACS International, a janitorial franchise. Both can be found on the franchise list on pages 158–59.) Developing your own franchise is an attractive alternative for business owners seeking to grow their business without having to put up all the money. As a franchisor, the money you invest is basically limited to the amount it cost to develop your franchise company. Expenses such as renting space, hiring employees, and signing agreements with suppliers are paid by the franchisee.

It will cost about $100,000 to implement your own national chain of outlets. Now you see why your company has to be a somewhat profitable entity before you head down this road. This amount will pay for retaining an attorney, preparing the legal paperwork, and developing a marketing campaign for prospective franchisees, all of which will take about six weeks to complete.

## THE STEPS

**Step 1.** The first step is to determine how viable it is to turn your company into a franchise. Consider the following points when making your decision:

- Is your company already profitable? There aren't too many business owners out there who will want to invest their hard-earned money in a failing enterprise.
- What would be unique about your franchise company? Would it be easy for another entrepreneur to start a similar competing business?
- Is the business fairly simple to understand and implement? A straightforward franchise system will allow anyone regardless of their background to own and run one of your franchises.
- How and where will you obtain the funds for the start-up cost to develop your franchise company?

**Step 2.** Analyze the finances of your company. Will the company provide a profit for you as well as your franchisees? An industry rule of thumb: the franchise company should offer a potential 15 percent return on the franchisee's investment, plus a manager's salary.

**Step 3.** How easy is it to standardize and replicate the business modus operandi? The key behind a franchise is replication. So when people buy into your system they expect to obtain the same success you have achieved in the first outlet. Also, when the procedures are standardized, you can keep check on quality control and customer service within the business.

**Step 4.** Research other franchises. Compare the fees, royalties, and franchise offering circulars of existing franchises similar to yours. Contact the franchisor directly or refer to the reference books I've listed in the appendix. They should be available in the public library.

**Step 5.** Assess the market. Questions you'll need to answer: Does your company cater to a specific niche? Will this group be interested in your product or service? Can they afford to pay for it?

What's the best area for this type of franchise: North, South, East, or West? Suburbs or city?

**Step 6.** Design a step-by-step company manual. Create a manual that defines and describes the precise procedures to be followed to run the business. Take Body St. Lucia Body Products (our case study) as an example. When Connie Harper is ready to turn her business into a franchise, one area included in her manual would spell out where to buy the products and provide recipes for custom scenting products, so the franchisee would know exactly how many drops of scent are needed. The manual insures the quality control of the products of the Body St. Lucia franchise company.

**Step 7.** Have an attorney prepare the Uniform Franchise Offering Circular. Filing this document will cost anywhere from $20,000 to $50,000, depending on the complexity of your franchise.

---

### SISTER CEO SUCCESS STORY
#### *Valerie Daniels-Carter*
#### V & J FOODS, INC.
##### MILWAUKEE, WISCONSIN

Valerie Daniels-Carter, Sister CEO of V & J Foods, can vividly remember the day in December 1984 when she opened the first of her thirty-seven Burger King franchises. "I started the application process with Burger King in 1982. It took two years before we officially opened our first store." As Daniels-Carter looks back on that day, the wait was not in vain. From that small beginning, V & J Foods is now a mega-franchisee with Burger King franchises located throughout Wisconsin and Michigan. The company employs 1,300, predominantly African Americans, and had sales of over $30 million in 1995. The company has also been listed two years in a row on the *Black Enterprise* 100 list.

#### *Daniels-Carter's Advice to Sister CEOs:*

- First, narrow down the field. Ask yourself—what do you want to do? What level of commitment are you willing to give to your

---

business to make it happen? Realize it takes an enormous amount of time.

- Research the industry. When you're well-equipped with knowledge, that's half the battle.
- Look at several franchise companies before you make your decision. Think long-term and don't look at the short-term companies. These are fads that quickly go out of business.
- Contact the companies, but be wary of the minority programs; some of them are turnkey programs with limited profit potential.
- Once you own your franchise, know everything about it. I physically managed the store so I would understand the ins and outs of running the business.
- You need strong professional advisers in finance and legal. Hire someone who has a hunger drive like you to succeed. They will help you become successful.
- There will be tons of roadblocks—expect them. Whenever there is a problem, look at it from a solution point of view.
- Learn to delegate. It makes you a leader.
- You must have a family support network. My family is extremely supportive. When I first started my husband took on a second job to help me to raise the money for the initial franchise fee. My mother-in-law is a gem; there is no way I could manage raising my son without her. I never have to worry during the day because she takes care of him, and when I go away on business, they both travel with me.
- Take time to build a solid base. Be prepared for both success and failure.
- Faith—don't start your business without it.
- Give back. It is important to give back to the black community by serving on boards and in community organizations. Black women need to become role models to young teenage girls. Rarely do they see successful African American women in business.

### Sister CEO Action Steps

1. If you're interested in becoming a Sister CEO of a franchise, the first step is to begin researching the various franchises available, starting with the list on pages 158–159.
2. Read books, talk to franchise owners, and attend small business seminars and conferences in your area to meet franchisors looking for new franchises.
3. If you're already in business, consider turning it into a mega-franchise company to grow your business by following the seven steps on pages 166 and 167.

# Chapter 12

## Your Game Plan

> As any football player knows, if you want to score a touch-down you have to have a game plan.
>
> Denis Waitley,
> *author, motivational speaker*

As a Sister CEO starting a business, you need a plan to help you determine which direction(s) to take to get your business up and running. The written game plan serves four important functions. First, it serves as your "plan of attack" to get the business started. You can set goals, estimate the start-up costs and expenses, and decide how much you will charge for your services or products. Second, it serves as a guideline enabling you to to steer the business into profitable waters and keep it there. You can show how you plan to attract and keep customers. Third, the game plan will enable you to think through your business idea and work out as many potential problems as possible before they occur. And fourth, when you're ready to seek outside financing, the game plan will be given to potential lenders or investors who nowadays expect a high level of expertise and preparation from entrepreneurs searching for money. Lenders want to see a business plan showing that your entrepreneurial idea has been rigorously assessed and that you have carefully thought through the steps necessary to make the idea into a successful company. Without a game plan, you will find that your business will just wander aimlessly, without ever reaching any destination, because you haven't developed the road map to get you to the final destination, whatever it may be.

Many successful businesses have been started by entrepreneurs using the "seat of the pants" method; in other words, without a game plan. But these success stories are few and far between. And anyway, as their businesses grew, many found they had to write up a plan later in order to give the business some direction. So do it now in the beginning stages of your business to help you become more focused and reach success more quickly.

It isn't necessary for the game plan to be long and complicated, but it does have to be clear—to you and to any potential investors. And it must be written by you and not your accountant or attorney. This is *your* business and it should detail *your* strategy for pulling together the resources to start and successfully run your company. The value in your doing it lies in the research and evaluation process. If you delegate the task to someone else, you'll miss out on one of the most valuable lessons you can learn about running your business. This undertaking will force you to determine your direction, consider your competition, and plan how to market your product or service. An accountant can help you with your financial projections, but you must know how much it will cost to produce your product or service and how much you will spend on promotions and other business expenses.

For the computer-savvy Sister CEO, there are relatively inexpensive business plan software programs you can use to write your success game plan. Two of the most popular are BizPlan-Builder, from Jian Software, and Business Plan Toolkit, from Palo Alto Software. The BizPlanBuilder program provides a series of text templates for the company, product or service, market analysis, and financial spreadsheets. You just fill in the text using your word processor. Business Plan Toolkit also walks you through the process of writing a business plan, but it doesn't provide templates. It outlines the specific areas and goes through the questions you need to answer to complete the plan. Both programs provide a sample business plan to show you what the final product should look like.

In writing your game plan, let your instinct be your guide. Not only must it make sense financially, but it must also feel achievable on a gut level. Memorize it. Visualize it. Why? Because when you are clear and can see the plan in motion, it seeps directly into your subconscious mind to bring about the desired results. You become unstoppable and turn your burning desire into your will to succeed. When you have the will to succeed, the bulk of your perceived obstacles will dissolve on their own and turn into perceived opportunities.

Be sure to build contingencies into your game plan. In business, things rarely happen as we project them to happen. There are always unexpected developments and unforeseen problems, such as lack of money, sudden competition, and changes in the economy and the marketplace that will cost the business money. It's to your advantage to know ahead of time what these problems will be and to work out a strategic plan to overcome them.

Finally and most importantly, work the game plan. Small-business owners spend countless hours creating a game plan only to ignore it as they grow their business. Don't allow it to just sit in your file cabinet gathering dust. Use it! Continue to revise it at least every quarter, or better yet, monthly. Compare notes; tally your actual sales and expenses at the end of the month and compare them with your projected sales and expenses.

## Mapping Out Your Success Game Plan

Now you're ready to start writing your success game plan. Though each business game plan is unique, all plans should include the following components:

**Plan summary:** The summary gives an overview of your business. Lenders will review this section first to decide if they want to read the rest of the plan in detail. Therefore, your objective in the plan summary is to highlight the key points of your business and entice a lender to study the game plan further. Although this summary appears at the beginning of your success game plan, it should be the last part you write.

The plan summary should include the following key points:

- A brief history of your business or business idea.
- A description of your product or service, with emphasis on its

uniqueness, a characterization of the market it will fill, and an assessment of the competition.

- How the products will be made or services performed.
- A profile of your management team's credentials and expertise.
- A summary of financial projections.
- The amount of money you are seeking, why you need it, and how you plan to pay it back.

**Statement of purpose:** In chapter 2, one of the exercises required you to write down your business purpose. If you completed it, simply include it in this section. If not, you can do it here. Write a brief description of one or two paragraphs stating why you want to start this business and what you hope to achieve with it.

**Company and industry:** The goal of this part of the plan is to provide information on your company and to describe the industry. Include the following points in this section:

- Your current business or prospective business. Include a description of the product or service.
- Background of the business, when it was started, and the legal structure (e.g., sole proprietorship, corporation, partnership).
- Who the principals of the business are and what role they play.
- Trends in the industry your business is in.
- The competition: describe who they are and what their performance record is in terms of sales, profits, and market share.
- An overview of how economic, social, and technological issues will affect your business.

**Product or service:** In this section you describe your product or service more in depth. Discuss trademarks, patents, special features, and future development plans. Key points to include:

- What type of product or service your business will sell and how you plan to sell it. Include pictures and sales brochures as well.

- Any patents, trademarks, and copyrights. Discuss any other factors that will give your product or service a jump on the competition.
- Any new products or services you plan to develop.

**Marketing plan:** This section is the meat of your success game plan. It comprises two parts: market analysis and market strategies. In market analysis, you will show how you plan to turn your idea into a product or service that people will buy. In market strategies, your identify your target market(s) and outline how you will find and contact potential customers or clients. Concentrating on the needs of a specific segment and carving out a niche may mean the difference between success and failure. Answer the following questions to complete this part:

## *Market Analysis*

A. What is your target market? Who are the customers?

- The company will sell primarily to (check all that apply):
  Wholesalers _____
  Retailers _____
  Government _____
  Other (describe) _____

B. You will target customers by:

- Product/Service: What specific product or service?
- Geographic area: Which area?
- Sales: Will you target sales to African Americans? Hispanics? Mainstream America?
- Industry: What is the target industry (e.g., lawyers, physicians, teachers, etc.)?

C. What is the size of the market?
D. What is your share of this market?
   Who are your main competitors?
E. Why would customers choose your product or service?

F. How much will your market spend on your product or service this coming year?
G. List your strengths and weaknesses compared to your competition.
H. What economic factors will affect your product or service?
I. What is the growth potential of your market?
J. Is your product/service available for the international market? If so, what countries?

## *Market Strategies*

- What kind of image do you want your company to project?
- List the features you will emphasize.
- What are your sales and credit terms?
- How will you sell/distribute?
- How will you promote?
- How will you differentiate your offering from your competitors'?

**Advertising/promotion:** Discuss how you will inform customers and clients about your product or service. Select from the list below the advertising/promotion strategies that your company will use and explain how:

- Television
- Cable television
- Radio
- Direct mail
- Personal contacts (word-of-mouth)
- Newspapers
- Magazines
- Yellow pages
- Black sororities/fraternities
- Other black organizations
- Churches
- Infomercials
- Push carts in shopping mall
- Street vendors
- Flea markets

- Black hair salons and barber shops
- Black family reunions
- Other black businesses that are related
- What unique advertising/promotional ideas do you have?

**Management:** The credentials and expertise of your management team are important. Begin this section by preparing a profile of each of the members who are part of your management team. Describe their qualifications and duties.

**Sales/distribution:** Describe how you will sell your product or services—through sales representatives, black expos, conferences, mail order, etc. Include your monthly and/or annual sales projections.

**Manufacturing/operations:** Describe who will make your product or provide your service and how they will do it. What raw materials are needed and what is the cost breakdown? Explain your procedures for quality and inventory control. Describe the location of the business. Office? Home-based? Small business incubator?

**Advisory board/board of directors:** Identify your advisory board members or board of directors. Discuss how they will assist in the running of your company and list if any have invested money in your company. Even if your company isn't large, an advisory board of an accountant, attorney, and fellow entrepreneur is highly recommended.

**Schedule of activities:** Show a shedule outlining steps you will take and your timetable over the next three to five years to grow your business. Lenders are sticklers for organization and time and will hold you to your schedule of activities, so be realistic and don't underestimate the time it will take.

**Critical risks and problems:** There are risks and problems involved in any business and the best way to prevent them from overwhelming you is to plan for them and have a "Plan B" in place as a backup. In this section you can list any potential problems and outline possible ways for dealing with them or minimizing them in such a way that they won't have a detrimental effect on your business.

**Financial information:** If you are seeking money, you will describe in this section the amount, type, and purpose, e.g., loan, line of credit, equity, to upgrade product line, etc. Also, include information on your company's current financial status (enclose two to three years of financial statements). If your business is new, include your personal balance sheet along with a projected three-year cash flow. You may want your attorney to complete this task.

**Financial statements:** Your game plan should include:

- Projected Cash Flow Statement (see page 178).
- Projected Balance Sheet (see page 179).
- Projected Income Statement (see page 180).

**In a nutshell:** Your success game plan should describe:

- Your company and the industry and its trends.
- Your product or service.
- Your market.
- How your product or service will reach your target market.
- Who will run the business.
- How much money the company needs and what it plans to do with it.

### Sister CEO Action Steps

1. Begin writing out your success game plan. Don't try to do it in one day. You can't, and if you try, you will become discouraged. Take your time. It may take two to three weeks to write out a usable plan. The key to your success is not to skip over this important step!
2. Ask your attorney to complete the business financial projections.
3. Once it is finished, have it professionally bound at your local copy store.
4. **Work the game plan.** Refer to it often to keep your business focused and on track.

## *Projected Cash Flow Statement*

| | *Month 1* | *Month 2* | *Month 3* | *Month 4* |
|---|---|---|---|---|
| **CASH** | | | | |
| Beginning Cash | | | | |
| Cash Sales | | | | |
| Collections | | | | |
| Other Cash | | | | |
| **Total Cash Available** | | | | |
| | | | | |
| **EXPENSES** | | | | |
| Salaries and Wages | | | | |
| Other Employee Expenses | | | | |
| Utilities | | | | |
| Rent/Lease | | | | |
| Office Supplies | | | | |
| Telephone | | | | |
| Printing/ Photocopying | | | | |
| Misc. (including postage) | | | | |
| Advertising | | | | |
| Insurance | | | | |
| Auto/ Transportation | | | | |
| Travel/ Entertainment | | | | |
| Taxes/Licenses | | | | |
| Packaging/Shipping | | | | |
| Subscriptions/Dues | | | | |
| Bank Charges | | | | |
| Interest | | | | |
| Depreciation | | | | |
| Commissions | | | | |
| Decorating | | | | |
| Legal/Accounting | | | | |
| Other—List | | | | |
| **Total Expenses** | | | | |
| **Cash Available** | | | | |

**Payment on Debt** _____  _____  _____  _____
**Ending Cash** _____  _____  _____  _____

Source: U.S. Small Business Administration

## *Projected Balance Sheet*

**ASSETS**

***CURRENT ASSETS:***

Cash on hand and in bank        $_____

Accounts receivable        \_\_0\_\_

Inventory        _____

**Total Current Assets**        $_____

Fixed Assets:

Automobile        _____

Furniture, fixtures, and equipment        _____

Less allowance for depreciation        \_\_0\_\_

**Total Fixed Assets**        _____

***OTHER ASSETS:***

Deposit-utilities        _____

Deposit-lease        _____

Prepaid expenses-remodeling &
advertising        _____

**Total Other Assets**        _____

***Total Assets***        $_____

**LIABILITIES AND CAPITAL**

***Current Liabilities:***

Loan payable, due within 1 year        $_____

**Total Current Liabilities**        _____

***Long-Term Liabilities:***

Loan payable, 5 years, 10%     $_____

Less: Current portion above        _____

**Total Long-Term Liabilities**        _____

**Total Liabilities**        _____

**Proprietor's Capital**        _____

**Total Liabilities and Capital**           $_____

(A similar format will be used for projected balance sheets at the end of year one and year two.)

Source: U.S. Small Business Administration

## Projected Income Statement

| | 1st Year Amount | % of Sales | 2nd Year Amount | % of Sales | 3rd Year Amount | % of Sales |
|---|---|---|---|---|---|---|
| Gross Receipts | ___ | ___ | ___ | ___ | ___ | ___ |
| Cost of Sales | | ___ | ___ | ___ | ___ | ___ |
| **Gross Profit** | ___ | ___ | ___ | ___ | ___ | ___ |
| **EXPENSES** | | | | | | |
| Salaries and Wages | ___ | ___ | ___ | ___ | ___ | ___ |
| Other Employee Expenses | ___ | ___ | ___ | ___ | ___ | ___ |
| Utilities | ___ | ___ | ___ | ___ | ___ | ___ |
| Rent/Lease | ___ | ___ | ___ | ___ | ___ | ___ |
| Office Supplies | ___ | ___ | ___ | ___ | ___ | ___ |
| Telephone | ___ | ___ | ___ | ___ | ___ | ___ |
| Printing/ Photocopying | ___ | ___ | ___ | ___ | ___ | ___ |
| Misc. (including postage) | ___ | ___ | ___ | ___ | ___ | ___ |
| Advertising | ___ | ___ | ___ | ___ | ___ | ___ |
| Insurance | ___ | ___ | ___ | ___ | ___ | ___ |
| Auto/Transportation | ___ | ___ | ___ | ___ | ___ | ___ |
| Travel/Entertainment | ___ | ___ | ___ | ___ | ___ | ___ |
| Taxes/Licenses | ___ | ___ | ___ | ___ | ___ | ___ |
| Packaging/Shipping | ___ | ___ | ___ | ___ | ___ | ___ |
| Subscriptions/Dues | ___ | ___ | ___ | ___ | ___ | ___ |
| Bank Charges | ___ | ___ | ___ | ___ | ___ | ___ |
| Interest | ___ | ___ | ___ | ___ | ___ | ___ |
| Depreciation | ___ | ___ | ___ | ___ | ___ | ___ |
| Commissions | ___ | ___ | ___ | ___ | ___ | ___ |
| Decorating | ___ | ___ | ___ | ___ | ___ | ___ |
| Legal/Accounting | ___ | ___ | ___ | ___ | ___ | ___ |

|  | 1st Year | | 2nd Year | | 3rd Year | |
|---|---|---|---|---|---|---|
|  | Amount | % of Sales | Amount | % of Sales | Amount | % of Sales |
| Other—List | ___ | ___ | ___ | ___ | ___ | ___ |
| **Total Expenses** | ___ | ___ | ___ | ___ | ___ | ___ |
| **Net Profit/Loss Before Taxes** | ___ | ___ | ___ | ___ | ___ | ___ |
| **Less:** Income Taxes | ___ | ___ | ___ | ___ | ___ | ___ |
| **Net Profit After Taxes** | ___ | ___ | ___ | ___ | ___ | ___ |
| **Less:** Withdrawals (only if Proprietorship or Partnership) | ___ | ___ | ___ | ___ | ___ | ___ |
| **Undistributed Profit or Loss** | ___ | ___ | ___ | ___ | ___ | ___ |

Source: U.S. Small Business Administration

# Part Four

## Growing Your Business

# Chapter 13

## SISTER CEO
## MANAGEMENT STYLE

Make those under your authority successful and you'll get
an incredible ride on top of their rocket.

ANONYMOUS

Most Sister CEOs (myself included) start their businesses to have
complete control over their lives. Many of the women are maver-
icks who have left corporate America because they saw themselves
hitting the glass ceiling with no chance of ever becoming the CEO
of the company. However, once they started the business, many
soon realized that starting and managing a business are not one
and the same.

This is a problem not only for Sister CEOs but for most entrepreneurs. The majority have the skills to get the business up and running but lack the skills to manage and grow the company. It is
during this time you either learn how to do it yourself—not always
the best option since it takes time away from the area of your
expertise—or you hire an independent contractor or employee.

In this chapter, you'll learn how to manage and grow your company through a technique I've coined, "Sister CEO Management"—
a method by which black women can use their natural-born
talents and traits to manage and grow their business. I'll also cover
success strategies for growing your company, which include hiring
employees and forming joint alliances with big businesses. And

185

finally, I'll cover one of the most important areas in any business: customer service. Returning phone calls and letters, and delivering products and services promptly are only a few of the ways to build customer loyalty.

## Sister CEO Management—Our Special Style

Our African ancestors and Mother Nature herself blessed black women with some very special gifts—compassion, outspokenness, patience, tolerance, durability, tenaciousness, and creativity, just to name a few. We're excellent storytellers. We can do a thousand things at once, keeping track of everything for ourselves as well as for other family members. We know how to take care of everyone and encourage them to do better. And the list goes on. . . .

Interestingly enough, it is these traits that become powerful skills when transplanted into the business arena. As a Sister CEO calling all the shots in your own business, knowing how to promote cooperation, build rapport, network, clarify what people mean, and handle others' idiosyncrasies are especially important.

When you look at management in big business today you can see it is clearly outdated. The male-dominated "Do as I say because I'm the boss" days are long gone. That attitude is not conducive to running a successful business, so there is no reason for you to run your business that way. Therefore . . .

## Run Your Business Like a Woman and Not Like a Man

When I began my financial career with Dean Witter Reynolds, I worked in an office with eighteen other financial advisers. I was the only African American and the only woman financial adviser. I tried extremely hard to fit in. I wore blue pinstripe suits, white blouses, and bow ties. Surprisingly, I was highly accepted in the group and became "one of the boys." And my manager, Bill Phillips, who to this day I thank for my success, became my mentor.

While being one of the gang was okay for the first two to three years, I eventually began to notice I was losing my feminine side and became dissatisfied with how my business was going. I'm sure many of you who started your professional careers in the early '80s can relate to my story.

While it is important that Sister CEOs adopt some male traits, such as drive and business savvy, it isn't necessary to get caught up in a man's competitive, dog-eat-dog world and become harsh, over-bearing, and uncaring. We have a God-given talent that many men don't have—intuition. We need to appreciate this sixth sense and use it to succeed in business. Ask yourself how many times you have not followed your "gut" or "instinct" and screwed up. I've made costly business mistakes by not following my intuition. Need-less to say, I have learned my lesson and now listen closely when I get that uneasy feeling.

In a *Forbes* magazine article, "The Best Man for the Job Is Your Wife," eight women business owners were profiled, including Sister CEO Loida Lewis of TLC Beatrice International Holdings. All were widows who had taken over the family business upon the death of their CEO spouses. What was significant about the women was that they managed the companies better than their husbands had. Under their tutelage many of the companies grew more than twofold. Why were they so successful? Because they applied common sense and their feminine characteristics to running the business. As housewives they knew how to manage their time, their children, and their husbands all at the same time.

Loida Lewis, Sister CEO of TLC Beatrice, firmly believes that her homemaking skills enabled her to step in and take over with ease. She encourages women business owners to "run your business like you would your household. Budget and manage the money and cut costs where you see fit. That's really all it takes to succeed in business." She must be right. As of June 1995, the company reported net profits of $11.9 million on revenues of $1.9 billion, and it is the world's largest black-owned company.

## Management Success Strategies

Success in business is never guaranteed, but if you put cer-tain success strategies in place, you can increase your odds.

Here are ten success strategies for smartly managing your business.

1. **Monitor closely.** Take charge of every aspect of the business—from quality control in the manufacturing process to managing every detail of product fulfillment, shipping, and customer service.

2. **Take care of customers.** Focus on building an ongoing business centered on long-term relationships with satisfied customers or clients. Continue to offer new products or services. If you are in a service business, offer some new type of product to sell to your existing base.

   I'll use my massage therapist, Imani Kei, Sister CEO of Healing Connection, as an example. Imani is a wonderful masseuse and her massage room is heavenly—filled with candles and the sound of ocean waves or a babbling brook in the background. It's a serene environment where my stress level is immediately lowered. On one particular occasion I enjoyed the music so much I asked to purchase a copy of the tape. Unfortunately, she didn't have one. A light bulb went off in my head. I suggested to her that she sell tapes and candles, since she already had a built-in market with her existing clients. Many would want to create that same environment in their home and would gladly purchase the products if they were conveniently available. Well, I'm happy to say Imani took my advice and during the Christmas holidays put together Christmas packages of candles and tea, and soon she'll have tapes. This is known as providing a value-added product to your service business. It is an excellent way to create more income for your service business, particularly during a slow period.

3. **Keep up with the times.** In today's fast-changing, highly competitive world, standing still is the same as moving backward. If you don't go forward, others will zoom right by you.

   As a Sister CEO of a small business, you have an advantage that large businesses don't have—the flexibility to make quick changes to keep pace with the latest market trends. The world is filled with companies that failed to adapt to change. IBM is a prime example. Known as the "Big Blue" of the computer industry, IBM lost market share to Apple and other computer companies when it became complacent and failed to change.

Times are much different than they were twenty years ago. With the advent of the information age, technology is faster. It used to take ten to fifteen years for a product to be improved. That's been cut down to five years, and soon it will be two years or less. As a Sister CEO you must embrace the necessary changes, otherwise you will endanger your company and quickly become obsolete. As a black woman you must engage in a lifelong self-improvement program for yourself and your business, continually seeking more knowledge and newer methods. You have to be open to new ideas and never be satisfied when people tell you, "This is the way it has always been done." Many people are afraid of change and will do everything in their power to resist it. Don't allow yourself to tap into their fear.

4. **Offer a quality product or service.** Your business must provide a quality product or service with real value and present it in a quality way. The question you should ask yourself is, "What's the best quality I can give consumers at a price they can afford?" Then do whatever it will take to provide that quality at that price. Your company motto should be, "We Can Do It Faster, Better, and Cheaper."

5. **Empower your coworkers.** As a successful Sister CEO you must manage your business by empowering your staff. You need to feel confident enough to let go of some of your power by surrounding yourself with top-notch people and getting out of their way. According to Carol Williams, Sister CEO of Carol H. Williams Advertising, "You have to appreciate your employees by openly thanking and praising them for their efforts. You must share your dreams with your people, then they'll enjoy coming to work and giving the business all they've got, which in the long run improves your bottom line." Do you remember what it was like to be an employee? And how you vowed never to do this or that to your employees? It's time to put that into action!

If you're a new Sister CEO and initially can't offer big salaries and benefits, be sure to provide sincere appreciation, and a fun and relaxed work setting.

6. **Delegate responsibility.** Avoid burnout. Giving up the power is difficult for many Sister CEOs. You must remember, we've been taught to do everything—work, clean, cook, take care of the kids and Aunt Mamie all at the same time—so juggling duties is embedded in our genes. But as I said earlier, you don't become a successful Sister CEO alone, you need help—so give it up, girlfriend.

You need to delegate in order to free up your time to concentrate on the big picture. If you're too busy doing all the small detail work, your business will only grow so far. As a Sister CEO, you are the leader and your goal is to empower others as well. When you help your employees make money, don't forget it trickles down to you, since you are the CEO of the company.

Hire people whose strengths complement your weaknesses. If you're not good with managing money, hire some who is. Just be sure you always know what that person is doing.

7. **Take time to reflect.** When you find your business heading "south," get away for a few days to reflect and sort things out. You'll return with a better perspective. Focus on what's good about your business and what the negatives are. Your goal is to eliminate as many of the negatives as possible.

8. **Manage growth.** Too much business can also be a problem. It can cause a small business to go out of control trying to keep up with the demand for products or services. Keep a low profile and be careful about taking on new clients or projects unless you know you'll be able to service them properly. Refer them to a colleague until you're able to manage your growth.

Rid yourself of bothersome clients or customers. Life's too short and there are better customers out there. Also, ask your clients or customers to make a 50 percent deposit on the product or service they are purchasing. This will improve your cash flow and weed out "lookie-look" clients who will waste your time but not give you their business.

9. **Automate your business.** Technology has leveled the playing field for Sister CEOs. With technology, your business is capable of performing the same tasks as any big business.

10. **Make joint alliances with big businesses.** Creating strategic alliances with larger businesses is fast becoming a way for African American entrepreneurs to grow their businesses. Partnering with a big firm could give your firm a more secure foothold in your industry. With so much competitiveness in the marketplace, smaller companies are fighting for a decreasing number of contracts coming from government and private industry sources. Without teaming up, smaller business just can't always compete.

To find interested big businesses to form joint ventures with, contact the National Minority Supplier Development Council, Inc. (212-944-2430). The group sponsors seminars for the sole purpose of introducing minority firms to majority-owned businesses such as Procter & Gamble, Coca Cola, Pepsico, and others.

African American firms should also consider large minority firms as potential allies. Firms can either combine their resources, talent, and expertise to withstand the turbulent business arena, or remain as individual companies and eventually be driven out of the business altogether.

## Commonsense Customer Service

Businesses today need to pay more attention to the needs of customers who are demanding red-carpet treatment. Many firms are realizing that it isn't enough to win the client over with one sale; you must turn them into loyal patrons. And the way to do that is by commonsense customer service. Treat your customers the way you would want to be treated. Think of the many times you've hung up the phone after talking with the company's rude receptionist. Or decided not to do business with a particular firm because it took them three weeks to get the information out to you. These factors affect your business. And if they're ongoing, they'll be the demise of your business.

Customers today have too many choices of who they can do business with. So it is quite easy for them to say "next" without batting an eye. Therefore, if your company isn't on top of problems or concerns with existing clients, the likelihood of retaining them or getting referrals from them is nil.

With the help of my two assistants, Autry Henderson and Shirley Jackson, I identified three major gripes people generally have with businesses:

- **Providing impersonal telephone service.** The automation of phone services has depersonalized business. People today want human contact on the phone and highly resent the systems that transfer them all over the place only to end up in the wrong department. If you can't hire a receptionist to answer your phone, consider a message service company. The other gripes in this area include keeping people on hold for a long time, not returning phone calls as promised, and waiting for an employee to get off a personal telephone call to answer your question or to wait on you.

- **Not being on time for an appointment.** People are busy and don't have time to wait. My biggest gripe in this area is with hair stylists, doctors, and dentists. Let's start with hair stylists. I truly don't understand why we black women think we need to sit in a beauty salon for four hours to get our hair done. It's crazy, but many of us allow it and therefore the hair stylist doesn't do anything to change it. I can understand to a degree that they have to overbook in order to make up for last-minute cancellations, but if that's the case, have a Plan B in place if everyone shows up. Ask another stylist who may not be as busy to take a couple of your clients and split the fee. I bet many sistahs wouldn't mind another stylist doing their hair to avoid spending their whole Saturday in the waiting room. If a client doesn't mind the wait, so be it, but at least offer her an alternative and let her make the choice. And the same goes for doctors and dentists. If you want to keep your customers satisfied, this waiting around and not being on time has got to go! I guess you can see I'm a real stickler for time.

- **Allowing your employee to take a break when the line is out the door.** Banks are notorious for this. How often have you been next in line when the clerk decides to take a break? This infuriates me no end. Why isn't there someone available to step right in and take his or her place? This is simply a problem of management disorganization. And it doesn't take a genius to fix it. If it is planned properly, customers can get waited on in a decent amount of time and employees can take their breaks and lunches on time. And everyone is happy.

These are the major gripes we've uncovered, and I'm sure you can think of several more. As a Sister CEO, make sure you have a customer service marketing program in place to enable your business to build customer loyalty.

### Sister CEO Action Steps

1. Manage and grow your company like a woman and not like a man; use the Sister CEO management style.
2. Follow the ten management success strategies to increase your odds of succeeding in business.
3. Use commonsense customer service skills to build client loyalty. Treat them the way you want to be treated.
4. Be on time for your appointments!!

# Chapter 14

## MARKETING: LETTING PEOPLE KNOW YOU'RE IN BUSINESS

> The first law of modern business is no longer find a need
> and fill it, but imagine a need and create it.
>
> PAUL ZANE PILZER,
> *author, economist*

Although Diane Shelton, Sister CEO of West Love, a thirteen-year-old ethnic fashion boutique in Culver City, California, owns a storefront, she doesn't sit around waiting for customers to come to her. Instead, she goes to them. Shelton spends 50 percent of her time on the road selling her ethnic fashions at black organizations' annual conferences and expos. "You've got to let people know you're in business if you want to make any money," states Shelton.

Today's fiercely competitive marketplace calls for aggressive marketing strategies to let people know you're in business. Like Diane Shelton, you can't sit around twiddling your thumbs waiting for your clients to line up at your front door. Believe me, it won't happen. You sometimes have to go to them. But first you need to know who your customers are and develop a marketing plan to reach them. In fact, not having a marketing plan in place for your business will be one of the biggest obstacles to your success. You can have the most incredible new product or service in the world, but if no one knows about it or buys it, your business can't possibly succeed.

In this chapter, you'll learn how to market your product or services with low-cost marketing tips. It really doesn't take as much money as you may think to get the word out about your business. But it will take creative "chutzpa." If what you are offering is a high-quality product or an excellent service, and it fills a need, once you become well-known in your field you'll find your marketing efforts paying off with a snowball effect of free publicity and great word-of-mouth advertising, creating a tremendous amount of business for you.

## The New Trend: Ethnic Marketing

As you look at the major media campaigns today, there is a surge of marketing effort directed toward specific markets, particularly the African Americans, Hispanics, and Asian Americans. In the past, these groups weren't considered viable markets and were lumped together and expected to assimilate into mainstream America.

But time has proven this reasoning faulty. America is no longer a melting pot. African Americans, Hispanics, and Asian Americans want to maintain their cultural identity and are looking for products or services that will help them do that. Which is why I firmly believe that, as a Sister CEO, you are in an unique position to capture these markets, since you can already identify with them. Going after a specific niche and offering the best product or service is what will lead your business to success. Here are a few demographic statistics provided by Market Segment Research to prove my point:

- People of African, American Indian, Asian, and Hispanic descent now make up one-fourth of the U.S. population. This figure is expected to rise to over one-third by the year 2000. And in California and Texas, it is projected that whites will be in the minority by 2010.
- African Americans, now numbering 32 million, are expected to reach 40.2 million by 2010.
- The spending power of African Americans is projected to

increase from the current $400 billion to well over $600 billion by the year 2010.

- The U.S. Hispanic population is projected to surpass African Americans by the year 2010 with 40.5 million people.
- Black households spend more than three times as much on small appliances and twice as much on perishables as do non-black households.
- In a study conducted by Yankelovich Partners and Burrell Communications Group, 60 percent of black consumers feel that most ads are designed only for white people.
- More than three-fourths of African American consumers want to buy more products from black-owned firms, according to a study by the American Health & Beauty Aids Institute. Most African Americans base their buying decision on how the business is giving back to the community and whether or not this is the best value for their money.
- While African Americans comprise only 11 percent of the population, they buy 19 percent of all cosmetics and beauty aids, and 34 percent of all hair care products.
- Black families with incomes of $30,000 or more spend about as much as white families who earn $50,000.
- Half of the African American market is between the ages of twenty-five and forty-four, and 56 percent are women.
- Blacks watch 48 percent more TV than whites. (I don't know why; based on the majority of shows on TV today, they're quite boring if you ask me.) And, radio reaches 96.5 percent of all African Americans.
- Marketers believe that African Americans, Hispanics, and Asians in this country lag behind major U.S. trends by about five years in areas relating to health, fitness, and diet. (This I firmly believe, based on the issue I brought up earlier about how there aren't health food stores in the black communities.)

## Don't Let the White Guys Have All the Fun

We are a lucrative market and corporate America knows it. They are latching on to these niche markets like white on rice, with multimillion-dollar campaigns expected to approach the $1 billion level by the year 2000. Corporations like Revlon, Maybelline, J.C. Penney, Sears, Procter & Gamble, and K-Mart are making major commitments to target ethnic customers by offering ethnically oriented toys, books, clothing, artwork, linens, bedding, rugs, and various other products that these groups can relate to or are faithful users of. While you may not be able to compete and match the marketing campaigns of the big boys, at least take advantage and get in on the action by supplying them with these types of products made by *your* company. Later in this chapter, I'll discuss how to do that via different channels of distribution.

## Market Research

Whether you target African Americans or mainstream America, no group is homogeneous and therefore your marketing plan needs to state the specifics of your target market. You need to determine what group or groups will be most eager to buy your product or services, and then when, how, and for how much. The way to find out this information is by first conducting research on your prospective market.

Thorough, ongoing market research provides a wealth of information about your potential and existing customers and your competition, and will help you to create an identity for your product or service that separates it from your competition. As a Sister CEO you must continually evaluate your marketplace if you are to produce new products or additional services, or adapt to changing demands, increased competition, and new technology. You want to take this important information and use it to develop an effective marketing campaign. Remember: while trying to provide a product or service to everyone is noble, it isn't feasible. You can't be everything to everybody. Your objective should be to reach only the people who will buy your product or service.

### CONDUCTING THE RESEARCH

To begin your extensive low-cost research, start with the public library, where you'll find a lot of information ready-made. The next step is to hit the pavement and talk to folks who fall within your target market. You can get them to answer a questionnaire by any or all of the following three ways: personal interviews, direct mail, or telemarketing. The most efficient method is telephone interviews; you get a fast response and can cover a wide geographical range. The most effective is personal interviews, yet they cost the most and are labor-intensive. The least effective is direct mail; not many people take the time to return the completed questionnaire, so the response rate tends to be lower.

Following is a sample of a market research questionnaire you can use to conduct your study.

### *Market Research Questionnaire*

1. Are you:   Female _____   Male _____
2. Are you:   African American _____   Hispanic _____
   White _____   Asian _____
   Other (specify) _____
3. What is your age?   18–24 ____   25–34 ____
   35–44 ____   45–54 ____
   55–64 ____   65 or over ____
4. What is your martial status?   Married ____
   Single, Never Married ____
   Separated or Divorced ____   Widowed ____
5. How many children under the age of 18 live in your household? ____   Over 18? ____
6. What is your total personal income? (Include income from all sources: salary, bonuses, etc.)
   ____ Less than $30,000        ____ $30,000–$39,999
   ____ $40,000–$49,999        ____ $50,000–$59,999
   ____ $60,000–$74,999        ____ $75,000–$99,999
   ____ $100,000–$149,999      ____ $150,000–$249,999
   ____ Over $250,000
7. What is your total household income? (Include all sources: salary, bonuses, etc.)
   ____ Less than $30,000        ____ $30,000–$39,999
   ____ $40,000–$49,999        ____ $50,000–$59,999

    ____ $60,000–$74,999      ____ $75,000–$99,999
    ____ $100,000–$149,999  ____ $150,000–$249,999
    ____ Over $250,000   How much? _____

8. Do you own a home, condominium, or co-op as your primary residence? Yes ____ No ____

9. If yes, what is the current market value?
    ____ Under $100,000     ____ $100,000–$199,999
    ____ $200,000–$299,999  ____ $300,000–$499,999
    ____ Over $500,000   How much? _____

10. How familiar are you with (name your product/service)?
    ____ Very familiar     ____ Somewhat familiar
    ____ Not familiar

11. Which of the following are important to you when purchasing (name your product or service)?
Check all that apply.
    ____ Customer service    ____ Attractive product
    ____ Best price         ____ Easy to use
    ____ Product quality     ____ Dependability
    ____ Other (please specify)

12. How often do you purchase (name your product/service)?
    ____ Weekly      ____ Annually
    ____ Monthly    ____ Other (please specify)

13. Which of the following sources of information do you use to make a decision about purchasing (name your product/service)? Check all that apply.
    ____ Business magazines    ____ Catalogs
    ____ Radio          ____ Television
    ____ Friends        ____ Newspaper
    ____ Other (please specify)

## Developing a Marketing Campaign

After completing your market research, you should have a general idea of the demographics of your target market. The next step is to develop a creative marketing campaign to let everyone in that group who needs your product or service know about it, and do so in a way that convinces them to buy it *today*.

Large corporations with an ample supply of money have extensive marketing campaigns consisting of television, newspaper, and magazine advertising, radio spots on local and national radio stations, and nationwide promotional activity. So how do you, as a Sister CEO just getting started, give yourself and your product or service the marketing boost you need?

## THE THREE MARKETING AVENUES OF SUCCESSFUL SISTER CEO BUSINESSES

Initially, you'll need to use a variety of inexpensive marketing avenues to determine which is the best to reach your specific customer. After talking with several Sister CEOs about their marketing campaigns, I found the most successful businesses use one or more of these basic marketing avenues.

### 1. Inexpensive Marketing Tools

- **Marketing materials:** Develop a professional-looking marketing package consisting of your business card, stationery, and a brochure describing your business. You only have a few minutes to win a customer over and therefore need to project a certain image within that time frame. Don't spend a lot of money or order too many brochures initially. You'll find later that you may need to make changes as you go along.

  I wish someone had given me that advice when I had a graphic design company create my company brochure. I ordered far too many and spent over $20,000 on a brochure that is already out of date because of certain changes I had to make due to securities regulations. Until your business is up and running, I suggest you create your own marketing package. With the aid of a computer and desktop publishing software, you can actually create it yourself without the help of a graphic designer. Paper Direct (800-A-PAPERS) is the program I recommend. Not only can you purchase the software, but the paper for the business cards, brochures, and stationery as well. Later, as your company becomes profitable, you will want to project a different image and should consider hiring a graphic designer who can design a more professional-looking marketing package, complete with your company logo.

- **Newsletters:** A newsletter filled with information can be a great tool to keep you and your company in front of your customers and clients. Whereas brochures are tossed in the "circular file," newsletters are often read and possibly filed away.

    If you're not a natural writer, you have several options to choose from to publish your own newsletter. You can hire someone to write and produce it for you (as discussed in chapter 10, this is one of the businesses that a new Sister CEO can start). Another option is to use a computer and desktop publishing software. Paper Direct, the company I mentioned earlier, also has paper and a template to create your own newsletter. You just need to write the copy and insert it into the columns. The third choice is to write the newsletter yourself and have the local copy shop print it up.

- **Direct marketing:** Direct marketing includes direct mail, mail-order, coupon advertising, and telephone marketing. With this avenue you sell directly to your client or customer, attempting to make a sale immediately. With the advent of the busy consumer, direct mail is growing faster than any other type of marketing. People enjoy the convenience of being able to shop and purchase by mail. Look at the popularity of the home shopping networks. No one has time to go to crowded shopping malls, stand in line, and be waited on by salesclerks who hate their jobs. As people become busier they will turn more to companies that make their products or services available through direct mail.

- **Seminars:** Seminars are ideal for service-oriented businesses such as accounting, finance, law, and insurance to showcase your expertise to clients. It's a nonthreatening sales and educational tool to generate a larger client base for your business. You'll find opportunities to give seminars at colleges, associations, churches, YWCAs and YMCAs, cruise lines, department stores, and hotels. Again, it is necessary to target your market. Look at your client base, profile who they are, and start seeking places where they might be found.

When Sister CEO and business etiquette consultant Antoinette Broussard wanted to expand her business, she gave a business seminar on "How to Outclass the Competition" at the African American Women on Tour Conference. Her topic and leadership skills turned out to be popular. Several of the women asked for her business card at the conclusion of her presentation. It just so happened one of the participants worked for McDonald's Corporation and later hired Broussard to conduct a seminar.

To hone your speaking skills, consider joining Toastmasters and the National Speakers Association. Toastmasters is an international group that teaches the tools of speaking in front of audiences and gives you the opportunity to have your presentation critiqued. The organization has local chapters in fifty-two countries. The National Speakers Association is a trade association for professional speakers. The numbers for both organizations are listed in the appendix.

- **Books and workbooks:** Writing a book or developing a workbook will not only increase your credibility but become an ongoing source of income. You can sell your book at seminars, use it as a promotional piece to help you get free publicity in magazines and on radio and TV programs, and give it away as an incentive to new and existing clients.

  When I self-published *The Black Woman's Guide to Financial Independence*, I sold the book at my seminars as a learning tool to attract new clients. Thanks to free publicity in magazines, newspapers, and on radio and TV, not only did I get new clients but I sold over 30,000 copies.

  As you can see from my experience, getting your book published isn't as complicated as you think. You can publish a small, simply bound pamphlet using desktop publishing software and following the step-by-step advice of the book I used, *The Self-Publishing Manual*, by Dan Poynter.

- **Sampling:** People love to get something for free. Famous Amos launched his cookie business by letting people sample his cookies before they bought them. When he opened his first store, he walked up and down Sunset Boulevard in Los

Angeles and everywhere else he went handing out free cookies.

Several software companies also use this method, through direct mail, to introduce new software to the market. With ads in major magazines, they encourage you to call a toll-free number, pay a nominal shipping and handling charge, and receive a free copy of the program.

Participating in expos and trade shows is an excellent way to get customers to sample your product or service. It's not unusual for such shows to attract from 30,000 to 50,000 people. And, at many of them, you can not only generate leads but sell your product or service as well. Whenever I have attended the popular Black Expo, I always come home with a bag full of free or low-cost product samples. Many were from new companies just introducing their product to the market.

*2. Word of Mouth*

Once your business is established, word of mouth is by far the cheapest form of advertising. When you provide a service or product that is obviously so wonderful, your customers will want to naturally pass on the good word. Continue to network and talk to everyone you know about your business. Also make a determined effort to meet and talk with new people as well.

Another way to generate word-of-mouth advertising is to pass out your brochures or flyers to all your customers and ask them to give them to their family and friends. Don't be afraid to ask for referrals. Offer a free gift or a discount on your product or services for every new customer they refer to your business.

*3. Distribution Channels*

There are seven basic channels of distribution I recommend for a Sister CEO with a product or service business:

- **Retail stores:** With so many retail stores and discounters like Wal-Mart, K-Mart, Costco, and J.C. Penney in the marketplace, I'm not in favor of initially setting up your own retail store. It's expensive to set up shop and too difficult to compete with warehouse prices. It makes better business sense to supply your product to the stores instead.

To get your products on the shelves of these retailers will take lots of patience; it generally is a gradual process. Most large corporations test-market products in smaller regions before they go national. This method is actually beneficial to your company because you're able to succeed in a smaller area first and also receive feedback from customers on your product, enabling you to make necessary updates and changes before it reaches a larger audience.

Before you hit the big chains, you really should start right in your own backyard. Local, independently owned stores will sometimes take a chance on a new product. These stores can be easier to sell to because they are closer to the heart of the marketplace and their survival depends on catering to the needs of the community. If you have already been selling to friends and neighbors, you're in a stronger position to make a case for your product when you talk to the local store owner. You will need to convince that owner your product will sell and that you will help to sell it.

Persuade the store owner to carry your product by inducements such as offering a small inventory on consignment, providing free samples to customers, and creating an ad or direct-mail campaign featuring the product and the store.

By going through the mechanics of getting your product into the local stores, you'll learn a lot about what you need to do to succeed with the national retailers, in particular, how to price the product so that you and the retailer make a profit.

If your product sells well in one local store, that success can often be expanded to other local stores and eventually to a larger local or regional chain. Chains respect small-business owners who have successfully sold their products through local retailers.

Any and all creative means—that's what it will take in the beginning to get your product in the stores, so use all avenues. Find just one store that will help you sell your product, and build from there. Once the product sells on a local level, wider distribution will take care of itself. Resources with information on how to get your product into the retail stores are listed in the appendix.

- **Direct marketing:** Mail-order, direct mail, and catalogs are the three popular distribution channels of direct marketing.

Today, mail-order is a billion-dollar industry because more people are willing to buy by mail. Selling your product in this manner is ideal for home-based Sister CEOs. Before you consider this method, I suggest you study several of the classic mail-order books. Many will show you step-by-step how to start and what you need to avoid in a mail-order business. One of my favorites is *How to Start Your Own Business on a Shoestring and Make Up to $500,000 a Year*, by Tyler G. Hicks. The book is easy to read, fun, and informative.

A one-product business is perfect for mail-order. You can reach your targeted market through inexpensive classified ads and publicity (both discussed later in the chapter on advertising) and, once you develop a customer mailing list, you can offer new or related products.

Outside of being relatively easy to start, the beauty of mail-order distribution is that you can control its size and dollar volume by increasing the number of ads you place in newspapers and magazines. Yet, as with any endeavor, mail-order will grow in direct proportion to the amount of time and money you invest in the business. A good product and prompt delivery are the important keys to success.

Direct mail is similar to mail-order except that rather than using classified ads, you purchase targeted mailing lists and send a direct-mail packet consisting of a letter, brochure, order form, prepaid return envelope and curiosity "teaser" envelope to pique the customer to open the packet.

Not long ago I received a brown envelope similar to one sent by the IRS containing our tax refund checks. When I saw the envelope, I immediately opened it, thinking I had made a mistake on my tax return and they were sending me money back. To my great disappointment the letter turned out to be from a mortgage company wanting me to refinance my house. In honesty, I found the envelope to be misleading and actually think this method may backfire on the sender because everyone will have the same thought running through their head as I did. I quickly tore up the envelope and threw it away.

But I must admit, the envelope did serve its purpose by getting me to open it. It just made me mad afterwards.

The one drawback of direct mail is the expense of postage. With rates continually increasing, sending a large packet by mail can be expensive unless it is sent by bulk mail. Contact the main U.S. Postal Service office in your area to obtain a free bulk mail information packet.

To increase the response rate from customers who have received the packet, provide a toll-free phone number for orders. If you don't have the womanpower to answer the phone, hire an 800 toll-free service. They will provide you with the phone number and answer the phone for a fee. Check your yellow pages under *telephone answering service* and call several agencies to compare their services and fees. But remember, the rule of thumb on direct mail solicitation is that a 3 percent return is great!

Mail-order catalogs are not for Sister CEOs just starting a business. They're expensive to produce and you need to offer several products in order for it to pay off. If you currently own a retail store, you can offer a mail-order catalog to serve out-of-town and busy shoppers and expand your business.

After a major comeback, Jameela Bragg, Sister CEO of the four-year-old E-Scent-Ials Body Care shop in Oakland feels she's a bona fide entrepreneur. Since her store grossed over $100,000 in 1995, her goal for 1996 is to increase her sales by offering a mail-order catalog featuring the products she sells in her store. You'll read more of Bragg's success story in chapter 16, "The Balancing Act."

If you're interested in starting a mail-order catalog, research the market by getting your name on different mailing lists to receive catalogs. All it takes is to purchase one item from one mail-order company and they will sell your name to other companies. When you receive the catalogs, study the merchandise, pictures, copy, structure of the catalog, and the prices of the merchandise to give you an idea of how to structure your own.

The cost to produce a four-color catalog could run up to $10,000. Consider starting small with an eight-page black-and-white catalog. Talk to printers in your area to get firmer printing costs.

• **Expos and trade shows:** Expos and trade shows can be an effective marketing strategy for Sister CEOs who want to aggressively compete against bigger companies. When you exhibit at these events your customers can see your firm in the same perspective as your competitors. In addition, potential customers or clients can see where they can receive quality products and services at better prices.

The biggest complaint you will have in participating in these shows is the cost, which includes the initial fee to acquire space, booth design and construction, and pre/post-show marketing. But you need to see the big picture. The results could mean new clients, which leads to more money.

To capitalize on the events, you need to go with an agenda. Here are a few tips to make your shows successful:

1. Develop a thorough game plan before you go. Define your audience and determine which event will deliver the worthwhile results. Then, design your marketing campaign to meet their specific needs.
2. Send out a unique and eye-catching preshow mailer to entice potential customers or clients to stop by your booth.
3. Design a booth that is visually exciting. Your objective is to lure people to your booth so that you can introduce them to your product or service. For example, if your product is child-related, hire a clown to pass out candy or take Polaroids of the children with the clown. You're guaranteed to have an exciting booth. Four years ago, at the Black Expo in Los Angeles, I lucked out when my booth was located next to Gladys Knight's hair care products. When she was there signing autographs, a line formed directly in front of my booth as women waited to get their autographs. I sold a ton of books as a result of that. Which brings me to another idea. If at all possible, get a celebrity to endorse your product or service at these events. The results are overwhelming. Now, of course the hard part is finding the celebrity. It will take plenty of networking and perseverance on your part. You

need to know someone in the higher ranks of the sports and entertainment business to find an endorser.

4. Host a before or after reception for top potential clients. Here you can meet and talk one-on-one in a relaxed environment.

5. Be a presenter. Give a talk or seminar that will establish your expertise and position your company as a leader.

6. Develop a mailing list of everyone who stops at your booth by offering a free drawing. When the event is over, follow up with everyone on the list by either phone or mail. If possible, get the list of all attendees from the producer of the event and add the names to your database.

- **Home shopping networks:** There are three major home shopping networks on which you can show your products: BET Shop, which caters to the African American market, HSN, and QVC, which targets mainstream America. It's only within the last few years that this distribution avenue has opened up for small businesses. And it's a channel you need to know to parade your wares to the mass market. A spotlight on a home shopping network would help you to reach millions of potential customers, possibly assist in securing a loan for the expanded production, and move your business into the big time.

    To get your product on the air, contact each of the networks and ask for the vendor information packet. Their addresses are listed in the appendix. Fill in the necessary forms and wait for a response. If they are interested they will ask for a sample. What they are looking for are quality products that can be demonstrated on air. Exclusive product launches and unique products offered for the first time are always of interest.

- **Network marketing:** When you hear the words network or multilevel marketing (MLM), you immediately think of Amway, Mary Kay, and Tupperware, and not a channel to distribute your products. Unfortunately, network marketing has developed such a sleazy reputation that very few African American entrepreneurs consider it as a means to expand their business. It's a shame too, because MLM is an over $68 billion industry that has proven to be one of the most powerful, cost-effective ways to reach consumers today and will continue to be even more so in the coming twenty-first century. What's also interesting is that women are the driving force behind this fast-moving industry. In existing MLM companies, women make up 75 percent of the distributors and hold the top positions.

To start your own MLM company takes money, a line of products, and network marketing expertise. The hot sellers are consumables such as vitamins, cosmetics, jewelry, and household products. To gain the experience of starting your own company, sign up for an existing MLM selling products similar to yours. Learn the business inside and out and interview successful distributors to find out what they did to become successful.

Read books on network marketing and contact the Direct Selling Association, the organizations' trade group.

- **Sales representatives/distributors:** If your company manufactures a product, you can hire an independent sales representative or wholesale distributor to sell it to the stores. Independent sales representatives earn a commission based on the amount of the sales, so they have an incentive to sell your product. The amount could vary from 5 to 15 percent. The major disadvantage is that most representatives sell anywhere from five to ten different products, some of which might compete with yours. Find out ahead of time what are the other products they represent. If one is similar to yours find another representative with noncompeting products. The best place to obtain names of independent representives is in the classified section of your industry's trade newspaper or magazine.

- **Airport concessions:** Guaranteed foot traffic, a captive and steady audience—what more could you ask for as a small business? These are the components that come with opening a business or distributing your product at the airport.

Airports are becoming success havens not only for many major businesses, such as Starbucks Coffee, the Body Shop, and food franchises, but for independent small businesses as well. The main reason is because airports want to provide travelers with a local flavor, thereby opening up opportunities for small companies.

To get your business or products in the door, first contact the airport and send a letter of interest; then set up a meeting with the property manager to discuss your concept and what the airport wants. Make sure your concept or product(s) will work well in an airport. In addition to food, businesses such as a gift shop, bookstore, toy store, or a store selling items travelers can carry work well.

Most airports must comply with a Federal Aviation Administration requirement that 10 percent of concessions be leased to minority and women entrepreneurs. This requires you to undergo a certification process; all contracts are awarded through a competitive bidding process.

For more information contact the Airport Minority Advisory Council at (301) 907-8027. This is a nonprofit trade association that helps minorities and women obtain contracts to do business with the airport. It also conducts workshops and seminars and has a newsletter that lists contracting opportunities.

## Going International

Ever dream about living on a tropical island? About abandoning the rat race of the city for warm breezes, clean white beaches, and an unspoiled, lush landscape?

Impossible, you say? Not according to Jackie Lewis, Sister CEO of Jackie's On the Reef, a holistic retreat in Negril, Jamaica. After twenty-one successful years in the fashion business, an unhappy Lewis decided to follow her dream and open a spa retreat for burned-out professionals seeking spiritual renewal. "Even though I had accomplished a great deal in my life, I still wasn't happy," states Lewis. "So to get away from it all, I went to Jamaica. While there I realized other people needed to work on themselves like I was doing, so I decided to build a retreat."

Starting a business or supplying your product or service in the Caribbean or overseas are marketing opportunities Sister CEOs should not overlook. Several countries want your business and are welcoming entrepreneurs with open arms. Take, for example, the U.S. Virgin Islands, which has enacted a comprehensive industrial development law under which qualifying businesses receive various tax benefits. Because it is a U.S. territory, it has a unique status which offers opportunities for investors and entrepreneurs. Other countries have similar benefits as well.

Japan and South Africa are other countries Sister CEOs need to consider, states Kathryn Leary, Sister CEO of The Leary Group, a New York marketing and communications firm that builds bridges linking black entrepreneurs to overseas markets. Her company has made trade connections in Japan for more than thirty U.S. minority-owned firms since 1991. And it is now turning its focus to South Africa. She publishes two newsletters, *Japan Watch* and *South Africa Watch*, that reach about 1,000 African American executives and educators.

Leary feels that Sister CEOs can accomplish more in the evolving global business environment by utilizing the "feminine" traits that are looked down upon by American corporations. "We are more nurturing, more relationship-oriented, and more adaptable," says Leary. "We also tend to listen better than most men. It is these unique skills that put us at a competitive advantage in the global business world."

To help all women understand how to do business overseas, Leary has teamed up with AT&T's school of business to create "Women in the Global Business Environment," a two-day symposium that teaches women how to identify and secure business opportunities abroad.

Leary and Lewis advise Sister CEOs wanting to expand their business overseas to stick to the following guidelines:

- Research and learn everything you can about the country you want to do business in.
- Contact the country's U.S. embassy as well as the U.S. Department of Commerce. Both agencies offer information to assist business owners with providing a product or service overseas.
- If at all possible, find a partner in the country, one with expertise so they can assist you with the right connections to get

through the red tape that's common when dealing with over-seas countries.

- Contact your state economic development agency. Many offer seminars, classes, and consulting services to assist your company in forging international business relationships.
- Contact SBA International Trade at (202) 205-6720 to find out about their trade missions abroad. You have to pay your expenses, but the agency provides a guide and will assist with the scheduling of meetings and trade shows.
- Check with your local library and bookstores on doing business overseas. Talk with other business owners who have conducted business there. With so many opportunities available, Sister CEOs must broaden their horizons and participate in the global economy.

## *Ten Low-Cost Sister CEO Marketing Action Steps*

1. Develop a mailing list of all your clients and send them a newsletter containing articles of interest to them.
2. Give out a sample of your product to entice buyers.
3. Offer a free gift with purchase. (This is how the cosmetic companies increase their sales. And I'm a sucker for it too.)
4. Write out a "hot" press release to get as much free publicity as you can (more in chapter 15).
5. Get yourself interviewed on radio and TV shows.
6. Host and produce your own cable TV show through cable access programs.
7. Write articles and get them published in local and national newspapers and magazines.
8. Write a book or a workbook. Self-publish it using your computer and desktop publishing software.
9. Offer to conduct a seminar at national conventions, trade shows, and expos.
10. Always go the extra mile and give the best service or product to your client or customer.

## Ten Low-Cost Advertising Tips for Sister CEOs

1. Network at social events.
2. Design and hand out brochures and flyers.
3. Exhibit at black expos, conferences.
4. Join professional organizations and send a flyer or brochure to the membership's mailing list.
5. Place an ad in *SuccessGuide* and the *Black Yellow Pages*.
6. Use classified ads in newspapers, magazines, and church newsletters.
7. Teach an adult education class.
8. Become active in the community as a member of the board of a local organization, or at your child's school.
9. Advertise and sell your products or services at black family reunions.
10. Barter your products or services in exchange for ad space.

# Chapter 15

# PUBLICITY VS. ADVERTISING

Cosmetics companies don't sell lipsticks; they sell romance (and sex).

BRUCE BARTON,
*advertising mogul*

Now that you know how to research your market and get your product or service into the hands of your client or customer, there are two additional important facets you need to include in your marketing campaign: publicity and advertising.

Many entrepreneurs erroneously think they are one and the same. They aren't, and there are real differences. First of all, advertising tends to be expensive and publicity is generally free.

This chapter is divided into three sections. In the first, I compare publicity to advertising. In the second, I show you how to design a publicity campaign and provide a sample press release for Body St. Lucia, Connie Harper's start-up company. And third, you'll learn how to plan an advertising campaign.

## Public Relations vs Advertising: A Comparison

How does public relations differ from advertising?

- You must pay for advertising; public relations is free. When you buy an ad in the newspaper you pay for the space; when a magazine or newspaper writes a story about you or your company, you don't have to pay for it, though you may incur some expenses drawing attention to yourself in the first place.

- When you advertise, you have complete control over the content, format, and timing of the ad as it appears in the media. *You* design the ad, since you are paying for it. With publicity, you can write anything you want in your press release, but the newspaper or magazine will decide what the story will say and when it will run.

- Advertising can be duplicated; publicity cannot. The same advertising can be duplicated as many times as you wish in a media source or in multiple media sources, broadening your exposure. But a press release will get attention only once. To get covered again, you will need to provide the media with a new story.

- People are skeptical of advertising and question claims made by ads. On the other hand, people tend to take what they read in the newspaper and magazines or hear on the radio as gospel. They believe if it is printed or broadcast on the radio, it must be true.

- Publicity coverage of your event or story can appear to be an endorsement of your product or service. If you were to say similar things about yourself or the company in an ad, it would look self-serving.

## Designing a Publicity Campaign

We live in a culture that is addicted to sensational, heart-throbbing, shocking, controversial, and scandalous news. It's evident in the popularity of the trashy talk shows and the tabloid newspapers. As a result, media newsmakers want attention-getting and provocative stories to publicize. So to get the news media to recognize your business, you will need to develop a publicity story with a unique story line or angle.

For example, if your business is a new health food store in the local community, you can elect to donate a portion of the proceeds from weekend store sales to the neighborhood homeless shelter.

215

To stimulate even further media interest, get the mayor of the city or another city official, or a local sports celebrity endorsing the importance of taking vitamins, to sign autographs. The appearance of any "star" is more reason for the media to be interested in telling your story in print or on television. While this example isn't provocative, the local media love sports and athletes and are also interested in stories that speak to the community.

## WRITING YOUR PRESS RELEASE

A press release is your initial method of communicating with media editors or producers. It is usually a one-page document announcing newsworthy information about you or your business that you would like to share by appearances on TV and radio, or by having a story written up in a magazine or newspaper.

There is a standard formula for writing an effective press release, according to Pat Tobin, Sister CEO of Tobin & Associates, a leading African American public relations firm in Los Angeles that boasts a client list that includes filmmaker Spike Lee, Reebok, Sony Music Entertainment, and Toyota Motor Sales U.S.A. Inc. The press release should be written precisely as you want to see the story in print. It must be written as if you are writing the article yourself, containing all the important information about your business. Oftentimes, the media will run the press release verbatim and will not add further information.

The formula for creating an interesting and informative press release is called the inverted pyramid. The stories are based on the information that answers the following questions: Who? What? When? Where? How? Why? By tailoring the order of these questions to reflect the emphasis of the story, you will include all the pertinent information the media will need to print your story. A sample press release for Body St. Lucia using the inverted pyramid formula appears on page 217.

***Press Release***

**BODY ST. LUCIA**
BODY & SPA PRODUCTS
2385 Aruba Street
Atlanta, GA 30301

*For Immediate Release*     *For more information contact:*
Connie Harper
Tel: 404-555-1285

### *Can't Get Away for a Vacation?*
### *Bring the Caribbean to You!*

Women today are stressed and burned-out. Working full-time and raising a family leaves little time for women to even think about taking a vacation to the Caribbean. Body St. Lucia Body & Spa Products solves that problem by bringing the exotic smells and natural products of the Caribbean to you—through their unique line of bubble baths, candles, soaps, and lotions with names such as Caribbean Breeze, Paradise Peach, and Tropical Mango.

Because of a woman's busy lifestyle, quiet time and solitude are difficult to come by, except in the bathroom. Which is the reason for the explosion in the luxury bath and body products industry—a $20 billion business.

And since women don't have the time to shop for these products, they can now purchase them in the comfort of their own home, with the Body St. Lucia mail-order brochure. We will ship out all orders within 24 hours. In addition, all new customers will receive a free booklet on "How to Pamper Yourself."

Busy women love escaping in a bath. Remember the famous "Calgon, take me away" commercial? Now they can escape to the Caribbean at any time without spending a lot of money, with exotic Body St. Lucia all-natural products.

## CREATING THE MEDIA KIT

The press release, along with a photograph of the products, a brochure, a bio on the owner and the company, previous articles published, and your business card makes up the media kit. This information should be well-organized and in an eye-catching folder to be sent to all local newspapers, magazines, TV and radio stations, and other targeted organizations. Packaging is very important; the more different or outrageous, the higher your chances of getting noticed by the media executives who can boost you into the spotlight of live radio or TV.

## Hiring a Public Relations Firm

In the initial stages of your business, lack of funds will require you to be your own publicist. But as your business becomes more successful, you may not have the time to put together your own publicity campaign and may need to hire an outside public relations firm.

A recommendation by a satisfied customer is worth its weight in gold. If you are unable to find a firm through a referral from someone you know, check the yellow pages. When you contact a public relations firms, ask for names of three clients. Call the clients and ask how happy they are with the firm, how long they have been working with them, and how successful are they today because of the business relationship.

As with any other professional service you hire for your business, have a written agreement or contract drawn up. The firm usually has a standard form they use for all their clients. It is highly advisable to have your attorney read it over. Make sure to put in a cancellation clause for terminating their services at any time. If you pay a retainer, ask for a monthly breakdown of all expenses, and ask for a copy of receipts if they are available. Small expenses such as the phone bill and mailings can get out of hand if you don't have a conscientious publicist. To prevent this happening, set limits on certain expenses and have the firm contact you before they spend additional monies. Also set a time frame for results. If after six months nothing is happening in the way of increased exposure or sales, it's time to find another publicist.

Your publicist's job, in partnership with you, is to help formulate a publicity campaign that will set you apart from your competitors.

After several years in business, Veronica Smith, Sister CEO of Design Veronique, hired a public relations firm to develop a new image for her company. Under their recommendations, her company took on a new name (previous name was My True Image), designed a new logo, created new stationery, changed her product catalog (by using professional models), and wrote a new press release that got her publicity in newspapers and magazines. "Thanks to our new image and recommendations made by my publicist, business went up 20 percent that first year and it is still increasing," states Smith.

## FEES

A public relations firm usually charges either by the hour or by the project. They charge for time spent interviewing you, designing the campaign and any new promotional materials, selecting the media sources, and following up with phone calls.

Depending on the expertise of the firm, the hourly rate can vary between $100 and $250. Many require a retainer of anywhere from $2,000 to $5,000. Short-term, this may seem expensive. However, the firm does not partake in the income generated from the publicity. So, in the long term, it may very well be worth it. Plus, you can observe how they create your campaign and follow suit on your own later.

You can keep the cost down by being prepared for all meetings. Read books such as *Guerrilla Marketing*, by Jay Conrad Levinson, and *Targeted Public Relations*, by Robert W. Bly; both are available at the public library. They will give you an idea of what to expect and contain ideas on how to organize your own publicity campaign.

## Using Advertising

As you read earlier, advertising costs money. So it is necessary to first develop an advertising budget for your campaign, particularly if you don't have much to spend. You want to use your advertising dollars as wisely as possible by using the media that will effectively target your market.

The advertising budget is generally 2 to 5 percent of projected gross sales. For example, if projected gross sales for the first year are $100,000 based on your business plan (figuring 5 percent), you would have $5,000, or about $417 a month, to work with.

## HIRING AN ADVERTISING AGENCY

As with publicity, when you're starting out, you don't have much money for advertising, so it will be difficult to attract a professional advertising agency. The majority of these firms work with companies that have several-thousand-dollar ad budgets. While you may not be ready to go this route, research and talk with advertising agencies to better understand the process.

## CREATING THE AD

The purpose of advertising is to get your target market to know that your product or service exists. A good ad campaign will create a desire for your products and a reason to do business with your company. The ad must persuade your customer to take immediate action by running out and buying your product or calling to make an appointment for your service.

There are six components of an effective ad:

1. The ad must be simple and easily understood.
2. The ad must be truthful.
3. The ad must be informative.
4. The ad must be sincere.
5. The ad must be customer-oriented.
6. The ad must tell who, what, when, where, why, and how.

For the ad campaign to have a significant impact, you must advertise in the same media regularly and continuously, even if it's on a small scale. One-time shots rarely pay off. So instead of buying one large ad space in a glossy magazine, purchase a small ad space in a newspaper and run it weekly. People like to see consistency, and once they've seen your ad several times they will eventually take notice. It takes time to build up awareness about your business.

## The Right Advertising Media

Not all ad media are created equal. You could have the best and most carefully thought-out ad campaign, only to lose its effectiveness by using the wrong media. Following is a list of different types of media that are available, with a brief description of each.

### WORD OF MOUTH

In chapter 14, I briefly touched on word-of-mouth advertising, but it's worth mentioning again, since it is one of the least expensive methods of advertising you can use for your business. One satisfied customer can convince several friends to do business with you, which gives you the opportunity to gain new customers and also attract the new customer's friends. This domino effect can quickly build a network of word-of-mouth customers, all of whom you have received from free advertising.

Keep in mind the reverse holds true too. If your product or service isn't up to par, you have the potential of losing several potential customers. These people will tell their friends about you, and it will be difficult to eradicate the negative word of mouth. This is why customer service is extremely important; without happy and satisfied customers, there is no business.

### PRINT MEDIA

**Newspapers:** A small ad in your local or regional newspaper is a good place to start your advertising campaign. If the newspaper has a certain section that targets your specific market, buy the space in that area to increase the probability of it being seen by your potential customers. For example, once a week most newspapers have a special food section. If you are in the food business, this is the area and day you should buy ad space. The one drawback of newspaper advertising is that you are competing for the reader's attention with a lot of other advertising.

**Magazines:** There are basically three types of magazines to advertise in: trade/organization, general interest, and specialty.

Almost every industry and organization has their own magazine or newsletter that is distributed to members at very little or no cost. The cost of advertising in these publications is low. If your business caters to one particular industry, advertising in their publication is excellent target marketing. Many public libraries subscribe to several trade journals. Most black sororities and fraternities also put out a quarterly magazine. Since these magazines are mailed out infrequently, contact a business owner who has already placed an ad there to get an idea of the response rate before you buy the space.

*People*, *Time*, and *Newsweek* are considered general interest magazines. The time to advertise in these publications is when your business appeals to the majority of the public and you have a national distribution channel in place. Unless your business is in the seven-figure range, this type of advertising is too expensive; a single page can run tens of thousands of dollars.

*Essence*, *Ebony*, *Black Enterprise*, *SuccessGuide*, and *Black Yellow Pages* are specialty magazines that target a specific market. Advertising in them will enable you to reach the consumer of your product or service more efficiently. For instance, if you're selling motivational audio tapes for African American women, you'll be better off advertising in *Essence* as opposed to *Glamour*, which is marketed to all women. Pricing in these magazines can be somewhat expensive. It depends upon the circulation and quality of the publication.

**Flyers:** Flyers can be an inexpensive and highly effective form of advertising for small-business owners. You can pass them out at conferences and meetings, or to people you meet on the subway or train. Plan your flyers carefully with attention to layout, message, and appearance. The design should match the image you are trying to create in your business. For instance, Connie Harper's Body St. Lucia flyer should have a Caribbean theme with sunset, palm trees, and water.

## TV AND RADIO MEDIA

**Radio:** Radio offers a way to get information about your business to a broad spectrum of people in your area. If you want to reach African Americans, this is the medium to use, since 96.5

percent listen to the radio. Every time I'm on the radio the response rate is phenomenal, with several call-ins for questions and book sales. There is cost in producing the radio ads—such as recording studio time—so include it in your advertising budget.

Several popular radio shows air during the early morning off-hours with huge listener audiences. Two shows in particular are *Night Talk* with Bob Law on American Urban Radio and *Front Page* on KGLH in Los Angeles. If you purchase ad time during these shows it will be heard by a large group of African Americans.

**Television:** Cable television has opened the opportunity for even the smallest business to take advantage of the power of advertising on TV. There are ad packagers who will help you with the entire process, from scriptwriting to buying the time for a set fee. Your local cable company can supply you with the names of the companies that provide that service.

## DIRECT MAIL; COUPONS

The 11 million African American households in the U.S. are an untapped direct-mail market, according to Andrew Morrison, president of NIA Direct, an African American direct-mail marketing firm in New York. Recognizing an opportunity, he has introduced the only co-op direct mailer that targets African Americans in the nation's top twenty-five markets; it includes a combination of coupons, radio, and retail support. He also has compiled a mailing list of 5 million, 90 percent of which are female households whose median age is thirty-five with an average income of $31,000. Some of NIA Direct's major clients include Procter & Gamble, Kraft General Foods, Home Box Office, *Heart & Soul*, and *Upscale* magazine. For the entrepreneur, there is also the NIA Small Business Builder's Package, which provides direct mail to small-business owners at a lower cost. Call the office at (212) 285-0865 to receive their information packet.

## ADVERTISING SPECIALTIES; PREMIUMS

Pens, calendars, coffee mugs, and notepads are low-cost but very effective business premiums on which you can display your name or logo while at the same time making an attractive gift for you to give to your customers or clients. There are many black-owned firms that supply these premiums. Check for names in resources such as the *SuccessGuide* or the *Black Yellow Pages* in your area.

## SISTER CEO SUCCESS STORY
### Carol H. Williams
CAROL H. WILLIAMS & PARTNERS ADVERTISING
OAKLAND, CALIFORNIA

The advertising business has never been the same since Sister CEO Carol Williams came on the scene. Formerly a senior vice president/creative director at Foote, Cone, and Belding in San Francisco, and vice president/creative director at Leo Burnett in Chicago, Williams, a creative genius in her own right, is famous for advertising campaigns such as Secret deodorant's "Strong enough for man but made for a woman" and Pillsbury's "Say hello to poppin' fresh dough." Today, Williams heads Carol H. Williams & Partners Advertising, an Oakland, California, advertising agency with such clients as Bank of America, Pacific Telesis and Clorox.

In the field for twenty-three years, Williams loves advertising and can't imagine doing anything else. She credits her rise to the top in the advertising field to her two bosses at her former firms who became her mentors. Both white men, they were staunch supporters and believed in her creativity. It was through their efforts that Williams at a young age was exposed to real business and many different types of people in her travels across the United States.

At the top of her field and in a new marriage, Williams made a tough decision that many women have had to face and took a one-year break to raise a family. While many on the corporate fast track may see this as a negative move, it was a blessing in disguise for Williams; when she decided to reenter the advertising business after the sabbatical, she found she couldn't go back to the status quo. "Finding a job wasn't an issue—there were plenty—but they were all the same, and I felt like I would be treading water. I knew I had to do something different," says Williams. It was at this point that Williams developed the burning desire to be her own boss. Using her contacts and working out of her home, she began freelance writing for other advertising agencies. Success came fast; after two months Williams needed assistance and hired her first employee, who wore the hats of many as a secretary, researcher, and account manager. It was also during this time that mainstream companies became interested in marketing products to the minority community. With years of experience under her belt, Williams was awarded larger contracts and provided research and assistance in helping big companies tap into the minority market. A year and a half later, with five employees, Williams knew she had reached a new level and moved her office out of her home and into an office building. Since that beginning she has never looked back. Now with thirty employees, over $26 million in billing revenues for 1994, and five Clio Awards for outstanding advertising, Williams remains focused and determined to be the best she can be.

## Williams's Advice to Sister CEOs:

- Before you decide to go into business for yourself, look deeply inside of yourself and determine what your dream is. As black women we must realize that we are like pilots—we are masters in control of our own fleet. Ask yourself: Are you willing to compromise your personal life in order to obtain your dreams? Because having your own business is a never-ending journey— you must love the challenge.
- Don't worry about not having a lot of money to start with. "I didn't have any money and I would not allow it to scare me. I knew if I gave the business my all, it would come, and to this day I continue to live by that philosophy."
- When it is time to hire employees, look for self-starters who share the company's vision and philosophy. In advertising it takes a team effort to pull an ad campaign together, so you want someone who has a passion for the business and loves what they do.

- Hire the best financial and legal experts you can afford. They have access to information that is instrumental in helping you manage and grow your business.
- Always set a profit goal for your company and put a process in place to reach it.
- Grow your business so that it has its own life and can continue on without you being there.

# Chapter 16

## THE BALANCING ACT

Strive for the greatest possible harmony and compassion in
your business and in your life.

OPRAH WINFREY

The first months, or even years, of running your own company will
require adjustments of all kinds. Sister CEO Barbara Bates recalls
the early lean days when she wasn't sure where the money was
coming from to meet the payroll. Pawning her jewelry was one of
the techniques she used. But what really saved her and made her
stick it out was faith, prayer, a supportive family, and a mission to
be her own boss. Today, Bates looks back on those days and
remembers the excitement and romance that went with them,
because it was during this time that she knew she could do it.

As a Sister CEO, when you first start your business, you will one
day find yourself in the same shoes as Bates and many of the other
women interviewed—financially strapped and unsure what to do.
This is the period when you will discover your ability to rise to challenges, substitute imagination for money, and affirm your commitment to your reason for becoming a Sister CEO. Yes, you will want
to give up and go back to a regular, stable 9 to 5. Don't. Instead call
upon your natural strengths of determination, persistence, and
sisterpower to get you through. And, if you find you must give
up your business because of financial or personal reasons, don't
despair. You can always start again. In fact, that is precisely what
Sister CEOs Jameela Bragg and Kathryn Leary had to do.

227

After five years of owning her own retail store, Jameela Bragg had to close it down for financial reasons. Bragg went back to work in corporate America with a goal to open her store again in three years. She sacrificed eating out and buying clothes, invested money in her company's tax-deferred retirement plan, and paid off all her credit cards. Bragg's determination paid off. In 1992, she reopened E-Scent-ials Body Care shop, and grossed over $100,000 in 1995.

For Kathryn Leary, the successful international marketing consultant you read about in chapter 14, it was necessary to shut down her advertising business after the dissolution of a partnership.

First and foremost, realize that Sister CEOs don't become successful overnight and must work through the hard and lean times. This is the nature of starting a business. And, as a black woman entrepreneur, you have a double challenge to deal with as well. But the biggest challenge every Sister CEO faced was the fluctuation of cash flow. They all agreed it is unnerving, especially when you've been accustomed to living for years on a predictable income. Here are a few success tips to get you through the tough periods:

- When your business is going through a down period, which it will do, just remember your original business vision. When you focus only on the problems of your business, you're apt to become derailed and lose sight of the opportunities that are still out there.
- Don't throw in the towel too early. Too many of us allow our short-term disappointment in business to prevent us from succeeding. It's rare when all of your business goals and dreams happen exactly as you want. Face up to what's going on, learn from it, and move on.
- Remain flexible and don't become too complacent. As your business is growing, you need to be able to change with the times. The success that you imagined may take a different route than you planned. You want to follow your business plan as closely as possible, yet remain flexible enough to change your plan as problems and opportunities come up. If you find your business heading in a different direction than was planned, that's okay. As a Sister CEO, you have to be

adaptable and willing to do whatever it takes to reach your business goals.

- Understand money. Take classes and seminars offered through community colleges and adult education programs. Read books on money management, such as *The Black Woman's Guide to Financial Independence* and *Smart Money Moves for African Americans* by Kelvin Boston. Both books provide the basics on money and cash flow management.

- Maintain a money cushion. Setting aside money may be difficult in the beginning stages, but it's a step you should not overlook. Set aside 10 percent of your monthly income in a savings or money market account for emergencies. Knowing you have this nest egg can be psychologically empowering, and that in turn makes it easier for you to make money.

- Have a list of quick ways to make money. Whether you pawn your jewelry, borrow from your relatives, or have a temporary job lined up, when the tight times appear, you want to be ready.

- When you don't have enough money to pay your bills, send a partial payment with an explanatory note. Entrepreneurship can wreak havoc on your credit bureau report. Many successful entrepreneurs have lost their cars or filed for bankruptcy before they became really successful. By following the advice in this book, you should be able to avoid this happening to you.

- Have faith. You must continue to pray and ask for guidance, and trust and believe in your business.

- Network with your mentor and members of your sisterhood to stay motivated and focused.

- Be clear about who you partner with. You need to know that partner well—like a spouse—because you'll be spending a lot of time together.

- Don't hire friends to work for you. Friendship becomes entwined with the power relationship.

- Sell or provide a service that people want.

- Never stop marketing your business.

- Reward yourself. If you've closed a big deal or made your monthly sales goal, don't forget to pat yourself on the back.

Treat yourself to a massage. If you don't want to spend any money, go to the beach or museum.

- Every morning, ask yourself: What will I do to reach my visions and goals today?
- Every evening, ask yourself: What did I do to reach my goals and visions today?

## Combining Your Business with Your Lifestyle

Balancing business and family is a continuing challenging task for Patricia Yarbrough, mother of two children and Sister CEO of Blue World Travel, sponsor of the successful annual African American tailor-made summer Caribbean cruises. But after seventeen years in business, Yarbrough believes she has it figured out, and her advice to other Sister CEOs is "Get help with the housework! Women have been brainwashed to think they need to do everything. Get help and don't feel bad about it. Plus you'll be employing someone—and they want to do it."

Juggling business and family will be difficult for you, especially if you're a single parent. Mixing business ownership demands with raising a family will take sacrifices to find that "happy medium." As a Sister CEO, you'll need to make important decisions about how to divide your time. The choices will not be easy and you'll find yourself feeling guilty when you'll need to choose business over family. You also must realize that you won't be able to do it alone. Like Patricia Yarbrough said, you'll need to get help, either by hiring someone or by relying on your spouse, significant other, family, or friends.

But in spite of the negatives, the Sister CEOs I interviewed with children said they would not give up running their own business, because the pros far outweigh the cons. Running their own show allowed them to have flexible hours, see their children more often, and include them in their business by providing them with part-time jobs.

Sister CEOs who were successfully balancing business and family found there were seven "pros" to being their own boss:

- A Sister CEO serves as a great role model, especially for young black girls.
- A Sister CEO can make up her own flexible time schedule.
- Children of Sister CEOs can visit the workplace at any time. And their visits enable them to learn about the business world.
- Children are encouraged to help in the family business, thereby helping them to develop positive work habits at an early age.
- Children who help their mothers at work develop a sense of sharing in a family project.
- Children develop a greater sense of responsibility and independence.
- Children understand and appreciate their mother more because they can see the great demands placed on her.

## Taking Care of You

You love your family dearly and will want to do everything in your power to make sure they are taken care of. But when you are in business, the one person you cannot forget is **You**.

A Sister CEO who neglects herself is not an asset to her company, nor to her family. As women, we strive so hard to be good wives, mothers, and business owners, yet we either forget—or don't take the time—to take care of ourselves. If you allow stress to intervene, not only will it take the joy out of your life, it could also prove harmful to your health.

Running your own business requires tremendous stamina and energy. Yes, it's tough to balance the demands of a growing business with personal need, but it is imperative that you do so in order to succeed. Most successful Sister CEOs work hard *and* play hard. And they are selfish about their personal time. The women made it a point to take care of themselves and although many admitted they didn't spend enough time with family, they took family vacations and took time out for R & R. In reality, sometimes the best thing you can do for yourself and your business is to get away to gain perspective on any problems.

The key is to remember your priorities. The purpose of your business is to provide happiness and security for your family *and* for you. If you find this isn't the case and you're frequently stressed out, it's probably time to rethink why you are in business.

As a Sister CEO, you must stay healthy by eating nutritious foods, exercising daily, and pursuing activities that reduce your stress. It's vital to unwind, relax, and rejuvenate your energy. Running a business is hard work. It's okay to give yourself some "TLC."

For the longest time, I felt guilty about taking time to relax. I naturally assumed that my business would fall apart if I wasn't at its every beck and call. However, nature always seemed to step in and take me out—with the flu—and force me to lay in bed for several days, relinquishing the tight control I had on the business. I now get a massage every week, exercise four times a week, and two or three times a year attend a women's "Renew Your Energy" retreat. In the last year, I've seen a vast improvement in my energy level and my health because I made the decision to take care of myself.

To help you combine your business into your personal life, here are a list of "Must Do" balancing-act lessons:

**Lesson 1: Mini-breaks.** Take mini-breaks throughout the day. They're refreshing and re-energizing. Take a walk outside or, if you're near a body of water, just sit by it with your eyes closed and meditate for a few minutes. Taking a few moments for yourself during the day can relax and help you to tackle the daily stresses of running your business.

I can't emphasize enough the need for Sister CEOs to take "time outs." If you don't, you'll quickly experience burn-out.

**Lesson 2: Exercise.** Exercising is the key to boosting your energy level and confidence. Also, you will find that after you exercise, your day will be more productive because your energy level will be high, your body will feel great, and you'll be motivated, relaxed, and invigorated all at the same time.

Take an hour to exercise every day. If you can, schedule it as the first activity you do in the morning. If you belong to a gym, take advantage of their early hours. Many open at 5 A.M. to accommodate busy professionals. And, don't use your children as an excuse not to exercise; many offer babysitting services.

For Carol Columbus-Green, Sister CEO of Laracris, working out is simply a part of her daily ritual. Every morning after dropping off her children at school she heads straight for the gym for her daily workout. "Exercising gives me the stamina to keep going. On days I'm not able to get to the gym, I have a workout machine in my office, so I really don't have an excuse not to exercise. Besides, it's something I do just for me and it makes me feel good."

**Lesson 3: Meditate daily.** Meditate in complete silence for thirty minutes in the morning and thirty minutes in the evening. Learn to rid yourself of the annoying mind-chatter. If business is bad and not going the way you expected, spend a day in complete silence. Don't listen to the radio or turn on the TV. Don't read a book, magazine, or newspaper and turn off the phone. Often you can find solutions to your problems—business and personal—when you eliminate outside noise pollution. Your mind is an amazing tool. Removing interference will allow you to focus and get a clear picture of the problem. In many cases, the problem isn't as big as you thought it was, and with a few minor adjustments it can be easily solved.

**Lesson 4: Learn to say no.** This is the hardest word for women to say, especially African American women. As Sister CEO Patricia Yarbrough said, we have been brainwashed into thinking we need to do everything for everybody.

To become a successful Sister CEO, the word will have to become a fixture in your vocabulary because there is no way in the world you'll be able to take care of everybody and run a business. You simply will not have enough time. You need to manage your time wisely. If something doesn't fall into the high-priority category, it can't be done.

**Lesson 5: Unwind at the end of the day.** Dip into a scented hot bubble bath at the end of the day to relax and unwind.

**Lesson 6: Support network.** Have a good support network nearby. If it isn't your spouse or significant other, enroll your mother, grandmother, or aunt for assistance in running errands, picking up the children, or occasionally cooking dinner when you need to work late.

## A Closing Message

I have heard or read that an author writes a book because he or she needs to know the information. As I look over the final draft of the book, I agree. I've collected all this information for you, but I wish I had known it when I first started my business. It would have been so much easier to turn to a book full of role models that look like me and read about their mistakes. Maybe I could have avoided some of the big ones I made along the way. Well, now I know. And I will continue to network with Sister CEOs to learn even more on how to become successful.

So, to close, I summarize with twenty Sister CEO Secrets to Success:

1. Be enthusiastic and optimistic. Keep your hopes high and don't allow racism and sexism to stop you from succeeding.
2. Work hard and play hard.
3. Keep your eyes and ears open for new profit opportunities. Talk to other black women who want to go into business and form a black women's networking group to give support to each other. Sisterhood is powerful.
4. Don't allow your sistahs Ms Doubt and Ms Fear to visit. Get rid of negative emotions and replace them with positive ones—ambition, drive, and helpfulness. The mindset you have going into your own business will determine whether you succeed or fail. As a Sister CEO, you cannot afford to allow obstacles to stop you from moving forward.
5. Start your business in your spare time. It's relatively risk free.
6. Work at home, at least initially, to cut costs. Obtain a separate phone/fax line, answering machine or voice mail, computer, printer, and software.
7. When working from home, set up a daily routine for starting and stopping.
8. Research thoroughly the industry you want to start your business in. The public library is full of information, and is in your own neighborhood.
9. Network, network, network! Tell everyone you meet about your business.

10. Reduce your debt, though more than likely your income will be uncertain at first. You may have to liquidate part of your assets to pay it off.
11. Build a cash reserve. Ideally, it should equal about six months' living expenses. If that's too difficult, a reserve of any size will help.
12. Plow as much revenue as possible back into the business in the beginning to help the business grow.
13. Have a "Plan B" in case your business goes through a rough period.
14. Know your marketplace. Continue to assess your market, your competition, and your ability to meet your client's or customer's need.
15. Live by the golden rule of customer service: Attention to the small details brings loyalty to your business.
16. Always act as a professional black businesswoman and treat your business like it's part of the family. If you're in business and no longer enjoying it, it's time to refocus and rethink if this is the right business for you.
17. Follow your intuition. Your gut instincts are often your best guide.
18. Involve your children in the business. Teach them to become entrepreneurs. It is the only way African Americans will gain economic empowerment.
19. Start your business in something you love and can have fun with. When you are passionate about what you do, the money will always follow.
20. Never give up on your dreams!

I know I have presented many ideas throughout the chapters of this book—all meant to show you that you *do* have the power to become a Sister CEO. Follow them and become successful beyond your wildest dreams. I wish you much success!

# YOUR SISTER CEO STORY, PLEASE

I am always on the lookout for stories of other successful and powerful Sister CEOs making their mark on society. If you are one or know of someone who is, and would like to include the story in a future edition of *Sister CEO*, please mail or fax me the story along with your name, address, and telephone number. Thank you in advance and I look forward to receiving your letters. Take care.

**BROUSSARD & DOUGLAS, INC.**
**499 Hamilton Avenue, Suite 140**
**Palo Alto, California 94301**
**Fax: (415) 688-1166**

# JOIN THE SISTER CEO™ CLUB!

Members will receive an official Sister CEO Membership Packet:

- Sister CEO Newsletter!
- Official Sister CEO T-Shirt!
- "The Sister CEO Ten Secrets to Starting Your Own Successful Business" cassette tape!

Keep up to date on the latest small business news and information! Learn to have fun, network, and be in business for yourself! All members will receive priority notice on all new Sister CEO products:

Seminars (various locations), videotapes, cassette tapes, books and more!

*Join today!*

For more information, write, fax, or E-mail to:

**The Sister CEO Club**
499 Hamilton Ave., Suite 140
Palo Alto, CA 94301
*Fax:* 415-688-1166
*E-mail:* Sister CEO @ aol.com

# Part Five

## APPENDIX

# Resources

## General and Governmental Organizations

**ABWE (ASSOCIATION OF BLACK WOMEN ENTREPRENEURS)**
Att: Dolores Ratcliffe
P.O. Box 49368
Los Angeles, CA 90049
(213) 624-8639

**AMERICAN ENTREPRENEURS ASSOCIATION**
2392 Morse Ave.
Irvine, CA 92714
(800) 421-2300

**AMERICAN ENTREPRENEURS FOR ECONOMIC GROWTH**
AEEG Coordinator
1655 North Fort Myer Dr., Suite 700
Arlington, VA 22209
(703) 351-5246
*Fax:* (703) 351-5268

**AT&T SMALL BUSINESS LENDING CORP.**
2 Gate Hill Drive
Parsippany, NJ 07054
(800) 221-SBLC
(800) 707-0609

**BAY AREA SMALL BUSINESS DEVELOPMENT CORPORATION**
3932 Harrison St.
Oakland, CA 94611-4537
(510) 450-1935
*Fax:* (510) 652-6017

**BOOMER MARKETING AND RESEARCH CENTER**
Att: Phil Goodman
P.O. Box 880609
San Diego, CA 92168-0609
(619) 291-5784

**BUSINESS FOR SOCIAL RESPONSIBILITY**
1683 Folsom St.
San Francisco, CA 94103
(415) 865-2500

**CALIFORNIA CHAMBER OF COMMERCE**
1201 K St., 12th Fl.
P.O. Box 1736
Sacramento, CA 95812-1736
(916) 444-6670

**CALIFORNIA SMALL BUSINESS ASSOCIATION**
5300 Beethoven St.
Los Angeles, CA 90066
(800) 350-CSBA

CALIFORNIA SMALL BUSINESS DEVELOPMENT
CENTER PROGRAM
801 K St., 17th Fl.
Sacramento, CA 95814
(916) 324-5068

ILLINOIS INSTITUTE FOR ENTREPRENEURSHIP
EDUCATION
28 East Jackson, Suite 1220
Chicago, IL 60604
(312) 939-3665

INC. BUSINESS RESOURCES
P.O. Box 1365
Wilkes-Barre, PA 18703-1365
(800) 468-0800, ext. 5197

INTERNAL REVENUE SMALL BUSINESS
WORKSHOPS PROGRAM
(800) 829-1040

JUNIOR ACHIEVEMENT
One Education Way
Colorado Springs, CO 80906
(719) 540-8000

NATIONAL ASSOCIATION FOR THE SELF-
EMPLOYED
P.O. Box 612067
Dallas, TX 75261
(800) 232-6273

NATIONAL BUSINESS ASSOCIATION
5025 Arapaho, Suite 515
Dallas, TX 75248
(800) 456-0440

NATIONAL FEDERATION OF INDEPENDENT
BUSINESS
53 Century Blvd., #300
Nashville, TN 37214
(800) 634-2669

*California office:*
980 9th St., 16th Fl.
Sacramento, CA 95814
(916) 729-7110

NATIONAL VENTURE CAPITAL ASSOCIATION
1655 North Fort Myer Dr., No. 700
Arlington, VA 22209
(703) 351-5269

NEDA BUSINESS DEVELOPMENT CENTERS
*Oakland*:
1212 Broadway, Suite 900
Oakland, CA 94612
(510) 271-0180

*Sacramento*:
1779 Tribute Rd., Suite J
Sacramento, CA 95815
(916) 649-2551

*San Francisco*:
221 Maine St., Suite 1350
San Francisco, CA 94105
(415) 243-8430

SMALL BUSINESS DEVELOPMENT CENTERS
409 3rd St. SW
Washington, DC 20416
(800) 827-5722

UNITED AMERICAN PROGRESS ASSOCIATION
701 East 79th St.
Chicago, IL 60619
(312) 955-8112

U.S. CHAMBER OF COMMERCE
1615 H St. NW
Washington, DC 20062
(800) 537-IBEX

U.S. SMALL BUSINESS ADMINISTRATION
Chicago District Office
500 West Madison St., Suite 1250
Chicago, IL 60661
(312) 353-4528

## Small Business Incubators

*Alabama*
BIRMINGHAM BUSINESS ASSISTANCE
NETWORK
110 12th St.
Birmingham, AL 35203
(205) 250-8000

242

*California*
OAKLAND SMALL BUSINESS GROWTH
CENTER
1919 Market St., Suite 250
Oakland, CA 94607
(510) 444-4495

SAN FRANCISCO RENAISSANCE MICRO
BUSINESS INCUBATOR
404 Bryant St.
San Francisco, CA 94107
(415) 541-8580

*Illinois*
INDUSTRIAL COUNCIL OF N.W. CHICAGO
2023 West Carroll Ave.
Chicago, IL 60612
(312) 421-3941

*Minnesota*
FRANKLIN BUSINESS CENTER
1433 East Franklin Ave.
Minneapolis, MN 55404
(612) 870-7555

*New York*
LATIMER WOODS ECONOMIC DEVELOPMENT
ASSOCIATION
395 Flatbush Ave.
Brooklyn, NY 11201
(718) 237-2585

*North Carolina*
WEST CHARLOTTE BUSINESS INCUBATOR
617 North Summit Ave.
Charlotte, NC 28216
(704) 377-0048

*Ohio*
REDWOOD DEVELOPMENT CENTER
815 East Mound St.
Columbus, OH 43205
(614) 252-0057

*Pennsylvania*
WEST PHILADELPHIA ENTERPRISE CENTER
4601 Market St., Suite 4000
Philadelphia, PA 19139
(215) 748-2145

*Texas*
HOUSTON SMALL BUSINESS DEVELOPMENT
CORP.
5330 Griggs Rd.
Houston, TX 77021
(713) 845-2400

## *Commercial and Professional Organizations*

AMERICAN ASSOCIATION OF HOME-BASED
BUSINESSES
P.O. Box 10023
Rockville, MD 20849
(202) 310-3130
(800) 447-9710

AMERICAN HEALTH & BEAUTY AIDS INSTITUTE
401 North Michigan Ave., 23rd Floor
Chicago, IL 60611-4267
(312) 644-6610

AMERICAN INSTITUTE OF BAKING
1213 Bakers Way
Manhattan, KS 66502
(913) 537-4750

AMERICAN SOCIETY OF INTERIOR
DESIGNERS
608 Massachusetts Ave. NE
Washington, DC 20002-6006
(202) 546-3480

BAKERY PRODUCTION AND MARKETING
ASSOCIATION
1550 East Touhy Rd.
Des Plaines, IL 60618
(708) 635-8800

BUSINESS NETWORK INTERNATIONAL
199 South Monte Vista Ave., Suite 6
San Dimas, CA 91773
(800) 825-8286

FRAGRANCE FOUNDATION AND OLFACTORY
RESEARCH FUND
145 East 32nd St.
New York, NY 10016
(212) 725-2755

243

GIFT & STATIONERY BUSINESS
ASSOCIATION
1 Penn Plaza, 10th Fl.
New York, NY 10119
(212) 615-2343

INDEPENDENT BUSINESS ALLIANCE
P.O. Box 1945
Danbury, CT 06813-9643
(800) 450-2422

INTERNATIONAL HEALTH, RACQUET &
SPORTSCLUB ASSOCIATION
263 Summer St.
Boston, MA 02210
(617) 951-0055

INTERNATIONAL MASS RETAIL
ASSOCIATION
1700 North Moore St., #2250
Arlington, VA 22209
(703) 841-2300

NATIONAL ASSOCIATION FOR HOME CARE
519 C St. NE, Stanton Park
Washington, DC 20002-5809
(202) 547-7424

NATIONAL ASSOCIATION OF MARKET
DEVELOPERS
P.O. Box 4446
Rockefeller Center Station
New York, NY 10185
(212) 355-1732

NATIONAL ASSOCIATION OF TEMPORARY
AND STAFFING SERVICES
119 South Asaph St.
Alexandria, VA 22314
(703) 549-6287

NATIONAL ASSOCIATION OF URBAN
BANKERS
1010 Wayne Ave.
Silver Spring, MD 20910
(301) 589-2141

NATIONAL BAR ASSOCIATION
1225 11th St. NW
Washington, DC 20001
(202) 842-3900

NATIONAL GOLF FOUNDATION
1150 U.S. Hwy 1
Jupiter, FL 33477
(407) 744-6006

NATIONAL INSURANCE ASSOCIATION
P.O. Box 53230
Chicago, IL 60653-0230
(312) 924-3308

NATIONAL MEDICAL ASSOCIATION
1012 10th St. NW
Washington, DC 20001
(202) 347-1895

NATIONAL OPTOMETRIC ASSOCIATION
2830 South Indiana Ave.
Chicago, IL 60616
(312) 791-0186

NATIONAL RESTAURANT ASSOCIATION
1200 11th St. NW
Washington, DC 20036
(202) 331-5900

NATIONAL SPEAKERS ASSOCIATION
1500 South Priest Dr.
Tempe, AZ 85281
(602) 968-2552

SNACK FOOD ASSOCIATION
1711 King St.
Alexandria, VA 22314
(703) 836-4500

TOASTMASTERS INTL.
23182 Arroyo Vista
Rancho Santa Margarita, CA 92688
(714) 858-8255

## Minority-Interest Organizations and Professional Associations

AFRICAN ASSOCIATION FOR AFFIRMATIVE ACTION
200 North Michigan Ave., #200
Chicago, IL 60601
(312) 541-1272

BLACK DATA PROCESSING ASSOCIATES
1250 Connecticut Ave. NW, Suite 610
Washington, DC 20036
(800) 727-BDPA
*Fax:* 775-1344

BLACK ENTERPRISE ENTREPRENEURS
CONFERENCE
Conference Department
130 Fifth Ave.
New York, NY 10011
(800) 543-6786
*Fax:* (212) 886-9600
*E-mail:* bebusin@aol.com

*BLACK ENTERPRISE* PEPSI GOLF & TENNIS
CHALLENGE
1751 Pinnacle Dr., Suite 1500
McLean, VA 22102
(800) 209-7229
*Fax:* (703) 905-4495

BLACK UNITED FRONT
700 East Oakwood Blvd.
Chicago, IL 60653
(312) 268-7500, exts. 144, 154

THE DOW JONES SPELMAN COLLEGE
ENTREPRENEURIAL CENTER
350 Spelman Lane, SW, Box 352
Atlanta, GA 30314
(404) 681-3643

*ESSENCE* MAGAZINE MUSIC FESTIVAL
1500 Broadway
New York, NY 10036
(800) ESSENCE

INTERNATIONAL BLACK WRITERS
P.O. Box 1030
Chicago, IL 60690
(312) 924-3818

JACK AND JILL OF AMERICA INC.
4761 Sylvan Drive
Savannah, GA 31405
(912) 356-2194
*Fax:* (912) 352-1814

JACKIE ROBINSON FOUNDATION
3 West 35th St
New York, NY 10001
(212) 290-8600

JUSTICE, UNITY, GENEROSITY AND
SERVICE, INC.
620 Southlake Dasha Dr.
Plantation, FL 33324
(305) 472-5282

LINKS, INC.
1200 Massachusetts Ave. NW
Washington, DC 20005
(202) 842-8686

MINORITIES INTERNATIONAL NETWORK FOR
TRADE
c/o Phelps Stokes Fund
10 East 87th St.
New York, NY 10128
(212) 725-3312

MINORITY ENTERPRISE DEVELOPMENT
PROGRAM
SBA Central Office
409 Third St. SW
Washington, DC 20416
(202) 205-6410

NATIONAL ASSOCIATION FOR THE ADVANCE-
MENT OF COLORED PEOPLE
4805 Mt. Hope Drive
Baltimore, MD 21215
(410) 358-8900

NATIONAL ASSOCIATION OF AFRICAN
AMERICAN CATHOLIC DEACONS
2338 East 99th St.
Chicago, IL 60617
(312) 375-6311

NATIONAL ASSOCIATION OF BLACK
ACCOUNTANTS
7249-A Hanover Parkway
Greenbelt, MD 20770
(301) 474-6222

NATIONAL ASSOCIATION OF BLACK
JOURNALISTS
11600 Sunrise Valley Dr.
Reston, VA 22091
(703) 648-1270

NATIONAL ASSOCIATION OF BLACK-OWNED
BROADCASTERS
1730 M St. NW, #412
Washington, DC 20036
(202) 463-8970

NATIONAL BAPTIST CONVENTION OF
AMERICA, INC.
National Baptist World Center
1700 Baptist World Center Dr.
Nashville, TN 37207
(615) 228-6292

NATIONAL BEAUTY CULTURISTS
LEAGUE, INC.
25 Logan Circle, NW
Washington, DC 20005
(202) 332-2695

NATIONAL BLACK BUSINESS COUNCIL,
INC.
1100 Wayne Avenue, Suite 850
Silver Spring, MD 20910
(301) 585-6222
*Fax:* (301) 565-3662
*E-mail:* nbbc@tnt.org

NATIONAL BLACK CHAMBER OF
COMMERCE
2000 L St. NW, Suite 200
Washington, DC 20036
(202) 416-1622

NATIONAL BLACK MBA ASSOCIATION
180 North Michigan, Suite 1515
Chicago, IL 60601
(312) 236-2622

NATIONAL BLACK NURSES'
ASSOCIATION, INC.
P.O. Box 1832
Washington, DC 20013-1823
(202) 393-6870
*Fax:* (202) 347-3808

NATIONAL MINORITY SUPPLIER
DEVELOPMENT COUNCIL, INC.
15 West 39th St., 9th Fl.
New York, NY 10018
(212) 944-2430

NATIONAL URBAN LEAGUE, INC.
500 East 62nd St.
New York, NY 10021
(212) 310-9000

OPERATION PUSH
(PEOPLE UNITED TO SERVE HUMANITY)
930 East 50th St.
Chicago, IL 60615
(312) 373-3366

U.S. AFRICAN AMERICAN CHAMBER OF
COMMERCE
117 Broadway
Oakland, CA 94607
(510) 444-5741

U.S. DEPARTMENT OF COMMERCE
MINORITY BUSINESS DEVELOPMENT
AGENCY
Maggie L. Faulkner, Business
Dev. Spec.
221 Main Street, Suite 1280
San Francisco, CA 94105
(415) 744-3001
FTS: 744-3061

U.S. HISPANIC CHAMBER OF COMMERCE
1030 15th St. NW
Washington, DC 20005
(202) 842-1212

## Women's Organizations and Professional Associations

ABWE (ASSOCIATION OF BLACK WOMEN ENTREPRENEURS)
Att: Dolores Ratcliffe
P.O. Box 49368
Los Angeles, CA 90049
(213) 624-8639

AFRICAN AMERICAN WOMEN ON TOUR
3914 Murphy Canyon Rd., Suite 216-B
San Diego, CA 92123
(619) 560-2770

AMERICAN ASSOCIATION OF BLACK WOMEN ENTREPRENEURS CORP.
815 Thayer Ave., #1628
Silver Spring, MD 20910
(301) 565-0258

AMERICAN BUSINESS WOMEN'S ASSOCIATION
9100 Ward Parkway
Kansas City, MO 64114
(816) 361-6621

AMERICAN WOMAN'S ECONOMIC DEVELOPMENT CORPORATION
*Los Angeles:*
230 Pine Ave., 3rd Fl.
Long Beach, CA 90802
(310) 983-3747
*Fax:* (310) 983-3750

*New York City:*
71 Vanderbilt Ave.
New York, NY 10169
(212) 692-9100

*Stamford:*
2001 West Main St., Suite 205
Stamford, CT 06902
(203) 326-7914

ASSOCIATION OF BLACK WOMEN IN HIGHER EDUCATION
Delores V. Smalls
c/o Nassau Community College
Nassau Hall, Room 19
One Education Drive
Garden City, NY 11530-6793
(516) 572-7141

ASSOCIATION OF PROFESSIONAL INSURANCE WOMEN
P.O. Box 98
Church Street Station
New York, NY 10008
(212) 238-9258

BLACK WOMEN IN CHURCH AND SOCIETY
c/o Interdenominational Theological Center
671 Beckwith St. SW
Atlanta, GA 30314
(404) 527-7740

BLACK WOMEN IN PUBLISHING, INC.
c/o Phelps-Stokes Fund Affiliates
10 East 87 St.
New York, NY 10128
(212) 427-8100

BLACK WOMEN'S AGENDA, INC.
1000 Vermont Ave. NW
Washington, DC 20005
(202) 387-4166

BLACK WOMEN'S AGENDA, INC.
3501 14th St. NW
Washington, DC 20010
(202) 387-4166

BLACK WOMEN'S FORUM
3870 Crenshaw Blvd., #210
Los Angeles, CA 90008
(213) 292-3009

BLACK WOMEN'S NETWORK, INC.
*Milwaukee:*
8712 West Spokane St.
Milwaukee, WI 53224
(414) 353-8925

*Los Angeles:*
P.O. Box 56106
Los Angeles, CA 90056
(213) 292-6547

**BUSINESS AND PROFESSIONAL WOMEN'S FOUNDATION**
2012 Massachusetts Ave. NW
Washington, DC 20036
(202) 293-1200

**DOLL LEAGUE, INC.**
170 Brayton St.
Englewood, NJ 07631
(201) 871-0857

**E GROUP**
Women's Self-Employment Project
166 West Washington, Suite 730
Chicago, IL 60602
(312) 606-8255

**FEDERATION OF ORGANIZATIONS FOR PROFESSIONAL WOMEN**
2001 S St. NW, Suite 500
Washington, DC 20009
(202) 328-1415

**GIRL FRIENDS, INC.**
5035 Heatherglen Drive
Houston, TX 77096
(713) 721-4645
*Fax:* (713) 721-4646

**INTERNATIONAL BLACK WOMEN'S CONGRESS**
1080 Bergen St., Suite 200
Newark, NJ 07112
(201) 926-0570
*Fax:* (201) 926-0818

**METROPOLITAN ATLANTA COALITION OF 100 BLACK WOMEN**
Women's Economic Development Agency
Nationwide Plaza
600 Peachtree St.,
37th Floor, Suite 3710
Atlanta, GA 30308
(404) 892-4008

**NATIONAL ASSOCIATION OF BLACK HOSPITALITY PROFESSIONALS**
P.O. Box 5443
Plainfield, NJ 07060-5443
(908) 354-5117

**NATIONAL ASSOCIATION OF BLACK WOMEN ENTREPRENEURS**
Att: Marilyn French-Hubbard
P.O. Box 1375
Detroit, MI 48231
(810) 356-3686
*Fax:* (810) 354-3793

**NATIONAL ASSOCIATION OF COLORED WOMEN'S CLUBS, INC.**
5808 16th St. NW
Washington, DC 20011
(202) 726-2044

**NATIONAL ASSOCIATION FOR FEMALE EXECUTIVES, INC.**
30 Irving Place, 5th Fl.
New York, NY 10003
(212) 645-0770

**NATIONAL ASSOCIATION OF MEDIA WOMEN**
213-16 126th Ave.
Laurelton, NY 11413
(718) 712-4544

**NATIONAL ASSOCIATION OF MINORITY POLITICAL WOMEN, USA, INC.**
6120 Oregon Ave., NW
Washington, DC 20015
(202) 686-1216

**NATIONAL ASSOCIATION OF MINORITY WOMEN IN BUSINESS**
906 Grand Ave., Suite 200
Kansas City, MO 64106
(816) 421-3335
*Fax:* (816) 421-3336

**NATIONAL ASSOCIATION OF WOMEN BUSINESS OWNERS**
1377 K St. NW, #637
Washington, DC 20005
(301) 608-2590
(800) 238-2233

NATIONAL ASSOCIATION OF WOMEN IN
CONSTRUCTION CONVENTION/TRADE SHOW
Att: Shelly Reeves
327 South Adams
Fort Worth, TX 76104
(800) 552-3506

NATIONAL ASSOCIATION OF WOMEN'S
BUSINESS ADVOCATES
100 West Randolph, #3-400
Chicago, IL 60601
(312) 814-7176

NATIONAL ASSOCIATION OF UNIVERSITY
WOMEN
1501 11th St. NW
Washington, DC 20001
(202) 232-4844

NATIONAL BLACK WOMEN'S CONSCIOUS-
NESS RAISING ASSOCIATION
1906 North Charles St.
Baltimore, MD 21218
(410) 727-8900

NATIONAL CERTIFICATION PROGRAM FOR
WOMEN BUSINESS OWNERS CORP. (WBOC)
18 Encanto Dr.
Palo Verdes, CA 90274
(310) 530-7500

NATIONAL COALITION OF 100 BLACK
WOMEN
38 West 32 St., #1610
New York, NY 10001
(212) 947-2196

NATIONAL COUNCIL OF NEGRO WOMEN,
INC.
1667 K St. NW, #700
Washington, DC 20006
(202) 659-0006

NATIONAL FEDERATION OF BLACK WOMEN
BUSINESS OWNERS
1500 Massachusetts Ave. NW, Suite 22
Washington, DC 20005
(202) 833-3450
*Fax:* (202) 331-7822

NATIONAL FEDERATION OF BUSINESS AND
PROFESSIONAL WOMEN'S CLUBS
2012 Massachusetts Ave. NW
Washington, DC 20036
(202) 293-1100

NATIONAL POLITICAL CONGRESS OF BLACK
WOMEN, INC.
600 New Hampshire Ave. NW
Washington, DC 20037
(202) 338-0800

NATIONAL WOMEN'S ECONOMIC ALLIANCE
1440 New York Ave. NW, Suite 300
Washington, DC 20005
(202) 393-5257

OFFICE OF WOMEN'S BUSINESS OWNERSHIP
U.S. Small Business Administration
409 Third St. SW
Washington, DC 20416
(202) 205-6673

ORGANIZATION OF BLACK DESIGNERS
717 D St. NW, Suite 500
Washington, DC 20004
(202) 659-3918

SOCIETY OF AFRICAN AMERICAN INTERIOR
DESIGNERS
P.O. Box 8537
Los Angeles, CA
(213) 960-1019

SOCIETY OF WOMEN ENGINEERS
120 Wall Street
New York, NY 10005
(212) 509-9577
(800) 661-1SWE

TOP LADIES OF DISTINCTION, INC.
1408 North Kings Highway
Suite 207B
St. Louis, MO 63113
(800) 883-8186

WOMEN OF COLOR AS WARRIORS OF LIGHT
P.O. Box 56078
Los Angeles, CA 90056-0078
(303) 443-3656

WOMEN IN COMMUNICATIONS, INC.
760 Market St., Suite 315
San Francisco, CA 94102
(415) 773-9472

WOMEN'S BUSINESS DEVELOPMENT CENTER
8 South Michigan, #400
Chicago, IL 60603
(312) 853-3477

WOMEN'S BUSINESS NETWORK AND
NEDA/MINORITY BUSINESS DEVELOPMENT
CENTER
P.O. Box 108
Berkeley, CA 94701
(510) 482-8583
NEDA: (415) 243-8430

WOMEN'S INITIATIVE FOR SELF EMPLOY-
MENT (WISE)
*San Francisco:*
450 Mission St., Suite 402
San Francisco, CA 94105
(415) 247-9473

*Oakland:*
519 17th St., Suite 520
Oakland, CA 94612
(510) 208-9473

WOMEN'S SELF-EMPLOYMENT PROJECT
20 North Clark St., 4th Fl.
Chicago, IL 60602
(312) 606-8255
*Fax:* (312) 606-9215

WOMEN'S WORLD BANKING
8 West 40th, St., 10th Floor
New York, NY 10018
(212) 768-8513

## Colleges, Universities, Alumnae Organizations, and Sororities

ALPHA KAPPA ALPHA SORORITY
5656 South Stony Island Ave.
Chicago, IL 60637
(312) 684-1282

ALPHA PI CHI SORORITY
P.O. Box 1337
Florence, AL 35630
(205) 764-4899

ALUMNAE RESOURCES
120 Montgomery St., Suite 600
San Francisco, CA 94104
(415) 274-4700
*Fax:* (415) 274-4744

BENNETT COLLEGE
900 East Washington St.
Greensboro, NC 27401-3239
(919) 273-4431

CHICAGO STATE UNIVERSITY
9501 South King Drive, ADM 313
Chicago, IL 60628
(312) 995-2400

CHI ETA PHI SORORITY, INC.
3029 13th St. NW
Washington, DC 20009
(202) 723-3384

DELTA SIGMA THETA SORORITY, INC.
1707 New Hampshire Ave. NW
Washington, DC 20009
(202) 986-2400

ETA PHI BETA SORORITY, INC.
16815 James Couzens
Detroit, MI 48235
(313) 862-0600

IOTA PHI LAMBDA SORORITY, INC.
P.O. Box 11509
Montgomery, AL 36111-0609
(205) 284-0203

KENNEDY-KING COLLEGE
6800 South Wentworth Ave.
Chicago, IL 60621
(312) 962-3200

LAMBDA KAPPA MU SORORITY, INC.
1521 Crittenden St. NW
Washington, DC 20011
(202) 829-2368

**PHI DELTA KAPPA, INC.**
8233 South M. L. King Dr.
Chicago, IL 60619
(312) 783-7379

**SIGMA GAMMA RHO SORORITY, INC.**
8800 South Stony Island Ave.
Chicago, IL 60617
(312) 873-9000

**SPELMAN COLLEGE**
350 Spelman Lane SW
Atlanta, GA 30314
(404) 681-3643

**ZETA PHI BETA SORORITY, INC.**
1734 New Hampshire Ave. NW
Washington, DC 20009
(202) 387-3103

## Internet Resources

### TECHNOLOGY & COMPUTER ORGANIZATIONS

**INFORMATION TECHNOLOGY TRAINING ASSOCIATION**
3925 West Braker Lane, #433
Austin, TX 78759
(512) 502-9300

**INTERNATIONAL COMPUTER CONSULTANTS ASSOCIATION**
11131 South Towne Square, Suite F
St. Louis, MO 63123
(314) 892-1675

**INTERNATIONAL DATA CORP.**
5 Speen St.
Framingham, MA 01701
(508) 872-8200

### ONLINE SERVICES

**AMERICA ONLINE**
8619 Westwood Center Dr.
Vienna, VA 22182
(800) 827-6364

**AT&T WORLD NET SERVICES**
295 North Maple Ave.
Baskingridge, NJ 07920
(800) 336-TRUE

**COMPUSERVE**
5000 Arlington Center Blvd.
Columbus, OH 43220
(800) 848-8199

**MICROSOFT NETWORK**
Microsoft Corp.
1 Microsoft Way
Redmond, WA 98052-6399
(800) 426-9400

**SMALL BUSINESS ADMINISTRATION ON-LINE**
(modem hookup)
(800) 697-4636
(900) 463-4636

### ONLINE AREAS

**AMERICA ONLINE:**
• The Entrepreneur Zone (*keyword*: ezone)
• HOC Online (*keyword*: hoc)

**COMPUSERVE:**
• Working from Home Forum (*keyword*: go work)

**MICROSOFT NETWORK:**
• HOC Online (*keyword*: go hoc)
• Janet Attard Business Know-How (*keyword not available*)

**WORLD WIDE WEB:**
• MCI Small Business Center (www.mci.com/smallbiz)
• Small Business Administration WWW Home Page (http://www.shoonline.sba.gov.)

The Gopher service:
(gopher://www.shoonline.sba.gov.)
SBA Technical Support
(202) 205-6400

## Software and Databases

### ACCOUNTING/BOOKKEEPING

MANAGING YOUR MONEY
Meca Software
(800) 288-6322

MICROSOFT ACCESS 2.0
Microsoft Corp.
(800) 426-9400

MICROSOFT MONEY FOR WINDOWS 95
Microsoft Corp.
(800) 426-9400

PEACHTREE ACCOUNTING FOR WINDOWS 3.0
(800) 247-3224

QUICKBOOKS 3.1
Intuit Inc.
(800) 816-8025

QUICKEN 6 (Macintosh)
Quicken 5 **(WINDOWS)**
(800) 816-8025

SIMPLY ACCOUNTING
Home Productions
(800) 773-5445

TURBO TAX FOR BUSINESS
Intuit Inc.
(800) 964-1040

### WORD PROCESSING, PRESENTATION, AND GRAPHICS SOFTWARE

MICROSOFT POWER POINT FOR WINDOWS 95
(800) 426-9400

PAGEMAKER 6.0
Adobe Systems Inc.
(800) 422-3623

PRINT SHOP DELUXE CD ENSEMBLE
(800) 521-6263

QUARKXPRESS 3.32
Quark Inc.
(800) 788-7835

SOFTWARE PUBLISHING CORP.
(800) 234-2500

WORDPERFECT 6.1 FOR WINDOWS
Novell Inc.
(800) 451-5151

### BUSINESS PLAN SOFTWARE

BIZPLAN BUILDER
JIAN Tools for Sales, Inc.
(415) 941-9191

BUSINESS PLAN TOOLKIT 5.0
Palo Alto Software
(800) 229-7526

MARKETING PLAN TOOL KIT
Palo Alto Software
(800) 229-7526

## Reference Books

BLACK WALL STREET
Dularon Entertainment, Inc.
P.O. Box 2702
Tulsa, OK 74149
(800) 682-7975

DIRECTORY OF DEPARTMENT STORES
Chain Store Guide Information
Services
3922 Coconut Palm Drive
Tampa, FL 33619
(800) 925-2288

SISTERS IN BUSINESS: THE BLACK
WOMEN'S BUSINESS DIRECTORY
International Black Women's
Congress
1081 Bergen St., Suite 200
Newark, NJ 07112
(201) 926-0570
*Fax:* (201) 926-0818

## Trade Shows

TRADE SHOW BUREAU
1660 Lincoln St., Suite 2080
Denver, CO 80264-2001
(303) 860-7626

## Airport Access

AIRPORT MINORITY ADVISORY COUNCIL
4733 Bethesda Ave., #200
Bethesda, MD 20814
(301) 907-8027

AIRPORTS COUNCIL INTERNATIONAL
NORTH AMERICA
1775 K St. NW, #500
Washington, DC 20006
(202) 293-8500

WORLD AIRPORT RETAIL NEWS
P.O. Box 30907
Palm Beach, FL 33420
(407) 863-7001

## Home Shopping Resources

BET SHOP
1 BET Plaza
1899 9th St. NE
Washington, DC 20018
(202) 608-2000

HSN
Merchandising Department
P.O. Box 9090
Clearwater, FL 34618-9090
(813) 572-8585

NIA DIRECT (direct mail/coupons)
139 Fulton St.
New York, NY 10038
(212) 285-0865

QVC
1365 Enterprise Drive
West Chester, PA 19380
(610) 701-8282

## African American Venture Capitalist Firms

BROADCAST CAPITAL FUND INC.
1700 K St. NW
Washington, DC 20036
(202) 496-9250

FAIRVIEW CAPITAL PARTNERS
190 Farmington Ave.
Farmington, CT 06032
(203) 674-8066

NATIONAL ASSOCIATION OF INVESTMENT
COMPANIES
1111 14th St. NW
Washington, DC 20005
(202) 289-4336

TSG CAPITAL GROUP
177 Broad St., 12th Floor
Stamford, CT 06901
(203) 406-1500

UNC PARTNERS
711 Atlantic Ave.
Boston, MA 02111
(617) 482-7070

## Securities and Investment Organizations & Associations

COUNCIL OF BETTER BUSINESS BUREAUS
4200 Wilson Blvd.
Arlington, VA 22203
(703) 276-0100

NATIONAL ASSOCIATION OF SECURITIES
DEALERS
1735 K St. NW
Washington, DC 20006
(202) 728-8300

NORTH AMERICAN SECURITIES ADMINISTRATORS ASSOCIATION
1 Massachusetts Ave. NW
Washington, DC 20031
(202) 737-0900

SCOR REPORT
P.O. Box 781992
Dallas, TX 75378-1992
(214) 620-2489

SECURITIES AND EXCHANGE COMMISSION
450 5th St. NW
Washington, DC 20549
(202) 942-7040

## *African American Investment Bankers*

APEX SECURITIES INC.
333 Clay St., Suite 1310
Houston, TX 77002
(713) 650-1122

BLAYLOCK & PARTNERS L.P.
609 5th Ave.
New York, NY 10017
(212) 272-7679

CHAPMAN CO.
401 East Pratt St., 28th Floor
Baltimore, MD 21202
(410) 625-9656

CHARLES A. BELL SECURITIES CORP.
44 Montgomery St., Suite 960
San Francisco, CA 94104
(415) 433-0270

DALEY SECURITIES INC.
616 Barrone St.
New Orleans, LA 70113
(504) 561-1128

GRIGSBY BRANFORD & CO., INC.
101 California St., Suite 200
San Francisco, CA 94111
(415) 392-4800

HOWARD GRAY & CO.
3050 Biscayne Blvd., Suite 603
Miami, Fl 33137
(305) 571-1380

L. C. RIDEAU, LYONS CO., INC.
911 Wilshire Blvd., Suite 2030
Los Angeles, CA 90017
(213) 895-5900

M. R. BEAL & CO.
565 Fifth Avenue
New York, NY 10017
(212) 983-3900

POWELL CAPITAL MARKETS INC.
40 Clinton St., Suite 200
Newark, NJ 07102
(201) 621-8050

PRYOR, MCCLENDON, COUNTS & CO.
1515 Market St., Suite 819
Philadelphia, PA 19102
(215) 569-0274

STURDIVANT & CO. INC.
223 Gibbesboro Road
Clementon, NJ 08021
(609) 627-4500

UNITED DANIELS SECURITIES INC.
170 Broadway
New York, NY 10038-4154
(212) 227-7723

UTENDAHL CAPITAL PARTNERS L.P.
30 Broad St., 31st Fl.
New York, NY 10004
(212) 797-2660

W. R. LAZARD & CO.
14 Wall St., 18th Fl.
New York, NY 10005
(212) 406-5855

## *Black Financial Institutions*

BOSTON BANK OF COMMERCE
133 Federal St.
Boston, MA 02110
(617) 457-4400

BROADWAY FEDERAL SAVINGS
& LOAN
4429 South Broadway
Los Angeles, CA 90037
(213) 232-4271

CARVER FEDERAL SAVINGS BANK
121 West 125 St.
New York, NY 10027
(212) 876-4747

CITIZENS TRUST BANK
75 Piedmont Ave.
Atlanta, GA 30303
(404) 659-5959

CITIZENS FEDERAL SAVINGS BANK
300 North 18th St.
Birmingham, AL 35203
(205) 328-2041

CITY NATIONAL BANK OF NEW JERSEY
900 Broad St.
Newark, NJ 07102
(201) 624-0869

CONSOLIDATED BANK AND TRUST CO.
P.O. Box 26823
Richmond, VA 23261
(804) 771-5200

THE DOUGLASS BANK
1314 North 5th St.
Kansas City, KS 66101
(713) 321-7200

4655 State Avenue
Kansas City, KS 66102
(713) 287-1012

DRYADES SAVINGS BANK, FSB
231 Carmelita St., Suite 200
New Orleans, LA 70130
(504) 598-7200

FAMILY SAVINGS BANK, FSB
3683 Crenshaw Blvd.
Los Angeles, CA 90016
(213) 245-3381

FIRST INDEPENDENCE NATIONAL BANK OF
DETROIT
44 Michigan Ave.
Detroit, MI 48226
(213) 256-8200

FIRST TEXAS BANK
P.O. Box 29775
Dallas, TX 75229
(214) 243-2400

FIRST TUSKEGEE BANK
301 North Elm Street
Tuskegee, AL 36088
(334) 727-2560

FOUNDERS NATIONAL BANK OF LOS ANGELES
3910 West Martin Luther King Jr. Blvd.
Los Angeles, CA 90008
(213) 290-4848

HARBOR BANK OF MARYLAND
25 West Fayette Street
Baltimore, MD 21201
(410) 528-1800

ILLINOIS SERVICE FEDERAL SAVINGS AND
LOAN ASSOCIATION
4619 South Dr. Martin Luther King Dr.
Chicago, IL 60653
(312) 624-2000

INDEPENDENCE BANK OF CHICAGO
7936 South Cottage Grove Ave.
Chicago, IL 60619
(312) 722-9456

INDEPENDENCE FEDERAL SAVINGS BANK
1229 Connecticut Ave. NW
Washington, DC 20036
(202) 628-5500

INDUSTRIAL BANK OF WASHINGTON
1317 F St. NW
Washington, DC 20004
(202) 722-2060

LIBERTY BANK AND TRUST CO.
3801 Canal St.
New Orleans, LA 60119
(504) 286-8817

MECHANICS AND FARMERS BANK
116 West Parrish St.
Durham, NC 27702
(919) 683-1521

SEAWAY NATIONAL BANK OF CHICAGO
645 East 87th St.
Chicago, IL 60619
(312) 487-4800

SOUTH SHORE BANK
4698 South Drexel Blvd.
Chicago, IL 60653
(312) 451-5900

TRI-STATE BANK OF MEMPHIS
180 South Main St.
Memphis, TN 38103
(901) 525-0384

UNITED BANK OF PHILADELPHIA
714 Market St.
Philadelphia, PA 19106
(215) 829-2265

## Franchise Resources

AMERICAN ASSOCIATION OF FRANCHISEES
AND DEALERS
1420 Kettner Blvd., Suite 415
San Diego, CA 92101
(619) 235-2556
(800) 733-9858

INTERNATIONAL FRANCHISE ASSOCIATION
1350 New York Ave. NW, Suite 900
Washington, DC 20005-4709
(202) 628-8000

WOMEN IN FRANCHISING INC.
53 West Jackson Blvd.
Chicago, IL 60604
(312) 431-1467

WOMEN'S FRANCHISE NETWORK
International Franchise Association
1350 New York Ave. NW, Suite 900
Washington, DC 20005
(202) 628-8000, ext. 7788
*Fax:* (202) 628-0812

# Bibliography and Recommended Reading

Beals, Melba. *Expose Yourself*. San Francisco: Chronicle Books, 1990.

Bly, Robert W. *Targeted Public Relations*. New York: Henry Holt and Company, Inc., 1993.

Boston, Kelvin. *Smart Money Moves for African Americans*. New York: G.P. Putnam's Sons, 1996.

Boyd, Julia. *In the Company of My Sisters*. New York: Dutton, 1993.

Brabec, Barbara. *Homemade Money*. Ohio: Betterway Books, 1994.

Brown, Carolyn. "More Than Window Dressing." *Black Enterprise*, September 1994, p. 103.

————. "Park Your Company Here." *Black Enterprise*, November 1995, p. 88.

"Business Profiles: Black Opal." *Black Enterprise*, November 1995, p. 106.

Celente, Gerald, with Milton, Tom. *Trend Tracking*. New York: John Wiley & Sons, 1990.

Chopra, Deepak. *The Seven Spiritual Laws of Success*. San Rafael, CA: New World Library, 1994.

DeAngelis, Barbara. *Confidence: Finding It and Loving It*. Carson, CA: Hay House, Inc., 1995.

Edwards, Sarah and Paul. *Working From Home*. Los Angeles: Jeremy P. Tarcher, Inc., 1990.

*Entrepreneur* Magazine. *Small Business Advisor*. New York: John Wiley & Sons, Inc., 1995.

Fraser, George. *Success Runs in Our Race*. New York: William Morrow & Company, 1994.

Hicks, Tyler G. *How to Start Your Own Business on a Shoestring and Make Up to $500,000 a Year*. Rocklin, CA: Prima Publishing, 1987.

Hill, Napoleon. *Think and Grow Rich*. Hollywood, CA: Wilshire Book Company, 1966.

Johnson, John J. *Succeeding Against the Odds*. New York: Warner Books, 1989.

Joy, Nicki, with Benson, Susan Kane. *Selling Is a Woman's Game*. New York: Avon Books, 1994.

Kirk, Randy W. *When Friday Isn't Payday*. New York: Warner Books, 1993.

Levinson, Jay Conrad. *Guerrilla Marketing*. Boston: Houghton Mifflin Company, 1984.

Lewis, Warren. *Franchise: Dollars & Sense*. Iowa: Kendall-Hunt Publishing, 1993.

King, Barbara. *Transform Your Life*. New York: Perigee Books, 1995

Milano, Carol. "How to Get Your Products onto Retail Shelves." *Black Enterprise*, November 1994, p. 100.

Parady, Marianne. *Seven Secrets for Successful Living*. New York: Kensington Books, 1995.

Ponder, Catherine. *The Dynamic Laws of Prosperity*. Marina Del Rey, CA; Devorss & Company, 1962.

Popcorn, Faith. *The Popcorn Report*. New York: HarperBusiness, 1992.

Poynter, Dan. *The Self-Publishing Manual*. Santa Barbara, CA: Para Publishing, 1989.

Rasberry, Salli, and Selwyn, Padi. *Living Your Life Out Loud*. New York: Pocket Books, 1995.

Rivers, Alicia M. "Business of Beauty." *Black Elegance*, December 1995, p. 17.

Robbins, Anthony. *Notes From a Friend*. New York: Fireside Books, 1995.

Ryder, Judy. *Turning Your Great Idea into a Success*. New Jersey: Peterson's/Pacesetter Books, 1995.

Shakspeare, Tonia L. "So You Want to Be a Franchisor?" *Black Enterprise*, September 1995, p. 88.

Sinetar, Marsha. *To Build the Life You Want, Create the Work You Love*. New York: St. Martin's Press, 1995.

Taylor, Susan L., *In the Spirit*. New York: Amistad, 1993.

"The 20 B.E. Best Franchises." *Black Enterprise*, September 1995, p. 67.

Waitley, Denis, and Witt, Reni L. *The Joy of Working*. New York: Dodd, Mead & Company, 1985.

Wallace, Ron, and Wilson, J. J. *Black Wall Street*. Oklahoma: Dularon Entertainment, Inc., 1992.

Wells, Valerie. *The Joy of Visualization*. San Francisco: Chronicle Books, 1990.

Wieder, Marcia. *Making Your Dreams Come True*. New York: MasterMedia Limited, 1993.

Wood, Andrew. *Making It Big in America*. Rocklin, CA: Prima Publishing, 1995.

Vanzant, Iyanla. *Acts of Faith*. New York: Fireside Books, 1993.

Vitale, Joe. *The Seven Lost Secrets of Success*. Ashland, OH: VistaTron, 1992.

## *Business Magazines*

BLACK ENTERPRISE

ENTREPRENEUR

FORBES

FORTUNE

INC.

SUCCESS

# Index